Between Worlds

A Study of the Plays of John Webster

Dena Goldberg

"Webster's iconoclasm was not the lonely experience of an alienated intellectual, but part of his generation's struggle to create the future. As such, the critical energy we find in the plays was sustained, not by ideological certainty, but rather by interaction with the great complexity of thought and action—much of it negative—that constitutes a pre-revolutionary movement. If Webster was part of a dying culture, he was also—and it is this that Webster criticism has almost consistently ignored—a member of the generation that prepared the way for the revolution of 1640" (Introduction).

Through detailed analysis of four plays, *The White Devil*, *The Duchess of Malfi*, *The Devil's Law Case*, and *Appius and Virginia*, Goldberg explores the relations between Webster and aspects of Jacobean social and intellectual history. Webster's satire of princes and prelates, his iconoclastic view of traditional philosophy, his trenchant analysis of institutions are seen as part of an intellectual movement that was undermining faith in the old order. Special attention is given to Webster's theatrical representations of legal practice and legal philosophy as key manifestations of the realities of political power. Webster's dramatizations of the judgment situation are shown to embody specific commentary on the legal system of his time, commentary that ranges in orientation from anarchist to reformist to revolutionary. Webster's irreverence for traditional ideals and institutions combines with a humanist sense of man's—and woman's—potential to make an important contribution to the pre-revolutionary movement.

Dena Goldberg teaches in the English Department of the Université de Montréal.

Between Worlds

A Study of the Plays of John Webster

Between Worlds
a study of the plays of
JOHN WEBSTER

Dena Goldberg

This book has been published with the help of a grant from the Canadian Federation for the Humanities, using funds provided by the Social Sciences and Humanities Research Council of Canada.

Canadian Cataloguing in Publication Data

Goldberg, Dena, 1935-
   Between worlds

Bibliography: p.
Includes index.
ISBN 0-88920-953-7

1. Webster, John, 1580?-1625? – Criticism and interpretation. I. Title.

PR3187.G64 1987   822'.3   C87-094113-5

Copyright © 1987
WILFRID LAURIER UNIVERSITY PRESS
Waterloo, Ontario, Canada   N2L 3C5

87 88 89 90 4 3 2 1

Cover design by *Vijen Vijendren*

Printed in Canada

No part of this book may be stored in a retrieval system, translated or reproduced in any form, by print, photoprint, microfilm, microfiche, or any other means, without written permission from the publisher.

Contents

Introduction 1

Chapter One
The White Devil: Law and the Challenge
of Human Nature 22

Chapter Two
The White Devil: Law and Power 43

Chapter Three
The White Devil and Jacobean Theories
of the Origin of Law 64

Chapter Four
The Duchess of Malfi: The Roots of Judgment 78

Chapter Five
The Duchess of Malfi, the Royal Prerogative,
and the Puritan Conscience 100

Chapter Six
The Devil's Law Case 113

Chapter Seven
Appius and Virginia 131

Chapter Eight
Conclusion: The Rule of Law 147

Works Cited 156

Index 162

Introduction

There is a dark side to the art of John Webster that has always been given its due by critics and directors. Charles Lamb saw Webster as one of the great gothic writers: "To move a horror skilfully, to touch a soul to the quick, to lay upon fear as much as it can bear, to wean and weary a life till it is ready to drop, and then step in with mortal instruments to take its last forfeit—this only a Webster can do."[1] Rupert Brooke was fascinated by "the world called Webster," a world in which people "kill, love, torture one another blindly and without ceasing," a world "full of the feverish and ghastly turmoil of a nest of maggots."[2] The emphases in contemporary criticism are a little different. Modern critics are less likely to see Webster's world as a nest of maggots than as a reflection of the decaying, constricted Jacobean world that Webster knew. If Lamb's approach echoes his generation's concern with individual emotional experience, and Brooke's reflects a post-Darwinian fascination with instincts, modern criticism has been especially sensitive to the poignancy of Webster's dramatic recreation of a dying culture, a society without workable values. The following excellent description of the world of *The White Devil*, the first of Webster's great tragedies, typifies the dominant tendency in modern discussion of Webster's work as a whole:

> Webster depicts a world lacking a clearly defined moral centre, a world in which the old values have grown decadent: the Court, courtly love, the processes of law, the Church, the moral imperatives of kinship have all been degraded. The only strengths and positive values one can find are within oneself, and even these prove in the end to be fallible.... The struggle to survive in this dark environment results in flashes of desperate poetry which contrast vividly, and often movingly, with the bitterly satirised corruption underlying everything.[3]

The darkness is now seen as the lack of clarifying ideology in a corrupt world. Webster depicts a society whose institutions are so corrupt and whose ideals are so false that individuals are forced to create their own values. But they find no definition of value that will survive the test of experience. The grim world that Webster creates on the stage—the torture, the suffering, the terror—becomes grimmer still when its inhabitants find no amelioration in traditional Christian comforts, or in any of the philosophical postulates that made life easier for some of Webster's contemporaries. In the words of Travis Bogard, Webster's plays imply no "positive ethic" to "attack" the overpowering evil they investigate; for "life, as it appears to Webster, is a moral chaos. Ultimately, no clarifying philosophy is possible, for man's mortality renders meaningless the very terms on which such a philosophy must be based."[4] Lacking such a philosophy, Webster's characters pass their lives in struggle and depart from this world (as one of them puts it) in a "mist."

Emphasis on Webster's nihilism in some of the most interesting criticism of the past thirty years has been a vital corrective to the kind of criticism that persists in seeing Webster as a stern Christian moralist, a view that originated as a defence against old-fashioned attacks on Webster accusing him of being an agent of the devil.[5] The complex texture of a Webster play is not reducible to any rigid moral scheme, a point on which most critics would now agree, even if many of them still underestimate the extent of Webster's rejection of traditional values. And yet the Christianizing persists, in both crude and subtle forms.[6] Indeed, both the nihilist and the traditionalist interpretations sometimes exist side by side, unreconciled, in the same discussion.

For instance, the same critic who finds no "positive ethic" or "clarifying philosophy" in the plays also says that Webster is an "explicit, ethically specific" playwright.[7] The critic here seems to be grappling with a set of impressions that add up to the paradoxical image of a writer whose plays are full of moral indignation, although he believes in no known moral system. The problem is made explicit by an editor of *The White Devil* who, seeing in that play a powerful "undermining" of the courtly code by which the characters live, wonders what is the source of the moral sense that makes such a critique possible; for

> there is nothing like a direct affirmation of Christian ethics. . . .
> There is no sense whatsoever of God. The positive values from which Webster's analysis and evaluation of aristocratic morality grow, like much else in the play, remain suppressed, implied, muffled. . . . When we ask the final questions 'Where did Webster himself stand? What did he value?' we too are 'in a mist.'[8]

It has occurred to me that our ability to grasp Webster's intellectual position has been blocked by an assumption that critical consciousness is dependent upon ideological certainty, that we can only evaluate what is around us if we are bolstered by some dogmatic faith. This inevitably gives rise to the question: how are we to account for the analytic power so clearly evident in the plays? If Webster had no faith, if he was floating around in a moral chaos, how did he manage to maintain so firm a perspective on his material? This, in turn, tends to lead back to the notion that he must have been grounded in traditional religious values.

The problem is resolved if we recognize that Webster's iconoclasm was not the lonely experience of an alienated intellectual, but part of his generation's struggle to create the future. As such, the critical energy we find in the plays was sustained, not by ideological certainty, but rather by interaction with the great complexity of thought and action—much of it negative—that constitutes a pre-revolutionary movement. In other words, if Webster was part of a dying culture, he was also—and it is this that Webster criticism has almost consistently ignored—a member of the generation that prepared the way for the revolution of 1640. A contributing member, too, for if it was the task of this generation, as Christopher Hill puts it, to "undermine men's traditional belief in the eternity of the old order in Church and state,"[9] then Webster's iconoclasm was at the centre of the intellectual life of his time.

Failing to perceive in Webster's work a dialectical union in which destruction and creation are intermingled, criticism has made too much of Webster's *fin de siècle* despair. In particular the criticism of the last thirty years has tended to interpret Webster's muscular nay-saying in the light of its own desperate search for something to hold onto as the foundations cracked. It has responded to the doomsday quality of Webster's plays with sympathy and imagination; what it has responded to less readily, perhaps because of its own stasis, is the life-giving quality of Webster's negations. My own view is that Webster's art (like some of the works of Gorky and Brecht) has that double nature which is so characteristic of pre-revolutionary art. At times extremely negative, expressive of the pessimism of a generation that has lost faith in old values and cannot foresee a future, at other times it is joyously iconoclastic, undermining truisms with sardonic exuberance. To the extent that it is of the past, Webster's art participates in the weariness and the sense of approaching death of the old order. But with the slightest shift of emphasis it becomes part of the future, by ensuring the wreck of the past while it simultaneously asserts that it is part of our nature to struggle, to refuse to give up. That is, the ambivalence in Webster's plays reflects the ambivalence of his historical position.

There are links between critical failure to define Webster's historical position and certain tendencies in discussions of the intellectual atmosphere of the early seventeenth century. Because it is such a difficult period to characterize definitively, historians are sometimes led to impose patterns created by splitting apart phenomena that can only be deeply understood in their interrelations. The patterns are useful, perhaps even necessary for awhile, if they enable the writer to isolate for attention some hitherto neglected aspect of this complicated period, but once that is accomplished, the detail must again be examined in the context of the whole picture.

One such pattern frequently shapes discussions of the impact of the new astronomy and other unsettling innovations on Webster's generation. Kicking off with a quotation from Donne's *First Anniversary* ("And new Philosophy calls all in doubt, / The Element of fire is quite put out"),[10] our historian (a caricature) traces a pattern of melancholia and despair as the inevitable response of people to the crumbling of ancient philosophical foundations. Burton's *Anatomy of Melancholy* is mentioned and reference is made to the preoccupation with death in Jacobean literature of all kinds. There may even be a reference to Donne's examination of the lawfulness of suicide in *Biathanatos*. I only object to this particular patterning because, in emphasizing fearfulness as a response to the expansion of the universe, it gives us a picture as partial as the image of Webster I have been discussing.[11] If Jacobeans were sometimes distressed by their own innovations, that is only one among many moods. The Jacobeans were nothing if not moody. The fact is that they went on innovating, and there is every reason to believe that they often enjoyed it.

I would even contend that the most exciting moments in late Renaissance literature owe their existence to that dizzying sense of infinite potential that alternates with despair as the response to the disintegration of authority. When Webster's Duchess of Malfi, in defiance of the restraints dictated by custom and enforced by the power of the church and state, sets out to live her life as she thinks proper, she expresses what she is doing in a figure that unconsciously pinpoints the exploratory spirit that is one of the really defining qualities of the age:

> wish me good speed
> For I am going into a wilderness,
> Where I shall find nor path, nor friendly clewe
> To be my guide. (I, i, 402-405)[12]

The image calls to mind early seventeenth-century voyages to the American wilderness; it also suggests the uncharted moral wilder-

Introduction

nesses embarked upon by Puritan heroines in the poems of Spenser and Milton. In its most intellectual sense, the figure expresses the adventure of those who were prepared to leave behind the comfortable idolatries of the past, although they had no revolutionary program to serve as a guide to the future, or even a clear conviction that there was to be a future. Webster was one of those, at his best as an artist when in a state of inspired disorientation, in which he shared with his audience a glimpse of the latent power and beauty in much that had been proscribed by the past.

The tendency of some historians to forget that intellectual disequilibrium can be invigorating probably bears some relation to the growing dread of the future in contemporary Western society. But this false splitting of negative and positive experience is also the inner ramification of the persistence, in some quarters, of a stereotyped idea of the Puritan revolution. When it can be taken to imply that revolutionary thoughts and actions were confined to one clearly defined group, the notion of a Puritan revolution (in itself indispensable to any understanding of the period) becomes a source of fragmentation, in which the splitting of positive and negative experience is externalized in the image of two groups moving in opposite directions. The two groups are variously characterized, but a typical polarization would associate the revolutionary fragment with optimism, clean living, hard work, belief in the future, short hair, and distrust of stage plays; in addition, of course, to liberalism, parliamentarianism, Puritanism, and land enclosure. On the opposite side would be those for whom the new philosophy had called all in doubt—decadent intellectuals grappling with melancholia, smoking American tobacco (that most recent innovation of the devil), and fearing the future—together with the avowed enemies of change, the corrupt, secretly Papist, economically conservative, sensual, self-indulgent, theatre-going, long-haired Cavaliers. Of course this is another caricature. Historians always point out that there were individuals who straddled both groups, and recent historians tend to repudiate such a picture altogether. But in one variation or another, this image of early seventeenth-century England persists, especially in literary criticism.

Given this view of the revolutionary faction, it is little wonder that Webster has never been included in it. The playwrights and the Puritans, we have been told, were at opposite ends of the political spectrum. And although this commonplace of literary history has recently been seriously challenged,[13] still one finds no striking affinity with liberalism or optimism in Webster's dark tragedies. But if we looked for an exhortation to clean living in Marvell's "To His Coy Mistress," we would be similarly disappointed. And whoever it was who wrote Puritan propaganda under the name of Martin Marprelate (thereby provoking one of the most spectacular witchhunts in England's history), they would have recognized more kinship with Rabelais, or with Tarleton the stage comedian, than with William Prynne the Puritan. William Walwyn, the Puritan pamphleteer who shared with Webster an urbane scepticism that both of them perfected by reading Montaigne, is as crucial a figure in his way as the Parliamentarian, Pym. One could go on and on. Obviously, one more example is not going to resolve anything, but I hope that in demonstrating that Webster's art has strong revolutionary elements intermingled with the pessimism and the sense of horror, I will be offering another piece of evidence against any facile drawing of lines in the pre-revolutionary period. The longer I study the Jacobean period, the more I am convinced that Christopher Hill is right to stress, in his *Intellectual Origins of the English Revolution*, the disparity of elements that ultimately worked towards the same end—the destruction of the old order in church and state. For if the Calvinist doctrine of election was a threat to the authority of the ecclesiastical courts, so too was the spread of a kind of radical scepticism that led to the evolution of ideas of toleration. And if the Puritan conventicle was a good workshop for revolutionary ideas, so too, as it happens, was the study of Sir Francis Bacon, a Lord Chancellor who sometimes accepted bribes. Then, as now, people did not always recognize their natural allies, or envision the future very clearly.[14]

The *fin de siècle* view of Webster has also been subtly reinforced by the tendency of literary historians to view life in terms of the rise and fall of literary genres. The view of Webster as one of the last of the great Renaissance tragedians inevitably suggests that he was one of the last of things in general, as if the world had come to an end with the closing of the theatres in 1642. Humanly speaking, of course, it makes just as much sense to think of Webster in connection with the *political* events that were to occur in that year, some fifteen years after he wrote his last play. This is particularly so if we remember that although the theatre was already in decline in Webster's time (in that both the audience and the number of great new plays were dwindling), it continued to be of great importance to many Jacobeans. Jonson, Middleton, and Chapman were still writing plays, old favourites by Shakespeare and Marlowe were sometimes revived, and taken all in all, the theatre in Webster's time offered as fine an ongoing discussion of history, politics, and law as any thoughtful young apprentice could desire. What I am saying is that there has never existed a finer instrument for the expansion of communal consciousness than the Elizabethan-Jacobean theatre, and that it was still very much alive when Webster wrote.¹⁵ So while it is possible to see cynicism in Webster's portrait of the Cardinal in *The Duchess of Malfi* as a dissolute, hypocritical opportunist, I would insist that the clarity and force of that characterization derive from another source. For there were many in Webster's audience who would have seen this Catholic prelate as another argument in support of their growing dissatisfaction with James' pro-Catholic foreign policy. There were many who would have seen Webster's Cardinal as an archetype of all princes of the church, whatever the denomination. In the context of the pre-revolutionary period, Webster's dramatic representation of organized religion was a political statement.¹⁶

Finally, the lack of a Webster biography has certainly not encouraged critics to see him as part of a historical process. Until the recent appearance of Muriel Bradbrook's *John Webster: Citizen and Dramatist*, Webster was a writer about whom astonishingly little was known, something of a disembodied spirit. Bradbrook has been able to locate Webster squarely in the mainstream of early seventeenth-century London life.¹⁷ The importance of the book lies primarily in its reconstruction of a plausible social milieu for this scion of the merchant class who wrote plays both before and after he succeeded to the family business in 1615. The concrete image that emerges of the writer in his environment should make it easier for students of Webster to envision his values as arising out of the specific conditions of his existence (it is somehow difficult to talk about a man who lived on Cow Lane and fathered five children as one who lived in a mist). In particular, the discovery that the Webster family was engaged—literally—in the carriage trade (the Websters were coachmakers) helps us to see how he could have been simultaneously preoccupied with and distanced from life at court.

It is the aim of this study of Webster's plays to stress their vital relation to the problems that Webster's generation faced. Perhaps the most important reflection of the tensions of his age in these plays is the conflict they express between the desire of the individual will to express and fulfill itself and the conflicting demands of the public world. Like most English Renaissance dramatists, Webster was deeply concerned about the contradictions, so sharply apparent in an emerging or dying bourgeois state, between individualism and social order. His most eminent fellow playwright, Shakespeare, almost invariably reconciled this conflict in favour of social order, although the pull of individualism is felt as a primary dramatic tension throughout his work. But the years between Shakespeare's apprenticeship as a writer and Webster's first great tragedy saw a general drift away from political optimism, as England moved into economic stagnation and political paralysis. By

1610 England was experiencing the sense of constriction that typifies a pre-revolutionary situation. The growth of monopolistic control of trade and industry, the increasingly blatant assertion of the royal prerogative, the experience of the mysterious crisis pattern of a capitalist economy, and the brutal oppression of political opposition were among the factors that created an atmosphere in which it was no longer easy for a sensitive writer to express optimism about the society. As Prince Hal was replaced on the mimetic throne by Octavius Caesar, the vision of a peaceful and dynamic society, in which individuals might best express themselves by acting in harmony with the state as a whole, gave way to a sense of conflict in which the maintenance of social order could only be achieved by the sacrifice of individuality.

Shakespeare's response to this changing situation varied, but on the whole he remained consistent in vindicating, sometimes narrowly, the priority of social order. It is in *Antony and Cleopatra*, with its sympathetic rendering of the opposition between personal fulfilment in love on the one hand, and political order on the other, that we most clearly sense how difficult it has become to maintain this position. It is here, and perhaps in *Coriolanus*, that Shakespeare most sensitively captures the conflict that many people were beginning to feel between the desire to play a role in public life and the recognition that the larger political world, monopolized by an increasingly corrupt court, no longer afforded scope for the expression of personality. It was a time of retreat into the more circumscribed world of the individual psyche. This is clearly evident in the literature of the time—in Donne's celebration of the self-contained world of love, in Herbert's withdrawal into his relationship with God, in the split we find in Bacon's work between the practical man of affairs and the philosopher dreaming of worlds to come. Even in drama, the most inherently social of literary forms, we sense a retreat into the shell of self. This is expressed in the stoicism of some of the plays of Jonson, Marston, and Chapman, with their emphasis on the ability of superior individuals to detach themselves from the corruption of the world. It is also expressed in a fading of the complicated socio-political tapestry against the background of which most earlier heroes and heroines acted out their individual tragedies (the point is less true of comedy, which, on the whole, concerned itself with less dangerous arguments). Middleton remained one of the great public writers of the Jacobean period, so much so that he had to leave town for awhile when the government responded to his anti-Spanish propaganda in *A Game at Chess* by issuing a warrant for his arrest.[18] And yet his great tragedy, *The Changeling*, is set against a background barren of everything but the inarticulate cries of madmen and idiots. It is as if Shakespeare had stranded Othello and Desdemona on the Isle of Cyprus, with no way back to the order of the mainland. Antony's retreat from the world of political reality was the retreat of many members of a generation for whom the mainland of social order had ceased to exist.

I am concerned here not with the frank escapism that increasingly characterized plays written for the private theatre, but with the work of writers who clung to the notion of the theatre as a public forum. In a very broad sense, the history of the theatre from about 1600 to 1625 parallels the personal struggles of men like Donne and Bacon to live coherent lives in spite of the pressures forcing them to separate their inner and outer worlds. This same struggle forms the major dialectic of Webster's plays. While some writers were retreating, Webster was writing the tragedy of the irreconcilable contradiction between public life and personal desire.[19]

The structure of this book reflects the two sides of the dialectic. Critical discussion has generally focused on Webster's two great tragedies, *The White Devil* and *The Duchess of Malfi*, and largely ignored the other plays that Webster had a hand in writing. While this makes sense from a purely aesthetic point of view, since these plays are clearly Webster's best, it does not allow us to appreciate his struggle, as an artist and a human being, to grapple with the contradictions he faced along with other men and women of his time. What I have attempted to do here is to set off the focus on individual passion and will in the two great tragedies against the emphasis on self-sacrifice and public order in two other plays by Webster. The picture is still incomplete because it largely ignores other facets of Webster's work, most notably his role in helping Thomas Dekker develop the genre of city comedy. The reader is referred to Bradbrook for a more comprehensive coverage of Webster's minor work than will be found here.

The structure of this book also reflects what a majority of critics and scholars believe to be the order in which the plays were written.[20] If our chronology is correct, we trace a growing commitment to public order at the expense of individual and personal satisfaction. In *The White Devil*, the first play that Webster wrote without a collaborator, the orthodox arguments in favour of suppression of the individual for the sake of the community are shown to be the ideological weapons wielded by the political and religious establishment to maintain itself in power. We are made to sympathize with those individuals whose passions and aspirations force them to defy this repressive establishment. We are also made to see that their defiance can only end in their own destruction. *The Duchess of Malfi*, which followed the first tragedy by a year or two, is similarly anarchistic. Here again we see the radiant individual destroyed by those who maintain order, yet winning a kind of moral-aesthetic victory over her enemies. But here the discussion is deepened. The Duchess' victory is not only poetic; she inspires men to avenge her death and so purge the world of some of the evil that has destroyed her. The rebellion of these men comes too late to save her life, or theirs, but it suggests a response to repressive authority that had not been suggested in *The White Devil*, where rebellion is totally individualistic and therefore doomed to failure.

The dating of the two tragedies is fairly certain. We are less confident in dating the two other plays that will be discussed here. It is generally believed that the next in order is *The Devil's Law Case*, a tragi-comedy, and the only other extant play written entirely by Webster. It is not a good play, but its very faults are interesting because, as I see it, they reflect an unsuccessful attempt to work out a reconciliation with the idea of social order as necessary for human life. A more successful attempt is made in *Appius and Virginia*, a tragedy that may have been written in collaboration with Thomas Heywood.[21] In both plays, the radical individualism of *The White Devil* and *The Duchess of Malfi* is negated and the needs of the community emerge as primary. This does not, however, involve an acceptance of a social order imposed by an arbitrary, repressive government. On the contrary, it involves an affirmation of the idea of social contract and of the responsibility of individuals to struggle against tyranny by whatever means are available. In *Appius and Virginia*, the only available means turns out to be revolution. The contradiction between personality and public order is not resolved. In fact, the contradiction is intensified by the fact that political resistance forces men to give up aspects of their basic humanity. But the dialectic is clearly stated, especially in the characterization of the two rebel leaders, Virginius and Icilius, who between them embody a dramatic dialectic of order and individualism, public good and private revenge, honour and passion.

One of the clearest manifestations of Webster's philosophical relations to other thinkers of the pre-revolutionary period is the fact that in all these plays the conflict between personality and social order is largely presented as a conflict between individualism and law. In fact, throughout Webster's work there is a striking preoccupation with legal issues. One immediately thinks of the arraignment scene in *The White Devil*, a classic demonstration of what happens before the lynching. Less obvious, perhaps, is the legal dimension of *The Duchess of Malfi*, where, as I attempt to show, Webster dissects the nature of judgment in his profound study of the relationship between the Duchess and Ferdinand. *The Devil's Law Case*, as its title indicates, takes up the subject once again, and the two contrasting trial scenes in *Appius* form the crux of its revolutionary statement. Webster's repeated dramatization of the judgment situation is not just good theatre, nor is it merely a way of symbolizing oppression. It is both these things certainly, but more fundamentally it reflects his concern with legal practice and legal philosophy as key manifestations of the realities of political power.

It is in analyzing the legal details of the trial scenes and the philosophical conceptions of law that underlie Webster's rendering of legal situations that we come closest to a specific appreciation of Webster's relation to pre-revolutionary and revolutionary thought. For throughout the pre-revolutionary period, and during the revolution itself, much radical thought channeled itself into criticism of the corruption, inequalities, and paternalism of the legal system. When Cromwell told Parliament in 1656 that the "one general grievance" in the nation "is the law,"[22] he was summing up at least fifty years of hard thinking. Webster's critique of law operates on two levels. In what we assume to be the earlier plays, there is a fundamentally anarchist rejection of all law as an absurd imposition upon human nature. At the same time, there is specific criticism, especially in *The White Devil*, of aspects of the Jacobean legal system. As Webster's anarchism gives way to a sense of the need for social order, his concern with details of the legal system becomes more urgent. My main reason for including *The Devil's Law Case* in this discussion is that it contains a detailed comment on features of the legal system that were of interest to reformers of his time.[23]

Oddly enough, it is in this play, where Webster's critique of the legal system and his portrait of a just court coincide with the views of the parliamentary radicals of the period, that Webster is at his tamest. For what is most revolutionary in Webster's work is not its endorsement of the program of an emergent bourgeois ruling class, but rather (leaving aside matters of structure and style) its expression of the intellectual vision that was an aspect of the revolutionary movement in its early phase. In Webster's work the key elements of that vision—irreverence for traditional ideals and modes of thought, and a humanist sense of the individual's potential—are powerfully interwoven. This is especially so in the two great tragedies, which juxtapose the inequalities of society with the equality of individuals. The idealisms and institutions that intervene between people and a sense of their worth are stripped of their traditional rationalizations, and we are confronted with the raw human energy that is the only real source of value.

The focus of this study, then, is Webster's dramatic treatment of the theme of individualism and social order, especially as it is expressed in commentary on the philosophy and practice of law in his time. In general, my method is first to look at each play as a coherent dramatic entity and then to deal with its themes more abstractly as they relate to the issues of the day. This makes for some repetition, but I felt that too much would be lost if I merely abstracted from the plays without giving some account of the way they are actually experienced by an audience. Even so, I am aware that I have sometimes moved too flatly through the dimensions of Webster's art. My concern has been to find a way of talking about the writer as part of history without reducing the plays to reflections, or history to a backdrop. Since the two plays we presume to be later than the great tragedies are less profound in their artistic impact, in dealing with them I have felt less compunction about moving rapidly into abstraction.

Other aspects of Webster's thought will emerge as important in the course of this book, two of which I would like to introduce at this point. Robert Ornstein, in his perceptive discussion of Webster in *The Moral Vision of Jacobean Tragedy*, suggests that Webster's iconoclasm may be seen as part of a revolt against the didactic rationalism of typical Elizabethan thought:

> Webster's attitude towards philosophical questions suggests derision rather than neutrality. He presents in art the skeptical, pragmatic nominalism of the late Renaissance, the weariness with meaningless abstractions and endless debates over words. In his tragedies the Elizabethan faith in didacticism—in the moral power of words—is blown away by the first gust of violence.[24]

In this study, Webster's anti-rationalism will be emphasized, and linked with the anti-rationalist, anti-idealist philosophical movement that was one trend in Renaissance thought. Webster will be seen as related to the group of Renaissance "heretics" that Hiram Haydn has assembled under the label "counter-Renaissance," that group of "otherwise dissimilar thinkers" who "share completely an anti-intellectualistic, anti-moralistic, anti-synthetic, anti-authoritarian bias."[25] Like the men that Haydn discusses (men as different from one another as Machiavelli, Luther, and Montaigne), Webster will be seen as concerned with "practice and fact, not theory: the particular, not the universal; the intuitive or instinctive or pragmatic, not the speculative or abstract or logical."[26] In making these connections, my purpose is to suggest that in Webster's finest work there is a union between a sophisticated scepticism that he shared with some of the important thinkers of the time and a democratic humanism that was part of his heritage as a popular English playwright. The link is a pervasive and passionate anti-authoritarianism that strikes me as the most characteristic quality of Webster's mind as manifested in his plays.

Webster's rejection of the orthodox Renaissance view of reason will be considered at length. What I want to call attention to here is the way in which his philosophical anti-authoritarianism expresses itself in an aversion to the form and content of didacticism and to all venerable, reassuring, and self-evident truths. Webster's profound disbelief in the relevance of abstract principles to the subtle phenomena of life explains one of the identifying features of his playwrighting—the fact that although his plays are embroidered with satire, fine sentiments, commonplaces of moral wisdom, and other abstractions of an "ethically specific" nature, these comments do not, in themselves, serve as a guide to the action of the plays. In fact, both the satire and the *sententiae* with which Webster's plays abound can only be evaluated by the audience in the light of the motives of the character who is speaking.[27] It will then be found that satire is often the mode of expression of characters who have qualms about the evil they are engaged in and find relief in reiterating their belief that evil is the way of the world. This does not negate the truth of the satire, but it does place upon the audience the burden of deciding how much truth there is in it. Thus if Flamineo, who is his sister's pander, says fine and witty things about the inconstancy of women, we are not necessarily to take his statement as Webster's. We must see what happens in the play.

This is very important. Again and again, critics cite the statements of Flamineo, Bosola, and other characters as evidence of Webster's supposed moral and satiric commentary. But it is precisely by underlining the partiality of such characters that Webster makes one of his important statements—that the more didactic the speech is, the more suspect is the message. This is truer of the sententious statements in the plays than of the satire; for while the satirists usually have hold of at least a partial truth, those who clothe their speech in the well-worn garments of conventional wisdom are usually either out of touch with reality or up to no good. When a Websterian character clears his throat and starts to lecture, that is a cue to the audience, not to take notes, but to beware the Machiavel. What Webster demonstrates again and again is that ideals—and other abstract formulas—tend to be evasions of reality, whether they are uttered by hypocrites who are hiding their real intentions behind fine words, or by those in power who understand that traditional moral pieties help to keep people in a state of subjection, or by conservatives victimized by a reality they no longer understand and trying pathetically to hold back its flow by shoring it up with neat and formal moralisms.

Let us consider a few examples. In Act IV, scene i of *The White Devil*, the Cardinal, Monticelso, is trying to discover what his friend, Francisco de Medicis, plans to do to avenge the murder of Isabella, Francisco's sister. Francisco replies, in terms that would satisfy any right-thinking, decent Jacobean, that he must refrain from violence because his personal vendetta might plunge his entire dukedom into war:

> Shall I defye him, and impose a warre
> Most burthensome on my poore subjects neckes,
> Which at my will I have not power to end? (lines 7-9)

Monticelso protests that he did not mean anything as open as that. A nice quiet poisoning would be more like it. Francisco responds in two images drawn from elementary Renaissance political ideology:

> Free me, my innocence, from treacherous actes:
> I know ther's thunder yonder: and I'le stand,
> Like a safe vallie, which low bends the knee
> To some aspiring mountaine: since I know
> Treason, like spiders weaving nets for flies,
> By her foule worke is found, and in it dies. (lines 24-29)

It is orthodoxy rampant—the Jacobean conservative's most treasured reasons for staying in his place, dignified by stately verse and underlined by the closing couplet. But Francisco is lying. And what is worse (from the point of view of our conservative spectator), he is *not* ultimately caught in his treacherous web. The cumulative effect of this kind of ironic undercutting is to place all expressions of humane wisdom in an ambivalent light. We are forced to perceive that such expressions are rhetorical formulas that may or may not impinge upon the real world. To live according to such dicta (as Cornelia, Marcello, and Isabella do) rather than according to a pragmatically derived understanding of reality is suicidal.

Webster's sceptical attitude towards codified wisdom is the source of much of the tension-relieving humour in the plays. For example, it was a Jacobean commonplace that extravagant jealousy in a husband might result in actual infidelity in his wife. The more you try to restrict the movements of a woman, it was sensibly argued, the more she is likely to rebel. When we encounter this idea in Webster, the speaker is Flamineo, who is urging his sister Vittoria's husband to relax his jealous vigilance, presumably for this good reason, but actually so that Flamineo's patron, the Duke of Brachiano, can get at her. So it goes with smart ideas in Webster's world. As the scene goes on, the foolish husband,

Introduction 15

Camillo, puts himself entirely into the hands of Flamineo, confessing that Vittoria has not slept with him for some time and begging Flamineo to use his brotherly persuasions to get her to his (Camillo's) bed. The witty Flamineo, anxious to please his master, Brachiano, by arranging a meeting between him and Vittoria for that very night, pretends to carry out the mission with which Camillo has entrusted him.

> FLAMINEO: I have almost wrought her to it, I find her coming, but might I advise you now, for this night I would not lye with her, I would crosse her humor to make her more humble.
>
> CAMILLO: Shall I, shall I?
>
> FLAMINEO: It will show in you a supremacie of Judgment.
>
> CAMILLO: Trew, and a mind differing from the tumultuary opinion, for *quae negata grata*.
>
> FLAMINEO: Right, you are the adamant shall draw her to you, though you keepe distance off.
>
> CAMILLO: A philosophical reason. (I, ii, 154-161)

The scene is essential Webster—the silly husband who is too much of a snob to gain even our pity; the marvelous Flamineo, wasting his mind in service to the aristocracy and staving off boredom by playing with this dupe of a brother-in-law; and underlying the horseplay, the serious satire of the "philosophical" reasons that Flamineo pulls out of his hat to appeal to Camillo's image of himself as a learned man. Notice that the reasons that impress Camillo are of several kinds. First, there is the homely wisdom that Flamineo expresses in his initial speech. Then Camillo joins the game and produces a learned Latin reason. Finally, Flamineo rounds it all off with a metaphysical conceit comparing love with the action of a magnet—a "philosophical" reason in the more limited Jacobean sense of "scientific." Webster is plainly saying that there is not much difference between a homespun English-speaking ass, an educated Latin-speaking ass, and a metaphysical fool who is deluded by his own analogies.

Perhaps the zaniest expression of Webster's attitude towards "philosophy" occurs in the final act of *The Duchess of Malfi*, when the mad Ferdinand decides to lecture the dying men around him on the relativity of pain:

> the pain's nothing: paine many times is taken away with the apprehension of greater, (as the tooth-ache with the sight of a Barbor, that comes to pull it out); there's Philosophy for you. (V, v, 78-80)

It is a whirlwind tour of the consolations of philosophy, whether Christian or Stoic. Beginning with a pretentious promise to offer words that will intercede between human beings and their suffering, Ferdinand, who is not all that mad, ends by conceding, with a giggle, that the best he can offer is the assurance that it could (and probably will) be a lot worse.

Another secondary theme of this study is Webster's dramatic handling of the related subjects of marriage, the family, and the position of women. Discussing Richardson's novel, *Clarissa*, Arnold Kettle comments:

> Tragedy occurs when a situation arises which men, at the particular point in development that they have reached, are unable to solve. Such a situation in the eighteenth and nineteenth centuries—and the problem is not yet answered—was the growing consciousness of women of the necessity of their emancipation... and the inability of class society to admit such freedom without destroying something essential to itself.[28]

This contradiction was already in evidence in Webster's time. Beginning as an expression of the evolution of the family business as an economic unit, a new conception of the family was emerging to challenge older aristocratic patterns. The Puritan doctrine of the family had important implications for women in that it emphasized "the wife as helpmeet and partner in the family joint-stock, whilst insisting on children's right to choose whom they would marry."[29] In support of the new "idealized view of the relationship of love and marriage," Puritan divines denounced arranged marriages and attacked the aristocratic institution of male infidelity.[30] Some women were also finding new support for their aspirations in the democratic tendencies inherent in radical Protestant theology. If every soul had to make its own covenant with God, it followed that women too must be responsible for their lives. How could they answer for lives over which they had no control?

The controversy over women's rights which expressed itself in the pamphlet literature of Webster's time as well as in the courts of law was thus deeply related to the economic and religious movements that were bringing about changes in the Jacobean social structure. Although the consolidation of these forces into a definitively bourgeois revolution ultimately pinned women into another confining role, Webster lived at a time when the limits of this revolution had not yet been defined. Webster's great tragedies grasp both the exciting potentialities of women and the "inability of class society to admit such freedom without destroying something essential to itself." Both plays centre around the struggle of their heroines to choose their own mates. Unlike Shakespeare's comic heroines, these tragic figures cannot outwit reality. Their freedom is shown to threaten those in power, who must destroy them.

Webster's respect for women is implicit in the characterization of his female protagonists.[31] Avoiding both idealization and vilification, Webster created characters whose existence is an implicit attack on traditional stereotypes of women as patient Griseldas, disobedient shrews, or robust, fun-loving, essentially placid girls. In *The White Devil*, Webster forces us to sympathize with a heroine who apparently prompts her lover to commit murder in order to legitimize their adulterous passion. Vittoria is no Lady Macbeth. She is forceful, but she is also sexual: a passionate woman who deliberately ignites desire. And Webster defies the laws of dramaturgy by making us sympathize with both Vittoria and her victim, Brachiano's patiently suffering wife, Isabella. By violently juxtaposing Vittoria's longings and Isabella's suffering, Webster makes us aware of the tragic position of women in a man's world.

The portrait of the Duchess of Malfi is even more radical in that it lacks the element of mystery associated with the vamp. Although we first see her through male eyes (the idealizing eyes of Antonio), the Duchess emerges from otherness and asserts a palpable materiality and a convincing self. Webster calls attention to the physical reality of the Duchess in a way that few dramatists would risk. One scene is devoted to showing her on the eve of childbirth, heavy, out of breath, green with nausea. In another scene (one of the most poignant in Jacobean drama), we see her searching her head for gray hairs and vowing to make all the ladies of the court powder their hair when hers begins to whiten. It is this same woman, feminine according to the notion of the time, who later achieves a heroic dignity unsurpassed by any male figure. The differences between Vittoria and the Duchess are so great that we are inclined to miss the fact that they both suffer tragedy for the same reason: because the establishment will not permit a woman to be both independent and (whatever is considered) feminine. Given Webster's feeling for women, it is not surprising that in *Appius and Virginia* the revolt is sparked by an attempted rape, the ultimate sexist act.

Notes to Introduction

1 *Specimens of English Dramatic Poets*, quoted by Don Moore, *John Webster and His Critics, 1617-1964* (Baton Rouge: Louisiana State University Press, 1966), p. 32.
2 *John Webster and the Elizabethan Drama* (New York: John Lane, 1916), pp. 161-162.

3 Clive Hart, ed., *The White Devil* (Edinburgh: Oliver and Boyd, 1970), pp. 2-3.
4 *The Tragic Satire of John Webster* (Berkeley: University of California Press, 1955), pp. 118, 131.
5 For an interesting survey of Webster criticism before 1964 see above, note 1.
6 See, for example, D. C. Gunby, "*The Duchess of Malfi*: A Theological Approach," in Brian Morris, ed., *John Webster* (London: Ernest Benn, 1970). According to Gunby, "Webster's plays reveal... an outlook not pragmatic but dogmatic, not sceptical but fideistic. And the faith upon which Webster's world-view rests is... that of Jacobean Anglicanism" (p. 181). Peter B. Murray also places Webster clearly within a Christian framework, seeing *The White Devil* as "a brilliant burst of flame illuminating the dark face of Satan" and *The Duchess of Malfi* as a demonstration of the value of "Christian-Stoic integrity of life" (*A Study of John Webster* [The Hague: Mouton, 1969], pp. 31, 153).
7 Bogard, pp. 9, 37.
8 Anthony Trott, ed., *The White Devil* (London: Macmillan, 1966), p. xxxiv.
9 *Intellectual Origins of the English Revolution* (London: Oxford University Press, 1972), p. 291. In a brilliant theoretical essay, Franco Moretti argues that such was the function of English Renaissance tragedy generally: "the historical 'task' effectively accomplished by [tragic form] was precisely the destruction of the fundamental paradigm of the dominant culture. Tragedy disentitled the absolute monarch to all ethical and rational legitimation. Having deconsecrated the king, it thus made it possible to decapitate him" ("'A Huge Eclipse': Tragic Form and the Deconsecration of Sovereignty," in *The Power of Forms in the English Renaissance*, ed. Stephen Greenblatt [Norman, Oklahoma: Pilgrim Books, 1982], pp. 7-8).
10 *The Poems of John Donne*, ed. Sir H. Grierson (London: Oxford University Press, 1933), pp. 213-214, lines 206-208.
11 Richard Bodtke, whose book on Webster is devoted to examining the writer in just such an intellectual context as I have been caricaturing, admits, in his Foreword, that his picture of the Jacobean mentality is partial: "The seventeenth century is notable for its yeasty ferment of new ideas in strong conflict with old ones, and the permutations of these conflicts in its philosophy and art is a bewildering kaleidoscope of response and adjustment." He justifies his simplification as useful to literary criticism: "The following discussion is not offered, then, as an inclusive picture of the period. It is intentionally restricted to that complex of feelings and ideas which finds its most insistent voice in the tragic drama of the period; for the tragic drama is most closely related in its world view to those ideas which, for convenience, are herein labelled *Jacobean*" (*Tragedy and the Jacobean Temper: The Major Plays of John Webster*, Salzburg Studies in English Literature [Salzburg: Institut für Englische Sprache und Literatur, Universität Salzburg, 1972], p. 3).

This strikes me as dangerous critical procedure. Once we admit that the Jacobean *zeitgeist* is bewilderingly complex, we are under some sort of obligation to resist any easy simplification. Inevitably, Bodtke forgets the very considerable qualification expressed in the Foreword, and we find him characterizing Webster's generation as "morally disturbed" (p. 177) and asserting that "most Jacobeans" had lost their "zest for life and their certainty of salvation" (p. 84). Bodtke's book traces a real and significant aspect of Webster's work and times, but his intentional restriction of the intellectual field results in distortion.
12 All quotations of the works of Webster are from *The Complete Works of John Webster*, ed. F. L. Lucas (London: Chatto and Windus, 1927).
13 See Margot Heinemann, *Puritanism and Theatre: Thomas Middleton and Opposition Drama under the Early Stuarts* (Cambridge: Cambridge University Press, 1980).

Introduction

14 Compare Mary Fulbrook: "A multiplicity of alliances were united in their opposition to a regime of which a variety of groups disapproved; the rapid passing of this early unity rendered evident the few bases for positive agreement once the crisis had erupted and developed. The Civil Wars in England cannot simply be reduced to a 'Puritan Revolution;' but Puritanism became involved, and made important ideological and organisational contributions; because of the particular structure of the regime in which it had been able to develop in shifting and ambiguous ways" (*Piety and Politics: Religion and the Rise of Absolutism in England*, Württemberg and Prussia [Cambridge: Cambridge University Press, 1983]), p. 176.

15 If the Red Bull Theatre held three thousand people, as has been estimated, then even a single performance of a play might have been seen by one out of every seventy Londoners, if we estimate the London population at about 200,000 (the figure for the Red Bull comes from Muriel Bradbrook, *John Webster: Citizen and Dramatist* [New York: Columbia University Press, 1980], p. 120; Heinemann gives the figure for the population of London in 1600 as 180,000 [p. 4]).

16 This point is well-expressed by J. W. Lever in *The Tragedy of State* (London: Methuen, 1971): "The sons of apprentices who hissed Webster's corrupt Dukes and Cardinals on the stage defeated the Cavalier armies in the field." Lever, who sees Jacobean tragedy "as a product of the intellectual ferment and spiritual upheaval which preceded the first great European revolution" (p. vii), was the first critic to place Webster in the pre-revolutionary context. His brief commentary on *The White Devil* and *The Duchess of Malfi*, though both original and provocative, has had little visible impact on Webster studies.

A more recent attempt to politicize discussion of Webster and his contemporaries is to be found in Jonathan Dollimore's *Radical Tragedy: Religion, Ideology and Power in the Drama of Shakespeare and his Contemporaries* (Brighton, Sussex: The Harvester Press, 1984). Dollimore's important and ambitious book constitutes an effort to correct a critical tendency to see Renaissance people as uniformly hog-tied by the Great Chain of Being. *The White Devil* is among the works singled out as radical. Since Dollimore's book appeared too late to affect my own work, I can only urge the reader to see it as complementary—especially in its concern with theory of ideology—to what I have attempted here.

17 Bradbrook's work benefits from the biographical research of Mary Edmond, as reported in "In Search of John Webster" (*Times Literary Supplement*, Dec. 24, 1976) and of Marc Eccles, in a letter to the same publication dated Jan. 21, 1977.

18 Gerald E. Bentley, *The Jacobean and Caroline Stage* (Oxford: Clarendon Press, 1941-68), vol. I, pp. 11-12.

19 The importance of this theme in Webster has been discussed by Robert Griffin, in what seems to me the most valuable of the Salzburg studies of Webster (*John Webster: Politics and Tragedy*, Salzburg Studies in English Literature [Salzburg: Institut für Englische Sprache und Literatur, Universität Salzburg, 1972]). Griffin focuses on the political dimension of Webster's art, and his conclusions parallel mine at some key points. But because the framework for his examination is that of political philosophy utterly divorced from historical events, far too much emphasis is placed, I feel, upon the influence of Machiavelli and far too little upon the actual conditions of existence in Webster's England.

20 For information on chronology, the reader is referred to Bradbrook. In dating *The White Devil* in 1612, *The Duchess of Malfi* in 1613 and *The Devil's Law*

Case in 1617 she does not depart from the general consensus of earlier scholars, give or take a year or two. G. E. Bentley takes a minority position in dating *The Devil's Law Case* before the two great tragedies (V, 1239ff.). The most difficult play to date is *Appius and Virginia*. There is a general feeling among scholars that the play was written either very early or very late in Webster's career (either before 1609 or after 1623), and there is a slight preference for the later period, but the evidence is not conclusive. Bradbrook favours 1622 and Fernand Lagarde argues fairly convincingly for a late dating (*John Webster* [Toulouse: Publications de la Faculté des Lettres et Sciences Humaines, 1968], pp. 278-281).

21 Most modern scholars accept the partial attribution to Heywood, even though his name does not appear with Webster's on the title page of the first edition (1654). However, cf. Bentley (V, 1247), who thinks that the attribution to Heywood is based on "simple impressionism."

22 Quoted by Hill, *Intellectual Origins*, p. 262. It seems likely that Webster studied law at the Middle Temple, which would help to account for his detailed knowledge (see Bradbrook, ch. 2).

23 Here I must indicate the wide divergence between my methods and conclusions and those of the only other Webster critic who deals extensively with law in Webster's plays. Ralph Berry, in *The Art of John Webster* (Oxford: Clarendon Press, 1972), defines *law* very broadly as "a simple retributive mechanism that punishes wrongdoers, as the ineluctable fate that awaits a sinful humanity. and as a moral and ethical code of human conduct—a central, albeit unfulfilled ideal" (p. 80). So conceived, law is found to be at odds with evil, the resulting tension being central to the three plays Berry studies, *The White Devil*, *The Duchess of Malfi*, and *The Devil's Law Case*. Given this rather ethereal definition, Berry does not concern himself at all with the theory and practice of law either in Webster's time or in Webster's plays. My own concern here is with positive human-made law, which I do not find to be in any clear-cut opposition to evil.

24 *The Moral Vision of Jacobean Tragedy* (Madison, Wisc.: University of Wisconsin Press, 1960), p. 34. It is interesting that in his recent definition of revolution, Perez Zagorin makes a point of including linguistic along with physical violence: "With violence in this fundamental sense [i.e., "force and coercion"]... we can also associate what may be called 'symbolic violence'—blasphemies in gesture, speech, and writing that, in deliberate transgression and reversal of prevailing social norms, are intended to destroy the sanctity or prestige of ruling persons and institutions and to proclaim the equality or superiority of subjects, the inferior, or the oppressed" (*Rebels and Rulers, 1500-1660* [Cambridge: Cambridge University Press, 1982], vol. I, p. 19).

25 Hiram Haydn, *The Counter-Renaissance* (New York: Scribner, 1960), p. xiii.

26 Ibid., p. xvi.

27 R. W. Dent, who has made a thorough study of Webster's *sententiae*, comes to the same conclusion. "When the totality of the play implies the contrary," he says, "we should not assume that Webster meant to imply any agreement with the cynical sententiae he borrowed for his malcontents, any more than we should feel that Shakespeare thought life 'a tale told by an idiot'" (*John Webster's Borrowing* [Berkeley: University of California Press, 1960], p. 30). More recently, Lee Bliss has studied Webster's subtle counterpointing of conflicting viewpoints in *The World's Perspective: John Webster and the Jacobean Drama* (New Brunswick, New Jersey: Rutgers University Press, 1983).

28 *An Introduction to the English Novel* (London: Hutchinson, 1951), vol. I, p. 66. I find Kettle's formulation more accurate than Juliet Dusinberre's contention

Introduction

that "the Elizabethan and Jacobean periods bred the conditions of a feminist movement" (*Shakespeare and the Nature of Women* [London: Macmillan, 1975], p. 80).
29 Hill, *Intellectual Origins*, p. 273.
30 Lawrence Stone, *The Crisis of the Aristocracy* [Oxford: Oxford University Press, 1967), p. 280. See Stone's whole discussion of this subject on pp. 269ff. In a recent study of the continuities and discontinuities between medieval and Renaissance ideas about women, Ian Maclean finds "a shift in emphasis from Scholastic to Renaissance" theological discussions of matrimony. In the latter, there is "a reassessment . . . which sets aside the Scholastics' grudging justification of marriage as a cure for concupiscence . . . and lays greater emphasis on its comfort and companionship" (*The Renaissance Notion of Woman* [Cambridge: Cambridge University Press, 1980], p. 19).
31 Webster's sympathy with women has been noted by Roger Stilling: "Fascination with woman is probably the basis of the whole complex evolution that made love a central concern of English Renaissance drama. But Webster is appreciatively fascinated, almost to the point of being a feminist" (*Love and Death in Renaissance Tragedy* [Baton Rouge, Louisiana: Louisiana State University Press, 1976], p. xx). Webster figures prominently in Simon Shepherd's *Amazons and Warrior Women: Varieties of Feminism in Seventeenth Century Drama* (New York: St. Martin's Press, 1981), the only feminist study of English Renaissance drama that does not focus on Shakespeare, and a book brimming over with insight and ideas. For students of Webster, chapter 8 is especially useful in that it sketches part of the literary context of Webster's major tragedies.

Chapter One

The White Devil: Law and the Challenge of Human Nature

I
Nature and Law

> Cupid is a treacherous god; he makes it his sport to wrestle with piety and justice; he glories in the fact that his power clashes with every other power and that all other rules yield to his.
>
> Montaigne

The White Devil is the tragedy of a society whose most brilliant and attractive people can find no honourable outlet for their creative energies. The main protagonists, Vittoria and her brother Flamineo, are alike in that in struggling to fulfill themselves—to impress their rich and potent personalities on the world—they are forced to commit illegal and immoral actions that ultimately lead to their own destruction. The ties that bind Vittoria are typical of her time. She is the victim of a marriage arranged by her family in a futile effort to reverse the trend of economic decline initiated by a spendthrift father. The strong implicit critique of arranged marriages is reinforced by the fact that Vittoria's lover, the Duke of Brachiano, is similarly trapped in a politically advantageous marriage to the sister of Francisco de Medicis. The attraction between these two frustrated people is inevitable. For Vittoria, especially, the attraction to Brachiano is an assertion of her own worth and of a capacity for life that, in all respects, cannot be satisfied by a man so inadequate as her husband, Camillo. The marriage between this charming, knowledgeable, high-spirited woman and the silly, impotent Camillo has (in Jacobean terms) offended the natural order in which like seeks out like; and in Vittoria's behaviour we see the inevitable struggle of nature to rectify the imbalance. The tragic paradox of her life is that her magnificent life force can only express itself in death—in the murder of the two people who stand in the way of marriage with Brachiano, and consequently, in her own destruction.

Flamineo, too, is blocked by a discrepancy between his aspirations and the means available for their fulfilment. Raised and educated as a gentleman (in spite of the dwindling resources of his family), Flamineo is caught between upper class expectations and the realities of the job market. When we meet him he has long since learned that public service, for the talented but poor, means subservience to the caprices and corruptions of the great men who constitute the state. For all his brilliance and his energy and his Latin, he can never hope to achieve any greater dignity than what is accorded to the Duke of Brachiano's personal lackey. The alternative is represented in the play by Flamineo's brother Marcello, a professional soldier; Flamineo likes to remind him that he is mere cannon fodder for the Duke. The church, that last outlet for genteel energies, is far from Flamineo's thoughts. When the Duke obligingly falls in love with Flamineo's sister, Vittoria, the young man sees a chance to gamble for the recovery of his class position. The bitterness with which Flamineo assumes the honourable office of pander is revealed in his answer to his mother's horrified rebuke:

> I would faine know where lies the masse of wealth
> Which you have hoarded for my maintenance,
> That I may beare my beard out of the level
> Of my Lord's Stirop. (I, ii, 304-307)

The feverish hysteria that dominates him towards the end of the play, as he stakes more and more on a dwindling chance of success, is the hysteria of the gambler who is playing for all or nothing. Flamineo is not blind to the odds against him. But he chooses to gamble at suicidal odds rather than reconcile himself to a loss of class status that for him is another form of death.

If Flamineo chooses to gamble, he is behaving like a true member of his class at a time when gambling fever was epidemic among the English upper classes. The highest stakes were to be won at court, where, as Lawrence Stone puts it, "the spectacular wealth that still came to the successful few blinded the many to the length of the odds against them." Stone estimates roughly that for members of the lower gentry (Flamineo's position) the odds would be thirty to one against success.[1] Flamineo is caught in a complicated historical situation. Throughout the sixteenth century, humanist education, supported by the experience of Henry VIII's reign, stressed service to the state as a gentlemanly ideal. The ideal served well during a period of rapid centralization, bringing an ever-increasing proportion of those who aspired into direct dependence upon the court. By the 1580s, in Stone's words, "the key to advancement lay at the Court, which... developed into the unique market-place for the distribution of an enormous range of offices, favours, and titles." What should have followed next was the development of a full-scale bureaucracy, but that was not to happen until later. As a result, an increasing number of well-educated young men, eager to serve the state in a lucrative and honourable capacity, found that they were a glut on the market. As competition grew fiercer, and as "the Crown's control of... powers of nomination slipped more and more into the hands of courtiers,"[2] the chances of a down-at-heels suitor like Flamineo were approaching the vanishing point.

In other words, the court was not exempt from the capitalization of master-servant relations that was taking place at all levels of society. In fact, during the reign of James, when the King and his best friends were trafficking on a large scale in titles of honour, the court was a centre for the exchange of human value into money. *The White Devil* expresses Webster's perception of the irrelevance of lingering ideals of courtly reward for honourable service in a period when relationships at court were based no longer on feudal service (or, as in Henry's time, on an alliance between the monarch and the gentry), but rather on competition in a labour market that heavily favoured the men at the very top. Webster's point of view is partly satiric. From beginning to end, the play weaves endless variations on the theme of the illusions and realities of life at court. But beyond bitterness and scorn there is sorrow, a tragic sense that the best minds of the generation are being wasted. It is the tragedy that occurs when the early capitalist sense of human potential comes into conflict with a constricting, static ordering of society.

The plight of Vittoria and Flamineo is very much the plight of the pre-revolutionary generation. Discussing the life of Sir Walter Raleigh, Christopher Hill concludes that "the frustration, the sense of great potentialities and small achievements, was only in part personal and temperamental; it was also an expression of the spirit of Raleigh's age."[3] Other examples immediately come to mind—John Donne, who also gambled on a marriage, and Thomas Hobbes, who thought dark thoughts about the aristocracy while running errands for the Earl of Devonshire.[4] It is significant that Stone finds a similar pattern of frustrated ambition in the lives of the rebels of 1601 and 1603.[5]

In *The White Devil*, the sense of waste is primarily expressed in the paradox of a life force that can only create death; and that life force is most significantly represented by the passion of Vittoria and Brachiano. Towards the end of the courting scene (I, ii), Flamineo's mind dwells, for a moment, on the naturalness of the passion he has been observing. Detached and cynical, Flamineo finds neither beauty nor love in the magnetic force drawing his sister and the Duke together. But because he sees sexual passion as a natural and necessary expression of an animal nature, he questions laws created to curb it:

> *Lycurgus* wondred much, men would provide
> Good stalions for their Mares, and yet would suffer
> Their faire wives to be barren. (I, ii, 336-338)

Here Flamineo is echoing an essay by Montaigne that Webster returns to for material several times in *The White Devil*. Montaigne states that "it is not enough that a man's will should carry straight. Weakness and incapacity legitimately break up a marriage." As an excuse for female infidelity, Montaigne urges the argument that, although women's appetites at least equal men's, wives have no way of knowing in advance whether their husbands' capacities will be great enough to satisfy them; or, to put it in his own apt phrase, when women marry, "they but a cat in a bag."[6] It is unfair of men, he argues, to define as criminal a passion which is naturally strong in women and which all their training serves to pinpoint as the essence of their lives. "Both we and they are capable of a thousand corruptions more harmful and unnatural than lasciviousness. But we create and weigh vices not according to nature."[7]

Montaigne's irreverent assault on the holy ideology of male superiority, with its corollaries of female submission and strict chastity, is echoed by Webster in *The White Devil*. Drama is indirect, and *The White Devil* especially so. And yet Webster obviously took pains to make certain things clear. We may be unsure of the extent of Vittoria's involvement in the two murders committed by Brachiano. Indeed, some degree of mystification seems to have been part of Webster's intent in characterizing Vittoria. But we cannot doubt that her actions are precipitated by the fact that she is saddled with an inadequate husband. That is the function of the vastly exaggerated figure of Camillo (as Roma Gill puts it, Camillo is the only character in the play who "elicits a response that is unfalteringly straightforward from first to last")[8]; that is why Webster portrays him at length just before the courting scene. As spectators, we may be tricked into feeling that Camillo is in the play to amuse us. We may not see that, in laughing at Camillo, we are implicitly asking the question: what is a woman to do with such a man?

The answer is given in the courting scene, as the grand, solemn ritualism of Brachiano's wooing of Vittoria overrides Flamineo's salacious counterpoint, conveying to the audience a sense of the inevitability of consummation:

> Let me into your bosome happy Ladie,
> Powre out, in stead of eloquence my vowes—
> Loose me not Madam, for if you forego me,
> I am lost eternallie. (I, ii, 195-98)

The last line, with its implication of the doctrine of salvation, expresses an almost religious obeisance to sexual love. Cupid is the god that matters in this play.

The relentless power of nature in the face of apparently insurmountable social barriers is strikingly expressed by Flamineo as he perceives Brachiano's determination to proceed at any cost:

> Wee are ingag'd to mischiefe and must on.
> As Rivers to finde out the Ocean
> Flow with crooke bendings beneath forced bankes,
> Or as wee see to aspire some mountaines top,
> The way ascends not straight, but Imitates
> The subtle fouldings of a Winters snake,
> So who knowes policy and her true aspect,
> Shall finde her waies winding and indirect. (I, ii, 341-348)

In this dynamic simile, Flamineo is expressing more than a characterization of "policy," for the image of the mountain-path and, even more obviously, the image of the river seeking out the ocean refer to the motivating force behind policy; that is, to the passion of the lovers. The simile is complex. What links the richly sexual image of the natural flow of rivers with the image of human aspiration is the implied statement that natural obstacles can be overcome by a combination of implacability and compliance. Rivers do not destroy what lies in their path—they mould it and are moulded by it. But the obstacles that bar the lovers' way are not natural, they are social. And so compliance becomes "policy"; and implacability, because it cannot mould, must destroy. Nature cannot be crushed, but, as a popular saying puts it, it can be made to "creep" where it cannot "go."

The tragedy that attends the consummation of the love between Brachiano and Vittoria is brought about by an irreconcilable conflict between nature and the social milieu in which nature seeks to manifest itself. The laws and the men opposed to the lovers are as responsible for the catastrophe as the lovers themselves. Here again, Webster echoes Montaigne: "The severity of our decrees makes women's addiction to this vice more exacerbated and vicious than its nature calls for, and involves it in consequences that are worse than their cause."[9] The social codes governing marriage (and, as the Cardinal implies, the willingness of the Corombonas to resuscitate their fortune by selling their daughter [III, ii, 246]) trap Vittoria in a relationship she never chose for herself. And the interference of those who are intent upon upholding these codes impels the lovers to take steps to secure themselves. When Brachiano furiously attacks Vittoria's mother, Cornelia, for interfering with his seduction of Vittoria, he warns her that she is now to blame for "all ensuing harme" (I, ii, 300). This is not an idle expression of anger, but an attack upon the philosophy of respectability which—because Vittoria is not impervious to it—now forces him to commit more harmful acts in order to satisfy his desire. To spare Vittoria the opprobrium of adultery, he must commit the crime of murder. Cornelia's interference at this point may or may not be decisive for the action that follows. In either case, it is an example of the kind of social pressure against which Brachiano and Vittoria must struggle. What we sense above all in Brachiano's accusation here is frustration over a passion that is hemmed in on all sides by marriage and divorce laws, mores, and considerations of family honour. As the pressure increases, the passions finds increasingly devious and destructive means for its expression. To Cornelia's statement that "violent lust" is the origin of the catastrophe (I, ii, 210), we must oppose Brachiano's accusation of Cornelia, if we are to see how the tragedy comes about.[10]

In *The White Devil*, natural passion, whatever its moral worth, is demonstrated to be beyond the reach of the laws created to curb it. Brachiano expresses the futility of law with respect to love when he renounces Isabella, and she echoes him in expanded form:

> And this divorce shall be as truly kept,
> As if in thronged Court, a thousand eares
> Had heard it, and a thousand Lawyers hands
> Seal'd to the separation. (II, i, 258-261)

Nor is law merely futile, or neutral, for it is worse than unrealistic. In its imposition of a rational ideal upon a human factor which has nothing to do with rationality, it renders natural passion more harmful.

The dominant legal philosophy of Webster's age has been characterized as a belief that law is "a reflection of the divine reason governing the universe; a reflection of that part which determines the 'ought' addressed by that reason to human beings as moral entities."[11] In *The White Devil* Webster clearly challenges this conception of law on the grounds that human beings are apparently not moral entities, and that the 'ought' of reason only creates havoc when applied to the reality of human nature. He goes further. He suggests that the failure of this philosophy is due to the fact that what passes for reason has nothing of the divine about it, but is itself corrupt and destructive, more destructive than nature without benefit of reason and its laws.

The core of this attack in *The White Devil* upon human reason and the laws that it creates and enforces is an irony characteristic of Webster at his most sardonic. Its most important manifestation is the conflict between Brachiano and Vittoria, on the one hand, and the Cardinal and Francisco, on the other. When we are first introduced to the Cardinal and Francisco, they impress us favourably, unless we are sensitively attuned to Webster's sceptical attitude towards sententious speeches. If we are not, we probably respond positively to the Cardinal's first speech; for if its moralism and its rhetorical manner are rather musty, it nonetheless seems to express honest concern for Brachiano:

> It is a wonder to your noble friends,
> That you that have as 'twere entred the world,
> With a free Sceptre in your able hand,
> And have to th'use of nature well applyed
> High gifts of learning, should in your prime-age
> Neglect your awfull throne, for the soft downe
> Of an insatiate bed. Oh my Lord,
> The Drunkard after all his lavish cuppes,
> Is dry, and then is sober—so at length,
> When you awake from this lascivious dreame,
> Repentance then will follow; like the sting
> Plac't in the Adder's tayle: wretched are Princes
> When fortune blasteth but a petty flower
> Of their unweldy crownes; or ravesheth
> But one pearle from their Scepter: but alas!
> When they to wilfull shipwrake loose good Fame
> All Princely titles perish with their name. (II, i, 27-43)

In both style and content, it is just the sort of speech we would expect a cardinal to deliver under the circumstances. Francisco, too, answers our expectations by demonstrating appropriate concern for his sister, Isabella. And like the Cardinal, he expresses common wisdom when he deprecates Brachiano's passion for Vittoria as evanescent.

At the end of the scene, though, the author shocks us by revealing the depths of evil in these characters. Having sent Camillo (who is the Cardinal's nephew) out of town on a pretext, the Cardinal and Francisco are finally alone on the stage. The rationalizing habit persists, but the rags of self-justification finally fall away, revealing their naked selves. And the audience suddenly realizes that these two pillars of church and state are not really interested in correcting the situation after all, but, on the contrary, are luridly delighted at the prospect of Brachiano's downfall and totally unconcerned about the fate of Camillo:

> FRANCISCO: I faine would have the Duke Brachiano run
> Into notorious scandale, for their's nought
> In such curst dotage, to repaire his name,
> Onely the deepe sence of some deathlesse shame.
>
> MONTICELSO: It may be objected I am dishonourable,
> To play thus with my kinsman, but I answere,
> For my revenge I'de stake a brothers life,
> That being wrong'd durst not avenge himselfe.
>
> FRANCISCO: Come to observe this Strumpet.
>
> MONTICELSO: Cursse of greatnes,
> Sure hee'le not leave her.
>
> FRANCISCO: There's small pitty in't—
> Like mistle-tow on seare Elmes spent by weather,
> Let him cleave to her and both rot together.
>   (II, i, 382-393)

Revelation of the destructiveness of these characters continues as the play progresses, so that although at the beginning of the play we are convinced of the wickedness of Vittoria and Brachiano, by the end we probably prefer them (judging by the reactions of critics) to their persecutors. Employing a common dramatic device in an intense way, Webster forces us to switch sides, and, in so doing, to recognize the shallowness of our original impressions of the Cardinal and Francisco.[12]

Part of this shallowness lies in our initial response to these characters' view of natural desire. Webster forces us to re-evaluate our attitudes towards reason and passion (attitudes deeply ingrained in his audience) by making us realize that Brachiano and Vittoria, whatever their guilt, are neither perverse nor grotesque. This is more than can be claimed for the proponents of reason who, failing in their lukewarm efforts to perpetuate the form (they care nothing about the content) of the marriages in which the protagonists, as well as their own relations, are trapped, move with alacrity to the next phase of action—vengeance on those who have allowed emotions to supersede considerations of worldly profit and family pride. Webster simplifies the issue by ignoring the Medici Duke's reputation in real life for sexual intrigue. His characterization of Francisco clarifies, for dramatic purposes, the conflict he is presenting between vulnerability to passion and worldly success. For, after all, the words of wisdom uttered by the Cardinal and Francisco have a limited truth. Brachiano does fall because of passion, whereas the Cardinal and the Duke are both capable of maintaining their positions of power. The irony lies in the evaluation of these qualities, in our ultimate preference for those who destroy themselves by yielding to desire over those who do not permit their passions to interfere with business.

Nor is this really a matter of choosing between a lesser and a greater evil, for whatever is attractive about Brachiano is directly related to his dedication to passion. This is a direct contradiction of Francisco's chastisement of Brachiano for failing to control his animal nature: "a good habite makes a child a man, / Whereas a bad one makes a man a beast"[13] (II, i, 140-141). Ironically, it is his very devotion to passion above duty, or above anything, that enables Brachiano to transcend, to some extent, the morally neutral world he inhabits, by defining value as the freely chosen, equal relationship between a man and a woman. For the same emotion that causes him to murder his wife also forces him to abandon everything for Vittoria, a woman far beneath him in station and entirely dependent upon his good will for the fulfilment of her ambition to be his duchess:

> I'le seate you above law and above scandall;
> Give to your thoughts the invention of delight
> And the fruition; nor shall government
> Divide me from you longer then a care
> To keepe you great: you shall to me at once,
> Be Dukedom, health, wife, children, friends and all.
> (I, ii, 253-258)

What is perhaps most remarkable about this speech in the context of the play is that Brachiano means it, as the ensuing action proves.

The attitude towards love shared by Francisco and the Cardinal provides the definition of "reason" in the world of *The White Devil*. Were Brachiano as circumspect as they, he would keep Vittoria in her place and his own animal nature in its place. It is helpful to compare Francis Bacon on the same subject:

> They do best, who if they cannot but admit love, yet make it keep quarter, and sever it wholly from their serious affairs and actions of life, for if it check once with business, it troubleth men's fortune, and maketh men that they can no ways be true to their own ends.[14]

What man's ends are is made abundantly clear when Bacon says that "whosoever esteemeth too much of amorous affection quitteth

The White Devil: *Law and Human Nature*

both riches and wisdom."[15] Although Francisco and the Cardinal avail themselves of the rhetoric of idealism associated with the philosophical tradition of Aquinas and Hooker, the rhetoric is deceptive rather than expressive, masking the simple Baconian pragmatism that constitutes the real basis of their actions. For them, reason has been stripped of its traditional ethical and metaphysical associations and reduced to a means for the achievement of worldly goals. Reason must control passion, not because that arrangement places humanity closer to the angels, but because uncontrolled passion interferes with business. That is the only kind of reason operative in the world of the play, and to Webster it is antithetical to whatever poetry and beauty there may be in life. The very "hyperbole" that Bacon condemns as the natural and foolish language of love[16] is what raises some of the speeches of Brachiano above the generally nervous and cynical tone of the play.

In this sense, *The White Devil* echoes *Antony and Cleopatra*, in which, perhaps significantly, Shakespeare's often firm ethic gives way before a conflict that admits no resolution.[17] Brachiano and Antony are parallel figures in their sacrifice of statesmanship, power, martial glory, and a politically advantageous marriage to a dominating passion for a morally ambiguous, perpetually interesting woman. The justification of that passion, if it requires any justification beyond the fact that it must be, is simply its fulfilment; and the incomplete humanity of those like Octavius, the Cardinal, and Francisco, who are devoid of sexual passion. Whatever doubts Flamineo or anyone else has about the value of such passion, it is demonstrated to be a tremendous force, overcoming the scepticism and hostility of the world and the temptation to succumb to the world's point of view. Brachiano and Vittoria falter for a moment (IV, ii), just as Antony falters at times, allowing the world to rush in upon his consciousness and condition his view of Cleopatra. But this is temporary. The outside world is overcome, spiritually if not physically; Vittoria is not a whore; Brachiano does not repent his faith in her; she is not a coward snivelling over her lost purity, but a courageous sinner once again. If Flamineo is right, and this love is an illusion, it is an illusion that brings another reality into being; for it is capable of infusing into the egotistical Brachiano both the humanity and poetry to think of Vittoria as he is dying:

> Where's this good woman? had I infinite worlds,
> They were too little for thee. Must I leave thee? (V, iii, 18-19)

Thus, in Webster's portrayal of the opposition between those who are impelled by natural urges and those who stand for the subordination of such urges to reason and law, a moral preference is implied. Amorality is opposed to a morality which is utterly corrupt. For reason, in the world of *The White Devil*, far from representing the divine in humanity, is a tool with which the strong maintain themselves in power. This is the chief irony, that the staunch defenders of law and morality are ultimately exposed as destroyers. Once again, Montaigne's essay can be detected in the background: "We see that in places where faults are crimes, crimes are faults; that in nations where the laws of propriety are rarer and looser, the primitive and common laws are better observed."[18] Those who are so anxious to chastise Brachiano for his offenses against the laws of sexual morality do not stop to weigh their own actions in the light of the much more primitive and essential laws against the taking of human life; for their impulse, from the very beginning, is to destroy.

A subtle and moving variation on the theme of law and natural affection is embodied in Cornelia's predicament when she has to cope with the killing of one of her sons by the other. Her grief over the dead Marcello does not move her to avenge herself on the cause of that grief—much to the surprise of a vengeance-oriented court—because the stronger maternal impulse is to protect her remaining son, although he has violated all her notions of law and morality:

> One arrow's graz'd allready; it were vaine
> T'lose this: for that will nere be found againe. (V, ii, 67-68)

Cornelia is not expressing a thought; she is simply giving voice to a natural impulse that has overcome an otherwise inflexible social code. And the breakdown of this code, the destruction of a sense of right and justice that has been the chief support of her personality, leads to madness. Cornelia is the only one among the representatives of righteousness whose values are challenged in the course of the play. The absolute clash between law and nature which enacts itself within this single human being leaves her a crumpled wreck so pitiable that even Flamineo is moved.

Nature's challenge to law in *The White Devil* takes two forms. Webster demonstrates that law is ineffectual in relation to nature. Further, he poses the question whether nature is not, in itself, more benign than the laws that corrupt human reason creates, since those laws present restriction and destruction of life as their only solution to human problems. The play is not a paean to nature. But it is significant that the most attractive figure of the play, its dubious heroine, is the character who most wilfully blinds herself to everything but her own fulfilment in "that which was made for Man, / The world" (V, 63-64). Her self-love, her single-minded drive to live fully, her appreciation of the body as the "goodly pallace of the soule" (V, vi, 58) locate her as the most formidable of nature's champions in the play, an embodiment of the will to survive. This is not the grim survival of the Cardinal, but a survival of the whole self, expressing itself in a constant striving towards that which is not yet attained. Paradoxically, Vittoria's failure to repress her natural self ultimately leads to her total destruction. For society, as Webster sees it here, is essentially opposed to life, so that self-control alone is victorious, and impulsiveness of any kind is a form of self-destruction.[19]

Madeleine Doran has stated that some of the "confusions" in Webster and other Jacobean dramatists stem from a failure to assimilate or choose between two ethical patterns in their plays, one blaming fate for the hero's fall, the other placing responsibility "on his free choice of the dictates of passion rather than of reason."[20] The characters in *The White Devil* who choose passion do not seem to have reason, or *right* reason, as an alternative. Rather, they have to choose between passion and law. Nor is it a free choice, for nature asserts itself in spite of human attempts to subdue it. The result, I think, is not all confusion. Passion and reason are evaluated in a fresh way, and the tragedy lies in the necessary and paradoxical self-destructiveness, in Webster's world, of the drive to live.

II
Justice Without Reason

Elizabethans rationalized the administration of justice in the same way that they explained the function of laws. The idealized human animal whose innate reason was supposed to respond sympathetically to the imperatives of law had its counterpart in an ideal judge who was supposed to subordinate all personal interests and emotions to an ideal of rational justice. Just as man-made law was expected to reflect the eternal truths of the laws of nature and of God, the earthly courtroom was expected to approximate, within human limits, the court of Heaven.[21] Judges, said Bacon, "should imitate God, in whose seat they sit."[22] In an optimistic (or rhetorical) mood Montaigne wrote: "No one would hesitate to punish with death a judge who had condemned his criminal through anger.... It is no longer correction it is vengeance."[23] Webster himself gave voice to this commonplace idea of selfless, rational judgment in his prose Character of an ideal judge: "A Reverend Judge hates to wrong any man; neither hope, nor despaire of preferment can draw him to such an exigent: he thinks himself then most honourably seated, when he gives mercy the upper hand."[24]

The fact that judges often fell short of these expressed standards—that Bacon himself accepted bribes and that judges were capable of tremendous displays of vindictiveness towards a defendant—did not invalidate the standards themselves. Idealism defends itself by readily admitting that the flesh is weak. What did undermine the ideal was the fact that it existed side by side with an equally marked tendency to think of law as a form of vengeance, a tendency that was reinforced by certain prominent features of the legal system itself.

Legal historians emphasize the lasting effect of vendetta law upon the English system of criminal law:

> The fact that the private vengeance of the person wronged by a crime was the principal source to which men trusted for the administration of criminal justice in early times is one of the most characteristic circumstances connected with English criminal law, and has had much to do with the development of what may perhaps be regarded as its principal distinctive peculiarity, namely, the degree to which a criminal trial resembles a private litigation.[25]

In Jacobean times, the line between personal redress and legal remedies was still hazy. A century earlier, the Crown had begun to evolve an effective system of public prosecution for criminal cases, but an alternative method of procedure still existed, in which the injured party (in the case of murder, the nearest relative) took sole responsibility for proving the case against the suspect. In this kind of process, the accused could choose as the mode of defence the ancient wager of battle.[26] The persistence of this medieval form alongside the newer, more impersonal method of public prosecution is one of the more spectacular evidences of the fact that "the ancient connection between private vengeance and public prosecution" had hardly been severed in Jacobean times.[27] It is little wonder that dueling, open assault, and forcible entry on claimed lands continued to be common Jacobean events, in spite of stern governmental measures to curb them,[28] when the law itself authorized personal redress in the form of the wager of battle. This contradiction within the law was further exacerbated by the fact that the government was forced to legalize personal redress in sections of the country where its own powers were inadequate to maintain order.[29]

The penal code was another striking embodiment of the concept of law as vengeance. It has been estimated that as many as eight hundred people were hanged in England every year.[30] (The total population was under five million.)[31] Nor was this simply accepted as one of the many dreary facts of life. The significance of these figures for a sensitive person of the time can only be appreciated when one is aware that enlightened penal philosophy was already a reality in the time of James; that Coke and other members of Parliament were talking about reducing penalties on the grounds that the death penalty was not an effective deterrent.[32]

The ideal of judgment as detached and rational was further undermined by the combative nature of trial procedure in the period; for, in fact, there was no clear distinction between the functions of the judge and the prosecuting attorney. Judges participated in pretrial examination of witnesses and collection of evidence, and they were prepared to play a prosecutive role during the trial itself by means of constant cross-examination of witnesses and even by stepping down from the bench and giving evidence themselves.[33] "Judicial duty, in the year 1603," says Catherine Bowen, "meant bringing forward every damaging fact of character and circumstance which could be gathered in the King's favor." This was especially true in cases that particularly interested the state. "Ralegh's judges," as she points out, "plainly were part of the prosecution, determined from the start to prove the prisoner guilty."[34] The fact that disinterested objectivity was not the functioning judicial ideal in this period is perhaps most clearly manifest in the lack of any rules to prevent a judge from sitting in a case in which he had a personal interest.[35]

In part, *The White Devil* is a highly sensitive reaction to these contradictions. The idealized judge of the prose *Characters*, who embodies one tendency of Jacobean legal thought, has no place in the irrational world of the play. Instead, there is the figure of the Cardinal, angry, biased, merciless—an embodiment of the legalized vendetta. For the ideal of rational judgment is unattainable in a world in which reason is corrupt, and lacking such a rational basis, judgment is actually motivated by anger or hatred. One of the important functions of the arraignment scene is to demonstrate the link between organized, legal revenge and pure revenge, for the same characters and motives are involved in both forms of action. Vittoria's demand that the Cardinal choose between the roles of accuser and judge calls attention to the prosecutive nature of the Cardinal's judicial behaviour. And Flamineo, with the arraignment fresh in his mind, refers, in another context, to the hypocritically rationalized hatred which underlies justice:

>   if you will be merry,
> Do it i' th' like posture, as if some great man
> Sate while his enemy were executed;

> Though it be very letchery unto thee,
> Doo't with a crabbed Polititians face. (III, iii, 100-105)

Two forms of judgment and punishment are presented in *The White Devil*. Roughly, the Cardinal represents legal punishment, while Francisco, Lodovico, and Cornelia represent extra-legal judgment, people judging their fellows without any authority to justify them. But this distinction is only superficial. The Cardinal himself urges Francisco to contemplate revenge; Francisco is an active participant in the trial; and all the characters are motivated by something other than an objective desire for justice. The main difference between Francisco and the Cardinal has nothing to do with their attitudes towards law and order; rather it has to do with a personality difference that Francisco perceives when he says that Monticelso's "flax soone kindles, soone is out againe" (IV, i, 44). That is, the intensity of the pursuit of "justice" is dependent not upon sensitivity to good and evil, but upon the capacity to stay angry. The important point is that the Cardinal, as judge, is entirely motivated by his momentary inclinations rather than by an ideal, which is, after all, the only possibility in a dramatic world where reason, as I have stressed, is not a transcendental quality, but only another means towards selfish ends.

Webster's portrait implies more than the corruption of an individual judge. The Cardinal's conduct is perfectly appropriate to its time, if we consider his familial responsibility for Camillo as well as the leeway normally allowed a judge. Webster shows these ordinary aspects of legal procedure in a new light, though, by portraying the Cardinal in the role of plotter as well as judge. The conjunction of these two roles, together with Vittoria's comments on the proceedings, has the effect of emphasizing the role of vengeance in ordinary legal procedure. The details of the arraignment scene will be examined later. For the moment, I only wish to make the general point that the characterization of the Cardinal embodies an attack upon current idealizations of the judge and that Webster anticipates the modern Freudian criminologist who perceives that theories of criminal law are attempts to rationalize something that the law does not care to admit: "that, in the strongest degree, [criminal law] rests upon instinct and emotion, and therefore upon elements which have nothing to do with law and indeed appear to exclude it."[36]

The gap between rationalization and reality is revealed by Webster as he dissects the motives of the various pursuers of justice. In the preceding section, I pointed out that, while Francisco and Monticelso at first appear to be interfering in Brachiano's affairs for the sake of the people concerned, they soon reveal their interest in punishment for its own sake. The Cardinal is willing to sacrifice Camillo, whom he is supposedly championing, and both are willing to destroy what little affection may remain (as far as they know) between Isabella and Brachiano, by giving Brachiano and Vittoria more opportunity to commit themselves irretrievably to their course of action.

In both Monticelso and Francisco there is a connection between readiness to judge and the enjoyment of condemnation and punishment for their own sake. The Cardinal easily gets carried away by his own rhetoric, in the trial scene, as he indulges in a verbal lashing of Vittoria which has little relation to anything he can show to be true. He likes to make sonorous speeches in behalf of God. Vittoria's unexpected virtuosity at self-defence never, for a moment, causes him to question his judgment of her. Rather, he seems increasingly frustrated by her interruptions, her wit, the favourable impression she is making on the ambassadors. The scene isn't going quite as he had planned it. Righteous Wrath is stumbling over the script because Evil Incarnate is making points. Peremptorily, he passes judgment.

Francisco, even more ardently, is alive in the element of anger. His quick temper, his recurrent emphasis upon war and the indolence of peace, and the blossoming of his spirit and imagination as he enters upon the enactment of revenge, all are indicative of a personality that responds to the delight of righteous fury. Nor is the righteousness of this fury gravely important to him, once it has served to justify his initial commitment to revenge. For when he finally discovers, *after* he has murdered Brachiano, that it was indeed Brachiano who was responsible for the death of his sister, he responds to Lodovico's "Why, now our action's justified" with a speech that completes the revelation of his character:

> Tush for Justice!
> What harmes it Justice? we now, like the partridge,
> Purge the disease with lawrell: for the fame
> Shall crowne the enterprise and quite the shame. (V, ii, 277-280)

In the excitement of the moment, Francisco finally discards the rationalization and reveals the pure enjoyment of combat which has motivated him all along.[37] In this light, it becomes clear that the intricacies and ingenuities of Francisco's plan not only serve to fill out Webster's plot, but also reflect the manic exhilaration of the avenger.[38]

Francisco's choice of Lodovico for his accomplice is characteristic. There is no pretence here of assembling the forces of good against the forces of evil. Lodovico is used because he is a killer and Francisco cheerfully lures Lodovico into further damnation. In a way, Lodovico epitomizes the whole enterprise, because he is least inclined to rationalize what he is doing. It is interesting that Webster deliberately ignores Lodovico's historical connection with the Orsini family[39]; for by so doing he removes the possibility of justifying, or at least explaining, Lodovico's action in terms of a sense of duty to his family. What explanation remains? There is the attachment to Isabella, obviously not sufficiently developed to count for much. There is the desire for money and for the continued favour of the Medici duke. This explanation carries weight, but it still leaves something unaccounted for: the fact that Lodovico is conspicuously happy in his work.

Lodovico's actual motivation is established in the first scene of the play. Like Francisco, he is easily angered and, in addition, he is full of bitterness towards the society that he feels has injured him. This bitterness has no specific direction, but radiates outward towards anyone who happens to be around. When Lodovico is called upon to murder Flamineo, Vittoria, and Zanche, he has an opportunity to express some of the pent-up rage that is a permanent feature of his personality. That he is not particularly angry at them as individuals is clearly expressed when he says as he is about to direct the murder:

> Oh could I kill you forty times a day
> And use't foure years together; 'tweare too little:
> Nought greev's but that you are too few to feed
> The famine of our vengeance (V, vi, 199-202)

His appetite for murder, because it is unrelated to any specific object, can never be satisfied. In the case of Lodovico, motivation most clearly lies, not in an idea of justice, not even in sheer desire for vengeance, but purely in an urge to destroy. It is his form of creativity.

Fredson Bowers accurately pointed out that the avengers in *The White Devil* are "actuated neither by the pure religious frenzy of the Kydian hero revenger nor by the malicious self-interest of the Marlovian villain."[40] We see what actually does motivate the revenge when virtuous frenzy gradually is unmasked and, at the end, stark aggression is revealed at the core of motivation. It is important to stress that simple self-interest has little to do with these avengers. This is so much the case that Webster suppresses the historical reason for the murder of Vittoria, which was prevention of her inheritance of Brachiano's estate after his death from natural causes.[41] No such practical considerations underlie this revenge. The sinners are destroyed by the enormous forces of aggression that their violation of the social code has unleashed.

The White Devil: Law and Human Nature

This analysis partly explains why critical response to Vittoria and, to a lesser extent, to Brachiano is ultimately sympathetic. Not only is their initial motivation comprehensible and natural, but the underlying motivation of those who oppose them, however just and virtuous their rationalizations, is essentially destructive. Exposure of these underlying motives necessarily calls into question the validity of the rationalizations themselves and of the assumption that we have the right to judge our fellows. If counter-aggression exceeds the initial aggression, and if righteous indignation is the factor which unlocks the floodgates, then it is no longer possible to rationalize judgment in a way that will satisfy the need to feel that it transcends particular human emotion. In this light, Vittoria and Brachiano have an edge over their enemies, as human beings, in that they are relatively forthright about what they want and because their emotional drives are not all reducible to aggression.

It is possible to rationalize the existence of laws and courts without recourse to the concept of right reason. Webster himself, we shall see later on, attempted to deal with other possible approaches to law in *The Devil's Law Case* and *Appius and Virginia*. In *The White Devil*, however, there is no implied alternative to the dominant juridical philosophy of his time; there is only a negation of that philosophy. Justice is impossible because reason, the key element in the structure, is an ideal with no roots in the reality of human nature. This being so, all judgment and law rest upon mere human drives.

Notes to Chapter One

1 Lawrence Stone, *The Crisis of the Aristocracy* (Oxford: Oxford University Press, 1967), pp. 213-214.
2 Ibid., p. 191.
3 *Intellectual Origins of the English Revolution* (London: Oxford University Press, 1972), p. 239.
4 Christopher Hill, *Puritanism and Revolution* (London: Secker and Warburg, 1958), pp. 268-269.
5 Stone, *Crisis*, pp. 220-222. Discussing Essex's followers, Stone says that five of them—Rutland, Southampton, Sussex, Bedford, and Mounteagle—"were angry young men in a hurry, all in their twenties, all chafing at the infuriating grip on office retained by the Cecils. But they too were hard pressed financially, frustration and idleness having led them into courses of extravagant dissipation. The remaining two—Lords Sandys and Cromwell—were embittered men of middle age whose lives had been failures. For years they had hung around the Court or gone soldiering in Ireland in the vain hope of responsible and lucrative office; for years they had struggled with mounting debt, for years they had been selling up the family estates" (p. 221).

6 "On Some Verses of Virgil," in *The Complete Essays of Montaigne*, ed. and trans. Donald M. Frame (Garden City, N.Y.: Doubleday, 1960), vol. III, pp. 109-110. Unless otherwise specified, all quotations from the works of Montaigne will be from this edition.
7 Ibid., p. 81.
8 "Quaintly Done," *Essays and Studies* 19 (1966), p. 46.
9 Montaigne, "Virgil," p. 81.
10 For a very detailed analysis of the conflicting points of view on love in *The White Devil*, see Lee Bliss, *The World's Perspective: John Webster and the Jacobean Drama* (New Brunswick, N.J.: Rutgers University Press, 1982), pp. 101-105.

It may be necessary to note that the laws which define the plight of Vittoria and Brachiano reflect the real world of Jacobean England as much as they do the world of Catholic Italy. Vittoria would have had little to say about her own marriage in the England of Webster's time, since it was only in that period that the courts were beginning to establish "the general principle that the marriage contract ought to be the result of the free consent of the parties" (W. S. Holdsworth, *A History of English Law* [London: Methuen, 1922], vol. VI, p. 646). Similarly, the divorce law that forces Vittoria and Brachiano to resort to murder is not necessarily reflective of the divorce law of a Catholic country. During the Jacobean period, divorce could only be obtained by means of an act of Parliament, once permission had been granted by the ecclesiastical courts (Holdsworth, vol. 1, pp. 622-624). Since both the ecclesiastical and secular branches of the state in the play are unfriendly to Vittoria, it is not likely that she could obtain a divorce, no matter what the official religion.
11 Roscoe Pound, *An Introduction to the Philosophy of Law*, rev. ed. (New Haven: Yale University Press, 1954), p. 27.
12 This is a characteristic of Webster's dramaturgy. Ralph Berry sees this "faculty of presenting events to us that are constantly being revalued by later events" as the manifestation of Webster's "ironic vision" (*The Art of John Webster* [Oxford: Clarendon Press, 1972], p. 26).
13 In this speech, Francisco is contrasting Brachiano's "bad" habit of sexual self-indulgence with Brachiano's young son's precocious interest in the manly art of war. Francisco's conception of manhood as aggressivity and of sexuality as degrading—an attitude towards life shared by characters in other Webster plays—bears comparison with the ideology of the feud in *Romeo and Juliet* as analyzed by Coppélia Kahn. Kahn finds that "the conflict between manhood as aggression on behalf of the father, and manhood as loving a woman, is at the bottom of the tragedy, and not to be overcome" ("Coming of Age in Verona," in *The Woman's Part: Feminist Criticism of Shakespeare*, ed. Carolyn Lenz, Gayle Greene, and Carol Neely [Urbana: University of Illinois Press, 1980], p. 179).
14 "Love," in *Essays, Advancement of Learning, New Atlantis, and other Pieces*, ed. Richard Jones (New York: Odyssey Press, 1937), p. 29.
15 Ibid.
16 Ibid., p. 28.
17 Marilyn French observes a direct connection between the wavering values in this play and the characterization of the heroine: "So far is Cleopatra from the idealized Shakespearean heroine, young, nubile, chaste and constant, so far also from the heavy panting Venus of the early poems, that it seems that when he wrote this play, he got up and went into a different room, one he had never worked in before, and shut the door on everythign else he had done.... For a time, then, Shakespeare put aside his ordinary demands of the female, as well as his ordinary demands of the male: no character in the tragedy is either idealized or demonized.... What this means is that there are no absolute

values in the play (*Shakespeare's Division of Experience* [New York: Summit Books, 1981], pp. 253-254).
18 Montaigne, "Virgil," p. 112.
19 Robert Griffin points out that in both *The White Devil* and *The Duchess of Malfi* the "imperatives of the Machiavellian court" create "a climate where success, even survival, requires the suppression of natural instinct" (*John Webster: Politics and Tragedy*, Salzburg Studies in English Literature [Salzburg: Institut für Englische Sprache und Literatur, Universität Salzburg, 1972], p. 114).
20 *Endeavors of Art: A Study of Form in Elizabethan Drama* (Madison: University of Wisconsin Press, 1954), p. 359.
21 See Chapter Three of this book for a fuller discussion of these concepts.
22 *Essays*, p. 157.
23 "Of Anger," in *The Complete Essays*, vol. I, p. 423.
24 Lucas, vol. IV, p. 38.
25 Sir James Stephen, *A History of the Criminal Law of England* (London: Macmillan, 1883), vol. I, p. 245.
26 Ibid., pp. 248-249.
27 Edward Jenks, *A Short History of English Law*, 2nd ed. (Boston: Little, Brown, 1922), p. 343.
28 Fredson Bowers, *Elizabethan Revenge Tragedy* (Gloucester, Mass.: P. Smith, 1959), p. 31; *Middlesex County Records*, ed. John Jeaffreson (London: The Middlesex County Records Society, 1887), vol. II, p. xiii.
29 See, for example, *The Comlete Newgate Calendar*, ed. John Rayner and G. T. Crook (London: The Navarre Society, 1926), vol. I, pp. 34-35.
30 Catherine Bowen, *The Lion and the Throne* (Boston: Little, Brown, 1957), pp. 64-65.
31 H. D. Traill, ed., *Social England* (London: Cassell, 1895), vol. IV, p. 141; Keith Wrightson, *English Society 1580-1680*, Hutchinson Social History of England (London: Hutchinson, 1982), pp. 122-123.
32 Catherine Bowen, *The Lion and the Throne* (Boston: Little, Brown, 1957), p. 442.
33 See Stephen, *A History of the Criminal Law of England*, vol. I, p. 497 and Bowen, *The Lion and the Throne*, pp. 143-186.
34 Bowen, *The Lion and the Throne*, p. 192.
35 H. H. Marshall, *Natural Justice* (London: Sweet and Maxwell, 1959), p. 34.
36 Paul Reiwald, *Society and its Criminals*, ed. and trans. T. E. James (New York: International Universities Press, 1950), p. 199.
37 The importance of sheer anger as motivation in this play has not been appreciated. In this connection, it is interesting that one of the few scenes in *Westward Ho* that is almost universally attributed to Webster (III, ii) is a piece of genre-painting depicting the violence of courtiers.
38 It is frustrating to have to confine my remarks about Francisco to those which relate to the subject in hand. It would give me great pleasure to explore the many facets of this rich character—poet, playwright, player, consummate hypocrite and manipulator, psychologist, philosopher. But that would be another book. I believe that Francisco would remain, for all that, the character glanced at in this chapter. True, he calls up his sister's image to spur him to revenge. But his response to her "ghost" is first to philosophize about the natural origins of phenomena considered supernatural, and then to dismiss the apparition because, as he puts it, "What have I to do / With tombs or deathbeds, funerals or tears, / That have to meditate upon revenge?" (IV, i, 109-111).

39 Gunnar Boklund, *The Sources of The White Devil* (Uppsala, Sweden: Lundequistska Bokhandeln, 1957), p. 139.
40 Bowers, *Elizabethan Revenge Tragedy*, p. 182.
41 Boklund, *The Sources of The White Devil*, p. 135.

Chapter Two

The White Devil: Law and Power

We have been considering a challenge to law that stems from ideas about our nature and relation to the universe. As I said earlier, Webster's philosophical anti-authoritarianism is related to a more directly political attitude towards autocratic power. Thus, while on one level *The White Devil* tends to dismiss law altogether as a philosophical impossibility, on another, more immediate, level it embodies a critique of specific aspects of Jacobean law and, in so doing, of the structure of Jacobean society. Before looking at this aspect of the challenge to law in *The White Devil* it will help to review some features of the Jacobean legal system.

Anyone who has ever risen when a judge enters the courtroom may find it hard to believe that one of the major differences between law in Webster's time and in our own is the far greater paternalism of law in the earlier period. Although we are still asked to look upon judges as our friends—as the kindly, experienced, reasonable people they sometimes are—the law nonetheless recognizes, in the implicit form of safeguards, that judges make mistakes. But law in monarchic society necessarily reflects the suspension of disbelief that makes monarchy possible. There is really a vast difference between our relativistic view of law as dependent upon what happens when such fallible elements as a jury, a judge, a lawyer or two, and a precedent interact and the view of law (maintained by James in the face of growing opposition) as the expression of the will of a monarch who is himself God's representative on earth. Given our present atomized view of the law, protection of individuals against the malfunctioning of one or another of the unpredictable elements that go into a legal decision seems natural. The law is a machine with parts that can malfunction. It is much more difficult to talk about protecting the rights of the individual in a court presided over by God's deputy; for theoretically, the monarch, as the source of all law, was the judge in every case, the actual trial judge being his representative. And the theory became practice when the King exercised his very wide powers to influence the decisions of judges, to transfer cases from one court to another, and to reverse the decisions of any court.[1]

In other words, in Jacobean England, the Bench was literally the King's, and the judges who sat upon it were assumed to be discharging the King's duty to protect his people. If a judge failed in this duty, he would have to answer to his monarch, just as the King would ultimately have to answer to God. Thus the only protection individuals needed was the right to appeal to the King in case of an injustice. This meant that judges exercised a power in their domain that paralleled the power of the sovereign in his. Although jury trial was established procedure in some courts, the function of the jury then should not be confused with its role today; for not only could the judge reverse a conviction or demand that the jury reconsider an acquittal,[2] but if the jury stubbornly persisted in a verdict of acquittal against the recommendation of the judge, its members might be fined, or even imprisoned.[3] The notion of judicial infallibility was further maintained by means of severe repression of public criticism. In 1615, Sir John Hollis and Sir John Wentworth were heavily fined and imprisoned for a year for "traducing the public justice" in connection with the Overbury case. The grounds for the conviction were as follows: Hollis had stated that had he been on the jury, he would have found it difficult to reach a decision; and both men had asked one of the convicted, at the time of his execution, to satisfy the world as to whether or not he had actually committed the crime.[4]

In criminal cases, defendants were thrown almost entirely upon the mercy of the presiding judge, since there was little they could do for themselves. They were not permitted to employ counsel; they were unable to see a copy of the indictment beforehand or obtain a list of the Crown's witnesses; and although they were occasionally allowed to call witnesses in their behalf, such witnesses were not permitted to testify under oath. It was up to the judge to decide whether defendants might meet their accusers face to face.[5] Essentially, defendants had no weapon but their tongues, and a good deal depended upon their ability to keep their wits about them and to summon up any knowledge they might have of legal procedure (which accounts for the considerable knowledge of law possessed by the general population of the time). If the judge was less than ideally paternal, if he was not disposed to bring up evidence for as well as against defendants, the defendants were helpless to

The White Devil: Law and Power

do anything but object to the proceedings, which was hardly likely to win the sympathy of the bench, but which might, at least, gain them support from the gallery. Since it was desirable for the Crown to gain approval of its judicial acts, particularly in cases involving public figures, a defendant's ability to play to the gallery was not an entirely negligible weapon, and in some cases, such as the trials of Essex and Southampton, it seems apparent that the defendants were concerned more with producing an impact on the audience than with impressing the bench. The fictional verbal battle between Vittoria and Monticelso in *The White Devil* is easily matched by Essex's dramatic creation of the role of innocence betrayed, a characterization not intended for the stage.[6]

In the preceding chapter I referred to the judge's right to function as prosecutor during a trial. We can now fit this into the context of the generally broad judicial power characteristic of the period. The judge could not only accuse the person he was judging; he could also conduct an inquisition. This was least true in the common law courts and most true in the ecclesiastical, in which the judge was not even constrained to present the defendant with definite charges, but might conduct a purely exploratory examination in order to trap the defendant into an admission of guilt.[7] Defendants in a common law court had the advantage of knowing what was charged against them, if not before the trial, at least during it.

To fully appreciate the helplessness of the Jacobean defendant, consider that judges were bound neither by strict rules of evidence nor by any "doctrine of binding precedent."[8] The Jacobean judge could and did admit any kind of evidence, from third-hand hearsay to unwarranted conclusions by witnesses. Character assassination, expressed with a picturesqueness that is a lost art, commonly made up the bulk of the evidence, and was often taken seriously. While there was increasing pressure to establish rules of evidence, it was still up to the individual judge to evaluate the testimony in any case.[9] As for the judge's obligation to observe precedent, there again no strict rule had been established. As Hill puts it, judges had "a pretty free hand to make what they pleased of the law." If a judge felt hampered by a statute, he could "appeal to custom or 'common right and reason' against it; or—vaguer still—he could construe it by 'the rule and reason of the common law!'"[10] I cannot resist quoting one of Hill's examples of how this latter process worked.

> When faced with a rule he did not like, such as the right of gilds to govern their trades, Coke quietly ignored the precedents, or turned them with another *dictum*—'at the common law no man

could be prohibited from working at any lawful trade, for the law abhors idleness ... especially in young men."[11]

Public acceptance of the kind of arbitrary power exercised by judges in Webster's time necessarily rests upon a popular image of the Crown and its representatives as reasonably impartial. But confidence was shaky. As early as 1592, Robert Greene expressed an opinion of law that was to be echoed many times:

> Howsoever right be, might carries away the verdict. If a poore man sue a gentleman, why he shootes up to the skie, and the arrow fals on his owne head; howsoever the cause goe, the weakest is thrust to the wall.[12]

An indication of the attitude towards the law of at least certain segments of the public is found in the cant of the underworld, in which the thief was called a "High lawier,"[13] and a thief's booty was called a "cheat,"[14] with satirical reference to escheats of property and the prevalent system of wardship and inheritance.

The courts themselves were well aware of the bias towards wealthy and powerful litigants, and sometimes even took steps to redress grievances of the oppressed. Thus, the Judges of Assize at Chester granted a new trial, in 1608, to a woman who complained of her treatment by the ecclesiastical court, claiming that her opponent had won "by reason of his great favor and friendship in the spiritual court, being a money man and your suppliant not able to contend in law with him."[15] The records of the Privy Council show that, in its role as court of appeals, it, too, occasionally acted upon its recognition of the ability of "persons of wealth and quality . . . to blind the eyes of Justice."[16] That redress was sometimes granted is largely attributable to the battle of the courts among themselves over spheres of jurisdiction, which made one court anxious to find fault with the decision of another. While this occasionally ameliorated the situation for the relatively poor and powerless litigant, it did not help to sustain an image of the law as rational paternal authority.

In fact, at its very philosophical basis, the law was unclear on the question of equality. If the Privy Council sometimes acted on the assumption that equality was desirable, at other times it openly accorded favourable treatment to persons of wealth and quality.[17] Inequality was built into other aspects of the complicated Jacobean legal system. Masters had wide power to punish their servants and apprentices.[18] Courts Leet, run by lords and gentlemen or their stewards, had power to regulate the behaviour of the commons in their spheres of jurisdiction and to judge and punish minor offences.[19] And "benefit of clergy" was still in effect in many types of crime, including manslaughter. Initially a medieval law ensuring that crimes by clerics would be judged in ecclesiastical rather than secular courts, *benefit of clergy* had come to mean, in Jacobean times, that any man who knew the "neck verse" (who could recite certain biblical verses in Latin) might avoid capital punishment for a first offence. It was entirely up to the authorities to grant or withhold this "benefit."[20] Thus, the very structure of the law was, in some respects, antithetical to the ideal of equality expressed by many of its practitioners. As far as we can tell, it was no surprise to the populace that, in the notorious Overbury case, the powerful criminals escaped punishment while their agents were hanged.

The feature of the legal system that probably did most to stimulate a cynical public attitude was the mercenary incentive that frequently, and quite openly, served as the basis for prosecution. The economic motive for pursuing the laws against recusancy (the failure to accept the official religion) is a blatant example; for a portion of the possessions of the recusant fell into the always gaping coffers of the Crown, and the State Papers often ingenuously refer to the "benefits of recusancy" to indicate the property gained in this manner.[21] Frequently, "benefits" of particular crimes were made over to individuals beforehand, for a lump sum, thus giving private parties a keen interest in seeing that the laws would be carried out in such cases.[22] In Greene's satirical pamphlet quoted above, he refers to this practice in an illuminating way. The upstart courtier, called "velvet breeches," boasts of his judicial severity:

> I am a severe sensor to such as offend the law, provided there be a penalty annexed that may bring in some profit; yea, by me the cheefest part of the realm is governed.

The upstart's opponent in this debate, a sturdy yeoman, reviles him for this passion for justice:

> Whereas thou saist thou art a severe sensour to punish sins, as austere as Cato to correct vice, of truth I hold thee so in penal statutes when thou hast begged the forfeit of the Prince; but such correction is open extortion and oppression of the poor.[23]

This behaviour on the part of their betters was evidently inspiring to the lower officials of the courts. Since these officials were dependent upon fees for their livelihood, they used their authority to extort as much as they could from those who were unfortunate enough to have to go to law. And since their enrichment depended on the volume of the court's business, they rarely refused to place a case on the calendar, no matter how petty or frivolous the plaintiff's suit appeared. This, in turn, afforded enterprising individuals with boundless opportunities for blackmail. By threatening to start an action in court, extortionists could force their victims to pay them a small sum in order to avoid the much greater expense of going to law.[24]

Finally, it is important in considering Webster and his contemporaries to be really aware of the implications of the "rogues and vagabonds" statutes enacted in the latter part of Elizabeth's reign and in the reign of King James. The average Jacobean could take little comfort in being poor but honest, for these laws made poverty and economic dislocation punishable offences, subject to imprisonment, whipping, and deportation. I have even come across one instance in which men were sentenced to death for being without means of support.[25] The obvious implication of this aspect of the laws was that if one had to choose between poverty and dishonesty, there was something to be said for the latter. In effect, the state made no clear legal distinction between poverty and crime.

By the time Webster wrote *The White Devil*, the inequalities and corruptions of the legal system had become the subject of public discussion, and the paternalistic view of law was under attack. It was a time when legal philosophy and the structure of the legal system were alike characterized by the flux and turmoil that precede great and fundamental change. The unpopularity of Stuart attempts to extend the royal prerogative created a need for definition and analysis, and led to a critical attitude towards legal institutions in general. Equity law was attacked as a "symbol and henchman of despotism,"[26] and in 1610 the judges declared it illegal for the Crown to create new offences and punishments by proclamation, a practice that, "used in moderation, had passed unchallenged under James's predecessors."[27] That it was not only the professionals who were critical is evidenced by the outspoken public reactions to such cases as the trials of Essex and Raleigh[28] and to the annulment of Frances Howard's first marriage.[29] And popular resistance to the accepted definition of felony expressed itself in "a humane reluctance on the part of many to come forward as witnesses."[30] All of this was preparatory to the great legal changes, especially in criminal procedure, that were to take place during the interregnum:

> From the year 1640 downwards, the whole spirit and temper of the criminal courts, even in their most irregular and revolutionary proceedings, appears to have been radically changed from what it had been in the preceding century to what it is in our own days.[31]

Webster's rendering of law in *The White Devil* participates in the critical and rebellious mood that preceded these changes.

Since *The White Devil* is set in Italy, I should, perhaps, anticipate the objection that English crime and law have nothing to do do with the play. Leaving aside larger issues, I will merely refer the reader to Monticelso's black book, which contains a catalogue of crime that must appear conspicuously English to anyone who is familiar with the pamphlet literature of the period. Even Francisco's meditation on the black book is just an echo of popular satire on the extortion practised by minor court officials (IV, i, 47-91). In the following discussion, I shall try to emphasize such parallels between the world of *The White Devil* and the realities of Jacobean law.

The chief objection in *The White Devil* to law as an adequate instrument for dealing with life is that the structure of law reflects the structure of power in the society. People are not equal before the law; they are treated in accordance with their rank, wealth, sex, and influence on those in power. This is established in a general way in the first scene, in which the dialogue between Lodovico and his comforters, revolving around this theme, sketches the social milieu in which Webster's characters are going to act. In answer to Lodovico's attacks—"Your woolfe no longer seems to be a woolfe / Then when hees hungry" (I, i, 8-9) and "In wonder then some great men 'scape / this banishment" (lines 38-39)—the comforters, who try, have nothing convincing to say. Rather, their crowning argument against Lodovico, "You terme those enemies / Are men of Princely ranke" (lines 9-10) reveals a propensity to accept inequality as a fact of life. Their difference with Lodovico is not only politic, it is philosophical; for, unlike him, they do not aspire to equality. They know that Lodovico has earned his punishment and the fact that equally guilty but more powerful people go free does not, for them, affect the justice of the sentence upon him.

From what I have been saying about Jacobean law, it should be apparent that their attitude is not simply attributable to cowardice and cynicism. Rather, it represents a prevalent philosophy in a period when criminals of high rank and influence were pardoned for murder, while the poor daily received the death sentence for stealing. Peacham's remark that a gentleman's punishment "ought to be more favourable and honourable upon his trial"[32] expresses a social law with deep roots in history. By making inequality before the law a recurrent theme in his play, Webster is giving voice to a way of thinking that was just then emerging to oppose the old social law.[33] It is dramatically consistent that those who speak against inequality in the play—Flamineo, Lodovico,

Vittoria—are the characters whose sense of equality with the rulers of society makes them struggle for self-fulfilment. We can understand those characters better if we bear in mind that they are burdened with a sense of equality which clashes impossibly with the ideas of status expressed by their rulers, ideas which determine the realities of the dramatic world in which they act.

There are critics, though, who tend to dismiss social forces as irrelevant to character motivation in *The White Devil*. Thus Clifford Leech says of Flamineo's death speech: "Like Vittoria, he is prepared to put some part of the blame on the corruptive power of great men, but this seems only a momentary weakening."[34] The reading seems particularly arbitrary in that Flamineo's statement is not just an inspiration of the moment, but a restatement of a theme that he and others have been harping on throughout the play. More than that, Flamineo's bitterness towards his betters really helps to explain his actions and underlies some of his most powerful statements.

Flamineo's argument with Cornelia in Act I, scene ii is his most detailed and direct expression of this theme. To his mother's outraged question—"What? because we are poore / Shall we be vitious?"—Flamineo replies, "Pray what meanes have you / To keepe me from the gallies, or the gallowes?" (I, ii, 307-309). Leaving aside the question of whether Flamineo's rationalization exonerates him, let us consider whether it is, at least, deeply felt by the character himself. Cornelia's ideal of honest poverty is certainly at variance with the spirit of the Jacobean legal enactments dealing with destitution, as Flamineo implies when he refers to gallies and gallows. His impatience with his mother reflects his stronger will to survive, which manifests itself in a more realistic appraisal of the rewards of poverty. We get a glimpse later on of the depth of Flamineo's fear of destitution when the image of debtor's prison makes its way into one of his comparisons: "Poor Lord, you did vow / To live a lowzy creature... Like one / That had for ever forfaited the day-light, / By being in debt" (III, iii, 110-113).

It is this fear, together with a sense of personal worth, that motivates Flamineo's ambition. He seeks power not so much for itself, but for the security he hopes it will bring with it. We sense this clearly at the point where he finally feels that the plot has succeeded:

> In all the weary minutes of my life,
> Day nere broke up till now. This mariage
> Confirmes me happy. (V, i, 1-3)

The happiness is illusory, but for one brief moment Flamineo is permitted to feel that he has attained a position that will keep him

The White Devil: Law and Power

above the reach of the forces which threaten and destroy those members of society who have nothing to interpose between themselves and the law.

As I have already pointed out, class background enters into Flamineo's motivation. Like Vittoria and Lodovico, he is one of the declassed, often mentioned in Jacobean writings as both symptom and cause of social disorder. The story is typical of the period. A member of the landed gentry, the father of Flamineo and Vittoria sold his land (perhaps to invest the money in commerce or in courting the upper nobility; we are not told). As Flamineo remarks to his mother, his father was lucky enough to die before the money was all spent. His children were less fortunate. For Flamineo, the effect of this class position is to intensify—perhaps originate—his sense of personal worth and, at the same time, to deny him the means of expressing it. His determination to raise his position at any cost is the outcome. At the root of his behaviour is a sense of personal injustice that obliterates, for him, all moral imperatives. The initial injustice of his loss of patrimony is reinforced by his later experiences of injustice at the hands of those upon whom his self-fulfilment depends, and the result is ethical breakdown and despair.

So if Flamineo's death speech refers again to the corruptive power of great men, it is because Flamineo has moments when he is objective enough to see that injustice leads to moral degeneration, his own included. To interpret this as a mere excuse is to assert that Flamineo's despair has no basis in the world of the play. But his despair over the condition of society is justified when the minor operatives in the revenge plot are led off to punishment while the prime movers, one of whom is now the Pope, go free. What Webster implies through his portrait of Flamineo is that inequality before the law is the source of a corruption that permeates the society. And Flamineo himself sees this at the end. Far from taking comfort in the thought that he has been a mere victim of great forces, Flamineo experiences deep scorn for himself as he realizes that he has been destroyed, body and soul, by social realities that he had vainly hoped, in his life, to transcend. This is no ordinary deathbed penitence. What he regrets is that, with all his wit and energy, with all his understanding of society, he has been taken in by tantalizing, unattainable goals, and that all his striving has gained him nothing but the knowledge of his own corruptibility.[35]

Seeing the sense of injustice as central to Flamineo's motivation enables us to answer another critic's objection that Flamineo represents "two incongruous, incompatible roles,—malcontent and tool-villain . . . without any ethical or psychological coherence between the two." Stoll's criticism rests on the assumption that it is impossible for a character to act immorally and speak morally without feeling some "contention of motives."[36] But if we examine the content of Flamineo's satire, we see that it is the utterance not of a "moralist" but of a man who is deeply embittered at his fellow men and, especially, at what they have done and will do to him. When he talks of the evil of great men, the subject of much of his railing, he speaks from his own experience, not from abstract moral principles. And it is the same sense of injustice that underlies his action as tool-villain, for Flamineo's moral indignation is the spring that releases him from moral responsibility towards others. The sense of injustice provides the psychological coherence that Stoll feels is lacking. Webster's characterization anticipates the modern criminologists who say that "the corruption of those in power breaks down the power of their inner representative, the inhibiting forces of morality."[37] Flamineo's moralizing, such as it is, is a constant reassurance to himself that he has chosen the right principle to guide his life—the idea that morality is absurd in an immoral world.[38]

The White Devil thus embodies a criticism of the structure of Jacobean society in the very characterization of one of its major figures. Legalized inequality, we are shown, inspires moral disintegration. Passive acceptance of inequality, on the other hand, leads to the frustration and self-destruction of Cornelia, the sycophantic opportunism of Lodovico's comforters, or the blind honour of Marcello. The question of ultimate moral superiority is not relevant. Webster presents the situation, defines the choices, and depicts the aftermath, but he does not judge. Rather, he leaves judgment to those characters who are concerned with maintaining their position of power and oppressing the upstarts who dare to challenge their ordering of society.[39]

Webster's attack on the social basis of law and his concomitant moral relativism are most fully expressed in his portrayal of the Cardinal and Vittoria, and in the scene in which these two figures directly clash. It is in the trial scene most of all that Webster emphasizes the paternalistic nature of Jacobean law, focusing his portrait on the figure of the judge. It is also in this scene that we find his most specific comments on the legal system, for although it may appear exaggerated to a modern reader, the scene actually embodies a pointed and particularized image of Jacobean justice.

In the trial scene, the Cardinal is shown to possess almost unlimited power by virtue of what appears to be a *carte blanche* from the Pope. That the Pope is interested in the outcome of these proceedings is revealed early, when Brachiano attempts to assume a nobleman's position on the bench and the Cardinal tells him:

> Forbeare my Lord, here is no place assign'd you
> This business by his holiness is left
> To our examination. (III, ii, 1-3)

Brachiano's answer, "May it thrive with you," is his bitter acknowledgment that, with the Pope backing the Cardinal, Vittoria's chances are not good.

The most striking feature of the Cardinal's behaviour as judge, at least to a modern audience, is his assumption of the role of prosecutor. It must be stressed that what Webster's original audience would have found remarkable is not Monticelso's behaviour, but Vittoria's criticism of it:

> If you bee my accuser
> Pray cease to be my Judge, come from the Bench,
> Give in your evidence 'gainst me, and let these [the ambassadors]
> Be moderators. (lines 233-236)

Vittoria must be seen here as the proponent of a progressive attitude that was to make itself increasingly felt in English legal practice and ultimately create a wide separation between the function of judge and prosecution. Defendants in a hostile court, as I have pointed out, could do little for themselves. But they could criticize the proceedings, and since they had no counsel to do this for them, they had to have some ideas of their own. It was Raleigh himself who had to argue the technical question whether one eyewitness was sufficient to convict an individual of treason.[40]

The Cardinal's role in the trial is further delineated by his personal economic interest in the outcome. He never denies the accusations levelled by Brachiano and Vittoria that his interest in Camillo's estate gives him a personal motive for wanting Vittoria out of the way (lines 161-165; 180-181; 221-224). The Cardinal's right to judge a case in which he is personally involved again reflects current English practice; for Coke was just then striving to legitimize what he called the "common law maxim" that "no man ought to be judge in his own cause."[41] This, together with his power to assign a verdict at will, completes the portrait of Monticelso's power. Accuser, judge, jury, and party to the case (as Camillo's avenger and possible heir), his power in the courtroom is godlike.

Webster's portrait of the courtroom is closely modelled on the actual structure of the English ecclesiastical courts. It was in the ecclesiastical courts that the judge could choose to proceed by "inquisition," a method of trial in which he himself acted as the accuser. It was also in the ecclesiastical courts that the judge was most likely to "proceed upon his own personal knowledge or on common fame."[42] His dominance in the court was not even theoretically checked by the presence of a jury or a defending lawyer,[43] and he had the power to imprison a defendant without delivering a formal verdict.[44] These characteristics of ecclesiastical justice are closely paralleled by Monticelso's court. And since it was the province of ecclesiastical courts in England to deal with such offences as "adultery, procuration, incontinency and drunkeness,"[45] it is likely that Vittoria's trial would have taken place in such a court, since, in spite of the suspicion of murder, the actual subject of the examination is immorality.

But it would be a mistake, I think, to conclude that the picture of Monticelso's court reflects a single branch of the Jacobean legal structure. Arbitrary imprisonment by the King's Council was probably more common than arbitrary imprisonment by the Christian courts.[46] The presence of a jury was not required in any of the equity courts, including Star Chamber.[47] And, as I have noted, the authoritarian position of the judge was characteristic of all courts. Furthermore, the introduction into common law procedure, during this period, of a system of pretrial examination tended to give the common law courts an inquisitorial quality which considerably lessened the difference between them and the prerogative and ecclesiastical courts.[48] Monticelso's court is really a dramatic abstraction based on aspects of the total legal system that Webster wished to emphasize—aspects which were particularly characteristic of the spiritual and prerogative courts, but which were also present in the common law courts. My conclusion that there is a double frame of reference here, as in so many aspects of this play, is supported by John Russell Brown's perception of the ambiguity of two statements made by Vittoria in the course of the scene. She refers to "this Christian Court" (line 132) at one point, apparently punning on the two meanings: "civilized" and "Courts Christian" (that is, ecclesiastical). Similarly, when she says that charity is seldom found in "scarlet" (lines 3-4), she might be referring to the scarlet of the Cardinal's robe, or the scarlet that symbolized the legal faculty.[49] The ambiguity of these remarks hints at the double reference of the scene as a whole.

In the trial scene, then, Webster demonstrates specifically the *realpolitik* of law, stressing the overwhelming odds against the defendant who is in some way offensive to the establishment. What makes the dramatic tensions here particularly legalistic is that Vittoria is not a dramatic emblem of innocence oppressed.[50] We are not asked to involve ourselves in a battle between weak innocence and powerful vice. Rather, because the two forces here opposed are both worldly-wise and capable of immoral acts, but vastly unequal in power, one of the prime sources of interest in this struggle is the attempt of the weaker figure to find some means of defence. That Vittoria is doomed in this scene is one manifestation of the fact

The White Devil: Law and Power

that she, with the rest of her party, is doomed in the play as a whole. This is later symbolized by the elevation to the papacy of her old enemy, the Cardinal. The trial is one of the means that those in power use against her, one expression of the force against which she futilely struggles. In this scene, she is a dramatic representation of the lonely figure against whom the state successfully employs its legal weapons. The fact that she is a woman, and therefore in an inferior position before the law, intensifies her symbolic position.[51] In its emphasis on specific aspects of legal procedure, Vittoria's defence is an expression of the growing awareness, in Jacobean England, that the legal system was, after all, vulnerable to change. In particular, her attempts exemplify what Bowen has described as "a groping after procedure which might give to the unfriended single prisoner fair chance against the solid power of the state."[52] As we analyze her defence, we shall see how closely her behaviour resembles that of defendants in real trials of the time. (Note that in the following pages Raleigh will appear in two roles: as hostile witness in the Essex trial and as defendant when he himself replaces Essex in the role of the accused.)

From the first, Vittoria's main goal is to make a favourable impression upon the audience, represented by the foreign ambassadors, in the hope that Monticelso will be sufficiently concerned about their opinions to take their reactions into consideration. In order to put on a good show, she has to rid the proceedings of the element of legalistic jargon, which can only operate as a barrier to real human communication, and so she immediately attacks the prosecuting attorney for his ornate and sterile oratory. The dialogue here echoes an episode in the Raleigh trial, when Sir Walter, like Vittoria, interrupted a torrent of obscure rhetoric with a few effectively simple words:

> ATTORNEY-GENERAL: Now, my Masters of the jury, I come to your Charge: treason is of four kinds; treason *in corde*, which is the root of the tree; treason *in ore*, which is the bud; treason *in manu*, which is the blossom; and treason *in consummatione*, which is the fruit...
>
> RALEIGH: Mr. Attorney, I pray you to whom, or to what end speak you all this? I do not understand what a word of this means, except it be to tell me news.[53]

Raleigh interrupts because, by making fun of the rhetoric, he hopes to please the crowd, and because he wants to make sure that the real issues will not be obfuscated in the course of the trial by what the Jacobeans called "fustian" (bombast). Vittoria's strategy is identical.

Having succeeded in forcing a change in the language of the court, Vittoria now addresses herself to the question of proof. To compensate for the lack of witnesses against her, Monticelso makes pictureque speeches, substituting loose and fanciful associations and vague hearsay for actual charges. Instead of proving that she has been unfaithful, he paints a general picture (a "character," to use the Jacobean term) of a whore, hoping that the ambassadors will associate that picture with the woman who stands before them. As I have pointed out, character assassination through hearsay ("Alas," says Monticelso, "I make but repetition, / Of what is ordinary and Ryalto talke" [lines 256-257]) was normally considered admissible evidence in the Jacobean courtroom, and in this case, the Cardinal's rhetorical ability certainly has an effect on the audience of ambassadors. The nature of Vittoria's defence is determined by the nature of the prosecution. Vittoria's only hope is to call attention to the quality of the evidence against her, to convince the auditors that such evidence is insufficient to convict her of anything. She tries to show them that the disquisition on whores is irrelevant to her. She makes the point that accusations without proofs reflect the character of the accuser rather than that of the accused ("As if a man should spit against the wind, the filth returns in's face" [lines 154-155]). And in the speech in which she asks the listeners to "summe up [her] faults" (lines 215-220), she attempts to pinpoint the gap between the implications of the Cardinal's rhetoric and the actual facts presented against her. Thus, the nature of the situation forces Vittoria to take a position which again places her among the critics of Jacobean legal procedure, as does her objection to the Cardinal's dual role of judge and prosecutor.

More traditional is Vittoria's attempt to discredit the witness against her, although here, again, she is asserting a new idea when she calls attention to his economic interest as a factor against his reliability. But for the most part, Vittoria relies on the old technique of answering his moral evaluation of her character by denigrating his. The contest of insult which ensues reflects the realities of law in a period when, even more than now, a person stood or fell by the word of the witness. Essex focused on this problem as he fought for his life:

> But, good my Lord, let me desire your Grace to note who they be, and in what state they be that testify thus against me; my Lord, they are men within the danger of the law, and such as speak with a desire to live.[54]

So fearful is he of Raleigh's testimony that he begins to attack his character as Raleigh is taking the oath: "What booteth it to swear

The White Devil: Law and Power   57

the fox?"⁵⁵ Vittoria uses animal imagery with identical intent when, in response to Monticelso's comment (as Brachiano leaves the courtroom) that her "champions gon," she replies, "The wolfe may prey the better" (lines 186-187).

Vittoria's particular problem is that the only witness against her happens to be her judge, so that in challenging the witness she necessarily finds herself challenging the authority of the bench. This is hardly politic, but not unprecedented. The directness of Vittoria's attack upon her judge should not prevent us from seeing its relation to Raleigh's more veiled and judicious aspersion:

> SIR WALTER RALEIGH: Brooke never loved me; and yet until his brother accused me, he said nothing: he hath been taught his lesson.
>
> LORD H. HOWARD: This Examination was taken before me. Did I teach him his lesson?
>
> RALEIGH: I protest before God, I meant it not of your Lordship nor any Privy Councillor: but when money is scant, men will juggle on both sides.⁵⁶

Vittoria, like Raleigh, could not hope to sway a judge by insulting him. The appeal is to the audience. And the audience for Vittoria is not only the make-believe audience, the ambassadors in the galleries, but also the real audience in the theatre, who, above all, must decide for or against her. It is primarily for the benefit of this latter audience that she delivers her final blow:

> It shal not be a house of convertites—
> My minde shal make it honester to mee
> Then the Popes Pallace, and more peaceable
> Then thy soule, though thou art a Cardinall. (III, ii, 300-303)

In its impact on the theatre audience, this speech is Vittoria's triumph. Its deliberate ambiguity is perhaps inspired by the superficial politeness of attacks on the bench in real trials, but, more important, this ambiguity expresses the essential relativity of Vittoria's defence. Because the Cardinal is guilty, she says, I am innocent. Because the bench is not objective, there can be no justice. She seems to believe this quite literally, although she is certainly being witty at the same time. For the moment, at least, she appears to be convinced of her own innocence, just as her brother more consistently feels himself exonerated by the evil he sees in high places. The injustices committed by the court—the basic injustice of Monticelso's role as judge and avenger—override Vittoria's sense of guilt and turn her into an embodiment of oppressed innocence, a "diamond" against a background of "darkness."

The psychological phenomenon that Webster recreates in this scene is sufficiently unfamiliar to cause critical difficulty. Unable to comprehend or believe in it, some critics dismiss Vittoria's behaviour as sheer hypocrisy, while those critics who are in one way or another moved by her performance (and they are in the majority) do not find her apparent conviction of innocence easy to explain. "It is in this scene, supremely," says Elizabeth Brennan, "that Vittoria defies analysis and challenges our judgment."[57] Granting that Vittoria is always somewhat elusive, it seems to me that some analysis is possible here. For the kind of transfiguration she undergoes has been observed again and again in the courtroom. Paul Reiwald, the judge-turned-criminologist, has observed and recorded many examples of ardent defences—apparently stemming from a real conviction of innocence—by undoubtedly guilty criminals. His explanation is illuminating for us. He sees the criminal's self-righteousness as a manifestation of the instinct of self-preservation borne up by a great hatred of the punitive force—the society—and a consequent sense of injustice. The criminal, he says, sees those who judge and punish him as a "malevolent opponent, who is just as evil as he, but who understands better how to conceal his vice and, moreover, has power on his side." This gives rise to a sense of righteousness so powerful that it momentarily obliterates everything else.[58] Vittoria's behaviour resembles her brother's in that her ethical sense is similarly transformed under pressure of injustice. In her case, the reaction is more spasmodic and extreme, but it is not confined to the trial scene. Her behaviour in the house of convertites scene varies the theme, as injustice transfigures her into the type of repentant sinner. For Vittoria, the world is very much a stage, but she is the kind of actor who lives her part.

The puzzling dramatic effectiveness of Vittoria's defence begins to become more comprehensible. If critics find their own sympathetic reactions to the defendant hard to explain or justify, at least part of the explanation lies in the power of Vittoria's conviction of innocence to influence those who are exposed to it. Knowing that she is guilty of at least some of the charges against her, we nonetheless identify with her because she is momentarily transformed into a symbol of impotence before a condemning, unjust authority, undergoing an experience with which we are all, somehow, familiar. Our reactions are not entirely irrational. We are philosophically impressed by her conviction that the guilty cannot judge the guilty. We see beyond the legalistic trappings of the situation to the real power struggle taking place. We dislike the Cardinal's rhetoric and his pretence of objectivity. And we are impressed by Vittoria's specific legal objections to the proceedings.

The White Devil: Law and Power

But all of this does not quite account for our absurd sense of Vittoria's innocence, a feeling that never quite leaves us throughout the rest of the play. It is this irrational part of our reaction that has to do, I think, with our own experiences of injustice.

In evoking this kind of reaction, Webster is making dramaturgical use of principles of human response that he might have observed in actual courtrooms. The changes in our reactions to Vittoria are no stranger than were the vacillations in public attitudes towards Raleigh. After Raleigh appeared against Essex, he was attacked by mobs in the street. A few years later, when he was convicted of treason in his turn, on less evidence than Essex and in a more openly hostile court, he was entirely forgiven by the English people and soon transfigured into a new hero.[59] The fluid interchange between the world and the stage which is characteristic of Elizabethan life is nowhere clearer than in Webster's recreation of a form of audience response originally experienced in a non-literary (although highly theatrical) situation. The popular dissatisfaction with Jacobean government that expressed itself in sympathy with those whom that government oppressed legally is paralleled by audience rejection of the Cardinal's authority and consequent sympathy for Vittoria in *The White Devil*. In both cases, sympathy stems not from a conviction of the defendant's purity, but from a strong reaction against the power possessed by a prosecuting authority of even more dubious virtue.[60]

Although the spell of the arraignment scene abates as the play proceeds, it never vanishes. In our eyes, Vittoria always retains the quality of helpless victim before the oppressive power of the law, even when the screen of legality is abandoned by those who seek to destroy her. For beneath the surface, there is no basic difference between legal and extra-legal punishment. This is what Webster reveals to us when he forces us to identify with Vittoria and see through her eyes. Behind the mask of paternal authority, we see hatred and anger, and, above all, the power to implement those feelings. The court may pretend to be concerned with Vittoria's correction, but we know, with her, that it desires her destruction. In this context, Vittoria, for all her "masculine vertue," is a mere child and woman and, whatever her guilt, we wish that she were better able to defend herself.

Thus, our empathy with Vittoria makes us stiflingly aware of the union of law and power in the world of *The White Devil*. And this awareness, in turn, increases our sympathy for her and for her brother, both of whom become somehow less guilty because of the failure of their world to provide real justice. Even Brachiano's guilt seems slighter in that it is his relative weakness, rather than moral inferiority, that dooms him to failure. Our sense of justice is offended by punishment that is meted out by culpable mortals who happen to possess the power to play god on earth. And this unequal justice is more than futile, it is destructive; for in creating cynicism and inspiring ambition, it produces crime, which it then proceeds to punish in an endless cycle. The Jacobean playgoer who nursed heretical thoughts and feelings about His Majesty's justice would have found those thoughts and feelings strengthened by an afternoon at the Red Bull Theatre.

Notes to Chapter Two

1 See Sir James F. Stephen, *A History of the Criminal Law of England* (London: Macmillan, 1883), vol. I; *Middlesex County Records*, ed. John Jeaffreson (London: Middlesex County Records Society, 1887), vol. II, pp. xxx-xxxi.
2 *Middlesex*, vol. II, pp. xxx-xxxi.
3 Stephen, *A History of the Criminal Law of England*, vol. I, p. 306. See also J. A. Sharpe, *Crime in Seventeenth Century England: A County Study* (Cambridge: Cambridge University Press, 1983), p. 23.
4 Stephen, *A History of the Criminal Law of England*, vol. I, pp. 338-339.
5 Sir William Holdsworth, *A History of English Law*, 3rd ed. (London: Methuen, 1922), vol. V, p. 193.
6 See David Jardine, *Criminal Trials* (London: M. A. Nattali, 1932), vol. I.
7 Holdsworth, *A History of English Law*, vol. I, pp. 605ff.
8 Christopher Hill, *Intellectual Origins of the English Revolution* (London: Oxford University Press, 1972), p. 251.
9 Holdsworth, *A History of English Law*, vol. V, pp. 193-194, and Stephen, *A History of the Criminal Law of England*, vol. I, pp. 336-337.
10 Hill, *Intellectual Origins*, p. 251.
11 Ibid., p. 233.
12 *A Quip for an Upstart Courtier*, in *The Harleian Miscellany* (London: Dutton, 1808-11), vol. II, p. 232.
13 Robert Greene, *A Notable Discovery of Coosnage* (London: John Lane, The Bodley Head, 1923), p. 38.
14 Thomas Dekker, *The Belman of London*, in *The Guls Hornbook* and *The Belman of London* (London: J. M. Dent, 1928), p. 113.
15 *Quarter Sessions Records of Chester, 1558-1790* (Cheshire, 1940), pp. 67-68.
16 *Acts of the Privy Council of England, 1613-4* (London, 1912), pp. 109-110.
17 Ibid., pp. 100, 175.
18 W. H. Manchée, *The Westminster City Fathers* (London: John Lane, 1924), pp. 124-127; *Middlesex*, p. xxvi.
19 William Goodman, *The Social History of Great Britain during the Reigns of the Stuarts* (New York: W. H. Graham, 1847), vol. I, p. 22.
20 Stephen, *A History of the Criminal Law of England*, vol. I, p. 462; Sharpe, *Crime in Seventeenth Century England*, pp. 145-146.
21 See, for example, *Calendar of State Papers*, domestic series, 1603-10 (London, 1857), p. 472.
22 See, for example, ibid., p. 402.
23 Greene, *Quip*, pp. 224-227.
24 Holdsworth, *A History of English Law*, vol. I, pp. 216-226, 424-428. On informing as a profession, see Sharpe, *Crime in Seventeenth Century England*, pp. 145-146.

25 Bertram Osborne, *Justice of the Peace, 1361-1848* (Dorset: Sedgehill Press, 1960), p. 24.
26 Peter Archer, *The Queen's Courts*, 2nd ed. (Middlesex: Penguin, 1963), pp. 38-39.
27 Osborne, *Justice of the Peace*, pp. 89-90. Cf. also p. 70.
28 Jardine, *Criminal Trials*, vol. I, p. 461.
29 Goodman, *Social History of Great Britain*, vol. II, p. 212.
30 Osborne, *Justice of the Peace*, pp. 55-56.
31 Stephen, *A History of the Criminal Law of England*, vol. I, p. 358.
32 Quoted by Hill, *The Good Old Cause* (London: Lawrence and Wishart, 1949), pp. 41-42.
33 See G. P. Gooch, *English Democratic Ideas in the Seventeenth Century*, 2nd ed. (Cambridge: Cambridge University Press, 1927), pp. 119, 128-129.
34 *John Webster: A Critical Study* (London: Hogarth Press, 1951), p. 51. Most critics have been less reluctant than Leech to recognize the importance of *milieu* in this play. Especially sensitive to the role of social forces are Griffin (*John Webster: Politics and Tragedy* [Salzburg: Institut für Englische Sprache und Literatur, 1972]) and Lever (*The Tragedy of State* [London: Methuen, 1971]). The former finds the question "May virtue in the conventional sense exist at all in the court?" central to the two major tragedies (pp. 108-109). And Lever explains Webster's use of apparently irrelevant spectacle, as in the scene of the Papal election, as giving "dramatic expression to the overriding theme of a corrupt society" (p. 86). Jonathan Dollimore's discussion of Flamineo's social position is very similar to what I am presenting here (*Radical Tragedy: Religion, Ideology and Power in the Drama of Shakespeare and his Contemporaries* (Brighton, Sussex: Harvester Press, 1984), pp. 242-244.
35 Robert Whitman sees the pursuit of unattainable goals as central to the construction of *The White Devil*: "By moving his characters, in each successive episode, seemingly closer to the goal they seek, and at the same time making that goal increasingly unattainable and unworthy, Webster both gives the action a real sense of dramatic development and intensifies the tragic discrepancy between what his characters, in their blindness, *would* be, and what they are" (*Beyond Melancholy: John Webster and the Tragedy of Darkness*, Salzburg Studies in English Literature [Salzburg: Institut für Englische Sprache und Literatur, Universität Salzburg, 1973], p. 91). I find Whitman's analysis very helpful in grasping the unorthodox aesthetics of the play. In concluding that "*The White Devil* is the tragedy of *contemptus mundi*" (p. 109), however, he seems to be positing an alternative stance that is barely glimpsed in the play itself.
36 Elmer E. Stoll, *John Webster* (Boston: Alfred Mudge, 1905), pp. 124-125.
37 Franz Alexander and Hugo Staub, *The Criminal, the Judge, and the Public*, rev. ed. (Glencoe, Ill.: Free Press, 1956), p. 10.
38 In arguing the psychological coherence of Flamineo's character, I do not mean to imply that standards of naturalism are applicable to Websterian (and other Renaissance) plays. In Webster's characterization there is, as Peter Thomson puts it, a "characteristic cross-reference between the ontological and the psychological" ("Webster and the Actor," in Brian Morris, ed., *John Webster* [London: Ernest Benn, 1970], p. 35). Or, in Ralph Berry's words: "The characters appear to switch from living *in* the experience to the attempted standing *outside* and drawing conclusions from it" (*The Art of John Webster* [Oxford: Clarendon Press, 1972], p. 29). In spite of this fragmentation, the profundity of Webster's psychological insight and his mastery of natural expression have, not unwarrantably, led to a recurrent use of the term "naturalism" in Webster

criticism. The definitive study of Webster's characterization has not yet been written, although a start in this direction has been made by Thomson and others. Such a study would have to take account of the marked histrionic aptitude of many of the characters.

It would also be able to build on the excellent work on dramatic character in the plays of other English Renaissance playwrights that has appeared in such studies as Michael Goldman, "Characterizing Coriolanus," *Shakespeare Survey 34* (1981); Stephen Greenblatt, *Renaissance Self-Fashioning from More to Shakespeare* (Chicago: University of Chicago Press, 1980); Robert Hellenga, "Elizabethan Dramatic Conventions and Elizabethan Reality," *Renaissance Drama*, NS 12 (1981); and Peter Ure, "Character and Role from *Richard III* to *Hamlet*," *Stratford-upon-Avon Studies* V, ed. John Russell Brown and Bernard Harris (London: Arnold, 1963).

39 It is here that criticism of the play is most divergent, with some critics contending that the play is to be understood in terms of traditional Christian values and others doubting or denying the relevance of such terms. It is noteworthy that even those who find an orthodox moral statement in the play agree with Elizabeth Brennan that "Webster challenged his audience to judge for themselves where good and evil lie in the characters of this tragedy and the act of attempting such judgment was not made easy for them" ("'An Understanding Auditory': An Audience for John Webster," in Brian Morris, ed., *John Webster*, p. 14). So difficult is this act of judgment that Peter Murray fears that although Webster is certainly on the side of the angels, the spectators, like the characters, "may be led to make false moral judgments" (*A Study of John Webster* [The Hague: Mouton, 1969], p. 32). Anders Dallby, who sees Webster as "an impassioned defender of the old world order," attributes the "confusion among modern Webster critics as to the moral values intended in the play" to oversubtlety on Webster's part. Webster uses a "sort of point-of-view technique, a strangely neutral, or seemingly neutral author's attitude," which results, on the positive side, in a "strangely modern texture" and, on the negative side, in the loss of a "quality of immediate clarity and moral conviction." The orthodox values are there, though, in the imagery: "The images are right; it is they that represent reality in this tragedy" (*The Anatomy of Evil* [Lund: Gleerup, 1974], p. 161).

Much energy and ingenuity has been addressed to the task of finding orthodox values in this play. For my part, I do not believe that Webster was incapable of expressing himself unequivocally when he wanted to. The fact is that the play has been profoundly disturbing to readers and spectators precisely because it does not lend itself to pious interpretation. Critical charity suggests that we credit Webster with having intended just that. I entirely agree with Roma Gill, who sees in this play a conscious and "skilled manipulation of the audience into unaccustomed and uncomfortable moral positions" ("'Quaintly Done': A Reading of *The White Devil*," *Essays and Studies* NS 19 [1966], p. 59).

40 See the account of Raleigh's trial in Jardine, *Criminal Trials*, vol. I.
41 Bowen, *The Lion and the Throne*, p. 315.
42 Holdsworth, *A History of English Law*, vol. II, pp. 619-620, Sharpe, *Crime in Seventeenth Century England*, p. 27.
43 Holdsworth, *A History of English Law*, vol. II, pp. 605ff.
44 See Bowen, *The Lion and the Throne*, pp. 88-89. Excommunication was a potent weapon. If the excommunicant did not submit within forty days, he was subject to imprisonment (Holdsworth, *A History of English Law*, vol. I, pp. 631-632).

The White Devil: Law and Power 63

45 Holdsworth, *A History of English Law*, vol. I, pp. 619-620.
46 Ibid., vol. I, p. 509.
47 Bowen, *The Lion and the Throne*, p. 108.
48 Holdsworth, *A History of English Law*, vol. V, pp. 191-192.
49 J. R. Brown, ed., *The White Devil* (Cambridge, Mass.: Harvard University Press, 1960), p. 71.
50 Critical discussion of Vittoria has, I think, been inordinately concerned with ascertaining precisely what admixture of good and evil goes into the making of her character. Thus, one critic expresses certainty that she is guilty of lasciviousness, but not of instigation to murder; another sees her as brave to the point of heroism; and a third (Dallby, *The Anatomy of Evil*, p. 131) is convinced that she is "Satan himself." The critical divergence on this issue stems, I believe, from the way Vittoria is presented to the audience, which is something like the way celebrities appear to the public eye, in fragments of reported or glimpsed behaviour subject to endless interpretation. Vittoria is always under the obligation to play a role; as Thomson says, she is the "observed" (whereas Flamineo is an observer) and therefore "consciously displays herself" (Thomson, p. 36). Given such a mode of presentation, the character inevitably remains to some extent enigmatic. When I say here that Vittoria is not innocent, what I mean is that she is at least guilty of conspiracy to commit adultery.
51 The confinement to a "house of convertites" (a detention centre for penitent whores) may be an indirect reference to another manifestation of legal discrimination against women. In 1609 the punishment for the moral offence of producing a bastard child was changed from the whipping of both parents to the confinement of the mother only to a house of correction (Osborne, *Justices of the Peace*, pp. 68-69).
    On the subject of the newly instituted houses of correction, see Sharpe, *Crime in Seventeenth Century England*, pp. 150-152.
52 Bowen, *The Lion and the Throne*, p. 223.
53 Jardine, *Criminal Trials*, vol. I, pp. 406-407.
54 Ibid., vol. I, pp. 349-350.
55 Ibid., vol. I, p. 330.
56 Ibid., vol. I, p. 429.
57 Elizabeth Brennan, ed., *The White Devil*, The New Mermaid series (London: Ernest Benn, 1966), p. xvi. Headway towards an analysis is made by J. R. Mulryne, who seems nonetheless to wonder at his own reactions: "Such is the force of her acting, such the climate of irresponsibility (we certainly do not regard Monticelso and Francisco as disinterested judges), that we almost believe her cries that justice has been ravished" (*The White Devil*, ed. J. R. Mulryne, Regents Renaissance Drama Series [Lincoln: University of Nebraska Press, 1969], p. xxv). Dallby, who is impervious to Vittoria's charms, says that "watching her effect on dukes and Webster critics alike is a frightening demonstration of the power of the white devil" (*The Anatomy of Evil*, p. 131).
58 Paul Reiwald, *Society and its Criminals*, ed. and trans. T. E. James (New York: International Universities Press, 1950), p. 268.
59 Jardine, *Criminal Trials*, vol. I, p. 461.
60 This analysis is not intended to exhaust the riches of the scene. See, for example, Griffin's interesting discussion of Vittoria's assertion "of what she feels to be her natural identity vs. the role assigned to her by the Court" (*John Webster*, pp. 85-86).

Chapter Three

The White Devil and Jacobean Theories of the Origin of Law

The White Devil is Webster's most purely iconoclastic play. With sardonic contempt for the pieties of his time, Webster draws a picture of human nature and social institutions that undermines the current philosophical orthodoxies without suggesting anything to replace them. It is the creation of a man who is both angry and amused at institutionalized deception, determined to reveal the true nature of the sacred institutions of marriage, the family, the church, the law and the state, and to demonstrate, in images of flesh and blood, the vacuity of the philosophical presuppositions used to support these institutions.

Chief among these presuppositions was the idea that human beings are essentially rational, that their nature is in accord with the principle of reason that guides the universe.[1] From Aquinas to Pico to Hooker, one of the fundamental philosophical assumptions was that people are distinct from other animals in their possession of a rational faculty that enables them to grasp the essential principles of right and wrong. Law, they said, is manifest throughout the universe, a reflection of the divine reason and harmony of the Creator. But while natural laws are obeyed passively and unconsciously by all the rest of creation, the human response to natural law is active, conscious, and rational. For people, natural law is not mechanical determination, but rather, as Hooker puts it, it is "the Law which human Nature knoweth itself in reason universally bound unto, which also for that cause may be termed most fitly the Law of Reason."[2]

This identification of the law of nature with the law of reason led to a notion of positive law as merely an artificial reinforcement of what all people might know by the light of their own understanding. As a very popular English essay on law put it, there is a law "written in the heart of every man, teaching him what is to be done, and what is to be fled."[3] The need for positive laws was easily explained in terms of Christian doctrine. The Fall had corrupted the human will so that people did not always do what they knew to be right. But the Fall had not eradicated the human conscience, and it was by the light of this conscience—or natural understanding—that people were to construct their positive laws. To test the quality of man-made laws, then, it was only necessary to apply the principle that "in every law positive well made, is somewhat of the law of reason, and of the law of God."[4] Legislators and judges alike were to be guided by this principle. "All national laws whatsoever," said Bacon, "are to be taken strictly and hardly in any point wherein they abridge and derogate from the law of nature."[5]

It is by virtue of this concept of human beings as moral and rational that Elyot was able to define a "public weal" as a "body living, compact or made of sundry estates and degrees of men, which is disposed by the order of equity and governed by the rule and moderation of reason."[6] Given the supremacy of reason, all things are possible. Positive law becomes a "reflection of the divine reason governing the universe,"[7] and nothing can be more perfect. Since the function of law is to recall fallen human beings to a sense of what it is that distinguishes them from the beasts, a well-ordered society will provide laws which, in their own reasonableness, appeal directly to our innate natural reason. Thus, laws should be framed with a mildness implied by Hooker when he reluctantly admits that "the corruption of our nature being pre-supposed, we may not deny but that the Law of Nature doth now require of necesity some kind of regiment."[8] In the tradition of natural law philosophy stemming from Aquinas, the state is, not an artificial structure designed to oppress and inhibit us, but rather a reflection of our natural desire to obey the laws of reason.

This sanguine view of human beings in society was reinforced by another assumption about their nature, the belief in a "social attraction engrained in human nature."[9] With such venerable authorities as Aristotle and Cicero to support it, the idea was taken as axiomatic by Hooker, Althusius, Grotius, and others, who saw this natural sociability as the great generative power behind human associations.[10] Bacon echoes Aristotle: "Whosoever in the frame of his nature and affections is unfit for friendship, he taketh it of the beast and not from humanity."[11] Concrete evidence for this theory was found in the apparent universality of the family, which Althusius called *consociatio naturalis necessaria*.[12] The widespread view was that the existence of the family was proof of a natural social instinct, and that all other associations, culminating in the sovereign state, had been built up by imitation of this basic unit. While the state itself might not be natural and necessary, it was at least made in the image of an institution that was.[13]

Thus, the idea of human nature as innately social and rational provided the foundation for a view of society and law as directly emanating from that nature. John Danby succinctly characterizes the harmonious interrelationship of reason, law, and nature in Elizabethan thought:

> The idea of Nature,... in orthodox Elizabethan thought, is always something normative for human beings. It is impossible to talk about Nature without talking also about pattern and ideal form; about Reason as displayed in Nature; about Law as the innermost expression of Nature; and custom which is the basis of Law and equally with law an expression of Nature's pattern; about Restraint as the observance of Law, and the way to discover our richest self-fulfilment.[14]

The qualification "orthodox" is important; for there were already intellectual countercurrents tending, each in its own way, to upset the traditional harmonies. The idealized image of nature was being challenged as inadequately grounded in observed phenomena. Carl Becker's definition of the "ghostly" image of nature in Renaissance philosophy implies the kind of criticism that was being directed against it:

> Design in nature was... derived *a priori* from the character which the Creator was assumed to have; and natural law, so far from being associated with the observed behavior of physical phenomena, was no more than a conceptual universe above and outside the real one, a logical construction dwelling in the mind of God and dimly reflected in the minds of philosophers.[15]

With the growing secularization of philosophy and emphasis on scientific observation and inductive logic, this ghostly image came increasingly under attack.

The various lines of this attack have been studied in great detail by Hiram Haydn, just as the traditional position has been presented by Douglas Bush, Theodore Spencer, and E. M. W. Tillyard.[16] (The reader who desires more information that I can include in this compressed discussion is referred to their books.) It is important to stress, as Haydn does, that what he calls the "Counter-Renaissance" is not a unified movement, but rather, a series of challenges—from various positions—to the orthodox view. What unites such diverse figures as Machiavelli, Luther, and Montaigne is not a common ideology, nor even a common interpretation of nature. Rather, it is a shared disbelief in the traditional image of nature and a "rebellion against their predecessors' exaltation of intellect and reason as the ultimate normative principle of every department of life."[17] Haydn summarizes:

> The world-views of the various schools of the Counter-Renaissance contain one important constant in their attitude toward Nature. However much they otherwise vary, and even contradict each other, they share a disbelief in the identity of, or complementary cooperation between, Nature and Reason. Whether an individual thinker or a given group within the Counter-Renaissance finds Nature "good" or "bad", he gives the lie to the traditional humanistic concept of the close and intimate relationship between Nature and Reason.[18]

Religious anti-rationalism provided one of the challenges. Within Catholicism, fideism was never dead. In his illuminating introduction to Milton's prose, Ernest Sirluck says:

> The fact is that although it is hard to find anyone bold enough to deny the existence of a natural law while heresy trials were a present danger, there was always a minority to whom it was simply evil.

As an example he cites John Colet, whose anti-rationalism is particularly interesting because it is not what we would expect from a humanist educator. Colet saw law as divided into two totally irreconcilable categories: divine law, which is revealed, and human law, which, as the expression of the corrupt nature of human beings, could create nothing but "injustice, folly, and death." The faculty by which people create laws, their "reason," is incapable of contact with divine law: "Human reason is the enemy and opponent of grace."[19]

It was possible to accept the main premises of natural law philosophy without accepting its conclusions. Admitting that God had given human beings the liberty to choose, and that he had set down eternal natural laws by virtue of which they had the potential to choose the good, one could go on to argue that they rarely realize that potential. Thus John Hayward:

> Certainly, of all the creatures under heaven which have received being from God, none degenerate, none forsake their natural dignity and being, but only man. Only man, abandoning the dignity of his proper nature, is changed like Proteus into divers forms. And this is occasioned by the liberty of his will.[20]

Ironically, it is the very gift of reason and choice, intended to raise human beings above the level of the beasts, that actually causes their debasement. This line of thought is perfected by Pascal, who took the traditional materials of natural law philosophy—the law of reason, and the idea of corruption by the Fall—and, by shifting the emphasis, stood the whole philosophy on its head: "Il y a sans doute des lois naturelles, mais cette belle raison corrompue a tout corrumpu."[21]

If anti-rationalism was a force within Catholicism in the Renaissance, it was the very essence of the Lutheran heresy. Abandoning even lip service to laws of reason and of nature, Luther declared reason to be the "whore of the devil. It can only blaspheme and dishonour everything God has said or done."[22] Since reason and nature are hopelessly corrupt, law must be seen, not as an emanation of human nature, but rather as an imposition upon it: "Man does not love but hates the law which forces him to what is good and forbids what is evil; his will, far from seeking the law, detests it."[23] Commenting on Luther's attitude towards reason, Robert Hoopes says:

> By "reason" Luther seems to mean only the logical faculty.... He ignores, or at any rate nowhere discusses, reason in the Christian humanistic sense of "right reason," that faculty in man which directs his thought *and* his behavior.[24]

If Luther "ignores" right reason, it is because, for him, no such thing exists. Just as it does not exist in the world of *The White Devil*.

The religious anti-rationalists rejected natural law philosophy primarily because, with their emphasis on the doctrine of the Fall, they found nature to be depraved. Another challenge came from more secular spirits who felt that nature's laws had not yet been ascertained. "Those who have taken upon them to lay down the law of nature as a thing already searched out and understood," said Bacon, "have herein done philosophy and the sciences great injury."[25] It is a quiet statement, the retention of the term "law of nature" rhetorically keyed to allay the reader's anxieties. But in cutting nature adrift from reason and leaving it as a free-floating body, the statement undermines the whole structure of natural law philosophy. The nature of nature is no longer to be deduced *a priori* from the character of the Creator, but is now to be understood through close observation of its particular manifestations. The assumption that people are rational should be re-examined and attention given to hitherto neglected aspects of human nature: "I find strange... that Aristotle should have written divers volumes of Ethics, and never handled the affections, which is the principal subject thereof."[26]

Among those who set out to handle the affections, Montaigne probably remains most interesting to modern readers and, judging from the number of borrowings, he seems to have had a considerable influence on Webster.[27] Abandoning the traditional hierarchical Christian framework, Montaigne denied that human beings possess any faculty that distinguishes them from the other animals: "We are neither above nor below the rest: all that is under heaven, says the sage, incurs the same law and the same fortune."[28] Our notion of ourselves as uniquely rational is nothing but the expression of a monstrous vanity. Montaigne did not deny the existence of some form of natural law, but his concept of natural law has nothing to do with Hooker's:

> It is credible that there are natural laws, as may be seen in other creatures; but in us they are lost; that fine human reason butts in everywhere, domineering and commanding, muddling and confusing the face of things in accordance with its vanity and inconsistency.[29]

For the notion that humans beings had been given even a potential faculty for creating positive laws in accordance with divine laws governing the universe, Montaigne had nothing but contempt. Laws are as various as the customs and traditions of societies, and they are as changeable as the ocean. The insistence on the immutable truth of certain laws is only another expression of pathetic human vanity:

> The laws of conscience, which we say are born of nature, are born of custom.... And the common notions that we find in credit around us and infused into our soul by our fathers' seed, these seem to be the universal natural ones. Whence it comes to pass that what is off the hinges of custom, people believe to be off the hinges of reason: God knows how unreasonably, most of the time.[30]

The concept of human nature as essentially rational, then, far from serving as a link between the human and the divine, only distorts our perception of ourselves and provides a handy rationalization for unreasonable actions. Absolute ethical postulates, and the positive laws that reflect them, are appealing in their apparent orderliness; but they have nothing to do with real life, which is—and must ever be—"a material and corporal motion, an action imperfect and disordered by its own essence."[31] To be at one with the universe is to accept our own disorderly and passionate nature.

The idea of a social instinct engrained in human nature received similar treatment by writers who felt that clear-eyed investigation revealed far different laws of human behaviour. Machiavelli explained the origin of political associations, not in terms of a natural social instinct, but rather in terms of the inability of isolated individuals to defend themselves against attack. "The little security which the natives found in living dispersed," he said, is what caused them to seek common shelter in political organizations.³² Bodin had a similar notion of the origin of political communities. Accepting the idea of the family as a natural social unit, he nonetheless denied that the state arose naturally out of the family. Rather, he postulated a version of Eden in which every man was master of his household and isolated from all other society, an Eden which man, unhappily, chose to abandon, thus unleashing the "force, violence, ambition, avarice, and the passion for vengeance" that inevitably led to armed conflict and subjugation. "Reason and common sense alike point to the conclusion," wrote Bodin, "that the origin and foundation of commonwealths was in force and violence."³³

The relevance of these ideas to orthodox political and legal philosophy is apparent. Roscoe Pound has observed that every system of legal philosophy reflects an attempt to postulate "some ultimate basis, beyond the reach of the individual human will, that stands fast in the whirl of change of which life is made up."³⁴ Elyot and Hooker, reflecting an authoritative tradition, had found such an ultimate basis in the natural laws of reason and sociability. For those who doubted the validity of these laws, the absolute foundation was shattered, and a rationale for law had to be sought elsewhere.

From Machiavelli on, there is a growing tendency to rationalize law as an aspect of the force necessary to preserve order, "a body of commands of the sovereign authority."³⁵ Since people are naturally anarchic, ambitious and irrational, the forms of social behaviour must be imposed upon them artificially or all society will disintegrate into chaos. "The nature of men is such," says Raleigh, "as will not endeavor any thing good, unless they be forced thereunto; for where liberty aboundeth, there confusion and disorder follow."³⁶ The aim of law is not to lead people to virtue by appealing to their conscience, but rather to preserve the state by frightening its subjects into submission. "The rod, which is the symbol of justice, ought never to be idle,"³⁷ says Richelieu. "This is more persuasive for most men than reason, which has little power over many minds."³⁸ The term "justice," once almost synonymous with the terms "nature" and "reason," has now become almost synonymous with the word "power."

In England, this tradition culminates in the post-Jacobean work of Thomas Hobbes, but Webster must have encountered it in the prolific, if less systematic utterances of James I. Anticipating Hobbes, James located the origin of all law in the sovereign power:

> So the trewth is directly contrarie in our state to the false affirmation of such seditious writers, as would persuade us, that the Lawes and state of our country were established before the admitting of a king: where by the countrarie ye see it plainely

prooved, that a wise king comming in among barbares, first established the estate and forms of government, and thereafter made lawes by himself, and his successours according thereto.[39]

Like Hobbes, James asserted that people are better off under the rule of the most tyrannical king than they would be in a state of nature:

> It is certaine that a king can never be so monstrously vicious, but hee will generally favour justice, and maintaine some order, except in the particulars, wherein his inordinate lustes and passions carry him away; where by the contrary, no King being, nothing is unlawfull, to none.[40]

But Hobbes was to base his political ideology on secular observation and analysis. James retained the analogy between king and God that had been commonplace for centuries and, by substituting an inscrutable Calvinist deity for his mild and rational predecessor, James buttressed his proto-Hobbesian ideology with a religious justification of absolutism:

> That which concerns the mystery of the King's power is not lawful to be disputed; for that is to wade into the weakness of Princes and to take away the mystical reverence that belongs unto them that sit in the Throne of God.[41]

Machiavelli, James, Richelieu, and Hobbes were alike concerned with rationalizing the consolidation of power into strong national units in sixteenth- and seventeenth-century Europe. In Webster's time, there was as yet no cogent philosophical response available to those who had discarded traditional natural law ideas but were opposed to absolute monarchy. Within thirty years of the composition of *The White Devil*, England was to be alive with new and revolutionary political ideas, theories of parliamentary sovereignty, of social contract, of natural rights. But positive political ideas germinate in action and in the stasis of 1610 it did not occur to anyone (or no one dared to suggest) that the true sovereign power in England might be said to reside absolutely in Parliament, or that all power ultimately rests with the people. Parliamentarian opponents of James' attempts to extend the royal prerogative did not propose new alternatives. Rather, they adopted a conservative posture, claiming that James was violating the time-honoured laws of England and the "fundamental" principles of its constitution.[42] With both Royalists and Parliamentarians claiming to be the true heirs of a hypothetical British constitution, the citing of legal precedents tended to replace ideas as the substance of the controversy, and political philosophy congealed into antiquarianism. Turning his back on the future he was helping to create, Coke rested his case on a variant of the argument from authority. To a philosophical and rebellious mind (like Webster's) with a deep distrust of authorities in general, Coke's rhetorical tactic would have been uninspiring.

Such were the alternative ways of rationalizing law in Webster's time, and in *The White Devil* he rejects them all. The focus of the attack is the orthodox view of human nature and the rationalization of law it generated. In *The White Devil*, there is no trace of the idealistic notion that humanity, by virtue of natural reason, can comprehend the basic laws of good and evil. The only kind of reason Webster recognizes as real is the reason of Machiavelli's fox. Monticelso and Francisco superficially stand for reason when they chastise Brachiano in terms of traditional rationalistic and hierarchical philosophy. They point out to him, as Hooker might have done, that he has violated the laws of nature by allowing his sexual desire to dominate his reason, and his personal impulses to dominate his political obligations, thus lowering himself to the level of a beast. But their stated belief in humanity's unique position in the universe does not enable Monticelso and Francisco to be better men than Brachiano. It merely gives them an excuse for revenge.

Webster's rejection of this idea of human nature is expressed in another important way. One of the prime tenets of thinkers like Hooker and St. Germain is that the laws of virtue and vice are firmly inscribed in the conscience of all people, so that they know what is right even if they are too corrupt to act accordingly. But the characters in *The White Devil* are singularly conscienceless. Flamineo experiences a moment of remorse when he sees his mother in a state of insane grief, but his reaction is spontaneous and emotional rather than ethical and conscientious. Flamineo's version of the golden rule (the law that was generally held to be most clearly accessible to natural reason) is to do it to others before they have a chance to do it to him. Vittoria is even more startlingly lacking in any basic moral sense. Her behaviour during the trial is marked by a conviction of her own innocence; her fits of remorse, whether sham or genuine, occur when remorse will serve as a potent psychological weapon, as in her quarrel with Brachiano in the house of convertites; and Webster blatantly disregards the historical accounts of Vittoria's penitence at the end of her life.[43] In fact, it would be very difficult to name a first-rate work of art in which major characters are less troubled by conscience than they are in *The White Devil*. Like Machiavelli and Montaigne, Webster seems disenchanted with the idea that the laws of nature "are written in the heart of every man."

Webster is equally unconvinced by the doctrine of humanity's innate sociability. In *The White Devil*, people come together purely for the purpose of mutual gain, and relationships exist only as long as they advance that purpose. This is manifest in the relationship between Flamineo and Brachiano, which is a grim parody of the feudal tie between lord and servant. In the totally individualistic world of *The White Devil*, society exists for the benefit of those who rule, and any coherence it possesses is attributable to the rulers' power to impose order upon the chaos natural to humans. For those who are not in power, the only hope is to remain serviceable to those who are. Thus, Lodovico is banished when his skill with a dagger seems, to his betters, to threaten social order, and then recalled when his particular talents are required. And Flamineo has no hold on Brachiano once he has served the latter's turn. Friendship, trust, mutual obligation—these are absent from the world of *The White Devil*.

At the core of Webster's negation of the idea of humanity's sociability is his portrayal of the "natural and necessary" institution of the family. The disintegration of the ties among the Corombonas is an emblem of the social chaos that prevails in general. In the background is the memory of a father who did not provide for his family and of the sacrifice of a daughter for the sake of the family's economic survival. From this proceeds Flamineo's rejection of his mother and his assumption of the role of pander to his sister. The disintegration is complete when Flamineo murders his brother and the two remaining siblings attempt to murder each other. As in *Lear*, the breakdown of family ties seems to be central to a total breakdown of order. If this most natural of human associations, this "image" of the state,[44] proves to be a feeble human artifice, then what hope can there be for the social order in general? In rejecting the family as a stable social unit, Webster is attacking the very foundation of the theory of humanity's sociability, and postulating a world in which social ties are artifical impositions that tend to fly apart when individuals pursue their natural bent. The very texture of *The White Devil*—the disappearance and reappearance of characters, the dialogues composed of alternating monologues, the failure of characters to interact or communicate, the intricacy and apparent randomness of the action—seems to express the chaos and loneliness that Webster sees as basic to the human condition. As Bradbrook puts it, "the characters magnetize each other, but egoism keeps them afloat in their uncomprehended orbits."[45] It is only in the love between Vittoria and Brachiano that Webster presents anything like a social impulse, but that love clearly does not generate sociability on a more general scale.

In rejecting the view of people as rational and social, Webster necessarily rejects the theory of politics and law based on this view. Society, such as it is, does not have roots in human nature, for human nature is essentially passionate and anarchic. The law of nature for humanity is not the law of reason; rather, it is a law of ceaseless striving for security, power, and sensual gratification. In such a world, there can be no distinction between law and force, because law has its origin in the force necessary to establish order. Thus, when Monticelso judges, he is not concerned with conscience, but with reason of state, as he clearly reveals when he tells Vittoria:

> your publicke fault,
> Joyn'd to'th condition of the present time,
> Takes from you all the fruits of noble pitty. (III, ii, 266-268)

In other words, the law, in *The White Devil*, is the absolutist imposition of order upon natural chaos. Paul Vinogradoff's analysis of the world according to Hobbes might almost be a description of the world of *The White Devil*:

> The force of Hobbes' argument depended on the fact that he had simplified the political problems to the utmost by reducing them to two factors—separate individuals, incapable of creating society, and the State, a "persona ficta", through whose compulsion the intercourse between isolated individuals became possible, but which was in truth the creation of individual brains. The atomism of individuals, disconnected in nature and connected by mechanical coercion, is the general principle in which both extremes are united.[46]

In *The White Devil*, the same gulf exists between individuals and the society in which they exist. The function of law is the suppression of individualism, sexual desire, ambition, and whatever else, being natural to humanity, leads to anarchy. For those who rule, the end of order justifies whatever means are used to attain it.

But whereas Hobbes makes the imposition of order more palatable by treating the state as an abstraction, Webster concretizes the state in portraits of individual members of the ruling class. The state, which in the seventeenth century was fast becoming a mystical and self-justifying entity to the prophets of absolutism, is no greater in *The White Devil* than the sum of its rulers. Reason of state is not a transcendent communal principle, but only the objectives of those who happen to be in power. And law is another way of maintaining power. England was well into the revolution before anyone became sufficiently liberated from the traditional reverence for law to state openly and without ambiguity that even "the best laws that England hath are yokes and manacles, tying one sort of people to be slaves to another."[47] But much the same point had already been made by Montaigne about laws in general:

> Lawes are nowe maintained in credit, not because they are essentially just, but because they are lawes. It is the mysticall foundation of their authority—they have none other—which availes them much: They are often made by fooles; more often by men who, in hatred of equality, have want of equity.[48]

Perhaps the influence of Montaigne helped Webster to be radically critical of law in advance of his time. Certainly, it was less dangerous to imply radical criticism in a play than to state it in plain prose. (Since even modern critics have occasionally read *The White Devil* as a sociological study of Renaissance Italy, we can suppose that the foreign setting helped to blind the censor in its own time.) In any case, law in *The White Devil* is stripped of its mystical authority and shown to be the property of the ruling class.

This, while Webster and Hobbes both explain the origin and existence of laws in terms of the Counter-Renaissance conception of law as an imposition on human nature rather than an emanation from it, for Webster this explanation does not constitute a justification. Seeing an innate conflict between human nature and social order, Hobbes chooses order. Webster, whose sympathies do not lie with the ruling class, chooses anarchy. Thus, he makes Vittoria, Brachiano, and Flamineo attractive to us exactly in proportion to their defiance of the law and disruption of the established order. Human nature may be amoral, but it is not improved by a tyrannical (and equally amoral) state. On the contrary, the laws of the state, together with the orthodox conception of nature used to rationalize the laws, only make things worse by turning natural impulses into criminal acts. On one level, the tragedy of *The White Devil* lies in the apparently irreconcilable contradiction between the actual flux and chaos of human nature and the human longing for peace and stability. Unlike Hobbes, Webster does not see a solution in political absolutism.

Writing about *Macbeth*, Franco Moretti says that the protagonist

> acts like Cesare Borgia but thinks like Hooker, and such is also the position of Shakespeare: the position manifest in his tragic structure, where the axis of actions (the plot) is governed by one logic and the axis of values (the paradigm) by another, without either ever succeeding in overwhelming or expunging the other.[49]

There is no one in *The White Devil* who thinks like Hooker, although, for various reasons, several characters talk like him. But Hooker is there in both paradigm and plot, as the ideology disintegrating before a strong blast of nay-saying.

Notes to Chapter Three

1. On this subject, see Theodore Spencer, *Shakespeare and the Nature of Man* (New York: Macmillan, 1942), Chapter I; Douglas Bush, *The Renaissance and English Humanism* (Toronto: University of Toronto Press, 1939); E. M. W. Tillyard, *The Elizabethan World Picture* (New York: Macmillan, 1944).
2. Richard Hooker, *Of the Laws of Ecclesiastical Polity* (London: Dent, 1907), vol. I, p. 182.
3. Christopher St. German, *The Doctor and Student*, rev. and cor. William Muchall (Cincinnati: R. Clarke, 1874), p. 5.
4. Ibid., p. 10.
5. "Case of the Post-Nati of Scotland," in *The Works of Francis Bacon*, ed. James Spedding, R. Ellis, and D. Heath (London: Longmans, 1857-74), vol. VII, p. 664.
6. Quoted by Spencer, *Shakespeare and the Nature of Man*, p. 16.
7. Roscoe Pound, *An Introduction to the Philosophy of Law*, rev. ed. (New Haven: Yale University Press, 1954), p. 27.
8. Hooker, *Of the Laws of Ecclesiastical Polity*, vol. I, p. 191.
9. Paul Vinogradoff, "Reason and Conscience in Sixteenth Century Jurisprudence," in *The Collected Papers of Paul Vinogradoff* (Oxford: Clarendon, 1928), vol. II, p. 296.
10. Ibid., vol. II, p. 299.
11. "Of Friendship," in *Essays, Advancement of Learning, New Atlantis, and other Pieces*, ed. Richard Jones (New York: Odyssey Press, 1937), p. 76.
12. Otto Gierke, *Natural Law and the Theory of Society*, trans. Ernest Barker (Cambridge, England: Cambridge University Press, 1934), vol. II, p. 277, note 36.
13. Ibid., vol. I, pp. 65, 72; vol. II, pp. 269-279.
14. *Shakespeare's Doctrine of Nature* (London: Faber & Faber, 1949), p. 21.
15. *The Heavenly City of the Eighteenth-Century Philosophers* (New Haven: Yale University Press, 1959), p. 55.
16. See note 1 to this chapter.
17. Haydn, *The Counter-Renaissance* (New York: Scribner, 1950), p. xv.
18. Ibid., p. 468.
19. John Milton, *Complete Prose Works*, gen. ed. Don Wolfe (New Haven: Yale University Press, 1963), vol. II (ed. Sirluck), p. 32.
20. *David's Tears*, quoted by Tillyard, *The Elizabethan World Picture*, p. 68.
21. Blaise Pascal, *Pensées Opuscules*, ed. Léon Brunschvicg (Paris: Hachette, 1904-14), p. 294.
22. Robert Hoopes, *Right Reason in the English Renaissance* (Cambridge, Mass.: Harvard University Press, 1962), p. 103.
23. Ibid., p. 101.
24. Ibid., p. 103.
25. Quoted by Haydn, *The Counter-Renaissance*, p. 272.
26. Ibid., p. 398.
27. I entirely disagree with Richard Bodtke's contention that it is a "peculiarly 'Jacobean' Montaigne of skepticism, despair, and a stoical attitude towards death whom we see hovering over the Jacobean drama," and that the "healthy naturalism for which we reverence him" caused the playwrights nothing but "despair and disenchantment" (*Tragedy and the Jacobean Temper: The Major Plays of John Webster*, Salzburg Studies in English Literature [Salzburg: Institut für Englische Sprache und Literatur, Universität Salzburg, 1972], p. 10). For more on Bodtke, see above, Chapter I, note 11. Here, as

The White Devil and Jacobean Theories 77

   throughout, Bodtke's view of the Jacobeans is too one-sided, as I am attempting to demonstrate.
28 *Apology for Raymond Sebond*, in *Complete Essays*, ed. and trans. Donald Frame (Garden City, N.Y.: Doubleday, 1960), vol. II, p. 137.
29 Ibid., p. 280.
30 *Essays*, vol. I, pp. 113-114.
31 Quoted by Haydn, *The Counter-Renaissance*, p. 259.
32 *The Discourses*, Book I, Chapter I, p. 106, in *The Prince and the Discourses*, ed. Max Lerner (New York: Modern Library, 1940).
33 *Six Books of the Commonwealth*, ed. and trans. M. J. Tooley (Oxford: Blackwell, 1955), Book I, pp. 18-19.
34 Pound, *An Introduction to the Philosophy of Law*, pp. 31-32.
35 Ibid., pp. 27-28.
36 Quoted by Haydn, *The Counter-Renaissance*, p. 413.
37 *The Political Testament of Cardinal Richelieu*, ed. and trans. Henry Bertram Hill (Madison, Wisc.: University of Wisconsin Press, 1916), p. 87.
38 Ibid., p. 85.
39 *The Trew Law of Free Monarchies*, in *The Political Works of James I*, ed. Charles McIlwain (Cambridge, Mass.: Harvard University Press, 1918), p. 62.
40 Ibid., p. 66.
41 Quoted by J. W. Allen, *English Political Thought*, rev. ed. (London: Methuen, 1960), p. 255.
42 See Sirluck, p. 12, and Christopher Hill, *The Century of Revolution* (London: Nelson, 1961), pp. 63-68, 176-179.
43 See Elmer Stoll, *John Webster* (Boston: Alfred Mudge, 1905), pp. 85-86, and Gunnar Boklund, *The Sources of The White Devil* (Uppsala, Sweden: Lundequistska Bokhandeln, 1957), pp. 46-47.
44 Bodin, quoted by Gierke, *Natural Law and the Theory of Society*, vol. II, p. 269, note 1.
45 Muriel Bradbrook, *John Webster: Citizen and Dramatist* (New York: Columbia University Press, 1980), p. 133. Compare J. R. Mulryne: "In general [Webster] seems to have mastered the incredibly difficult task, given the dramatic conventions of this age, of creating a theatrical expressionism that could register social and moral collapse" (*The White Devil*, ed. J. R. Mulryne, Regents Renaissance Drama Series [Lincoln: University of Nebraska Press, 1969], p. xix). Both these critics have excellent insights into the aesthetics of the play.
46 *Collected Papers*, vol. II, p. 295.
47 Gerrard Winstanley, quoted by Hill, *The Century of Revolution*, p. 177.
48 Quoted by Haydn, *The Counter-Renaissance*, p. 419.
49 "'A Huge Eclipse': Tragic Form and the Deconsecration of Sovereignty," in *The Power of Forms in the English Renaissance*, ed. Stephen Greenblatt (Norman, Oklahoma: Pilgrim Books, 1982), p. 31.

Chapter Four

The Duchess of Malfi: The Roots of Judgment

> FERDINAND: Where are your Cubbs?
> DUCHESS: Whom!
> FERDINAND: Call them your children;
> For though our nationall law distinguish
> Bastards
> From true legitimate issue: compassion-
> ate nature
> Makes them all equall. (IV, i, 40-44)

In *The Duchess of Malfi*, as in *The White Devil*, Webster distinguishes between those who judge and those who are essentially concerned with their own fulfilment. The actions which call forth judgment and the desire for revenge are similar: the consummation of a passion which is offensive to those in power, and at least suspect to society as a whole. Again, Webster's imagination is stimulated by the conflict between natural passion and the social codes which seek to repress it. But this time, there is no ambivalence in his statement of the theme, for his representatives of love are as clearly sympathethic as those who oppose them are villainous.

Clarity of values is manifest in the form of *The Duchess of Malfi*. In contrast, the structure of *The White Devil* is expressive of the relativism of its statement. The canvas of the earlier play is crowded and the pace exhausting. Our efforts to identify with a character or a group are repeatedly thwarted. When Vittoria has won us over in the arraignment scene, we are almost immediately asked to contend emotionally with the grief of Isabella's son. If we tend to identify with Flamineo, the responsive chord must be at

The Duchess of Malfi: *The Roots of Judgment*

least partially severed when he murders his brother. Even our distaste for the avengers is undermined when Francisco, in the mask of Mulinassar, becomes a sensitive observer of life. The play seems deliberately fashioned to threaten our system of values, whatever that may be. Webster seems to say: you can't even tell the good guys from the bad guys, so how can you pretend to know right from wrong?

In *The White Devil*, we are asked to see objectively. Although the major characters are all deeply conceived, they remain somewhat mysterious. We are seeing them from outside and, as in real life, their actions are often perplexing and unexpected, and never entirely understood. The tragic mode is panoramic, and characterization is episodic. The tragic mode of *The Duchess of Malfi*, on the other hand, is analytic. The major characters are thrown into high relief as Webster involves himself and his audience in profound character analysis of the judges and the judged. By the end of the play, there is little about the inner lives of these characters that has not been revealed. (Formally, the invasion of the characters' privacy is expressed in the large number of scenes that take place in private chambers rather than in public places like the court.) Out of these characterizations arises a profound condemnation of the judge, and the affirmation of a secular morality based on the identification of humanity with whatever is wild, free, and nonparasitic in nature.

The action of the play arises from the Duchess' situation as a young and beautiful widow who, since her husband's death, has been the ruler of her province. Her position, like Flamineo's, has important social implications. Rich widows were not uncommon in seventeenth-century England, and they were, almost by definition, a nuisance to men because they were the only women who were in a position to do as they pleased. From the male point of view, their existence tied up a lot of money and land that might otherwise be at the disposal of the men in the family. And they could refuse to be horse-traded a second time for the sake of the family fortune. On the other hand, they could, and often did, marry again to suit their own needs and desires, and this meant that the wealth at their disposal was alienated from the family and put at least partly in the hands of someone the family had not chosen, perhaps someone it despised. Lawrence Stone tells us that among the nobility, widows were usually eager to marry again, this time for love: "These women, now for the first time free to dispose of themselves at their pleasure, were often pathetically anxious to secure that domestic felicity which had hitherto been denied them."[1] He quotes the lines on the grave of Margaret, Lady Hastings, which tell a story common enough in the time:

> When choice of friends brought her to marriage-bed,
> With just renown she passed those her days,
> And though her youth were tied to age far spent,
> Yet without spot she lived and was content.
> Her second match she made of her own choice,
> Pleasing herself who others pleas'd before.[2]

Rich widows, then, were threatening to a paternalistic society not only in a directly economic way, but also, more profoundly, because they could liberate themselves from male domination by making their own choice among male suitors. It is in this second sense that the Duchess' marriage to Antonio is offensive to her two powerful brothers. Neither the Cardinal nor the Duke Ferdinand needs her money. But for reasons that Webster portrays in detail, they would rather have her dead than let her go her own way. The Duchess gives them cause. Not only does she choose to marry her steward (thus lowering herself to the level of the bourgeoisie by taking a husband who is her business partner), but also, by marrying him secretly, she inevitably makes herself the subject of scandal. From her brothers' point of view, the Duchess is too careless of appearances, too willing to let her reputation take care of itself as long as she knows that what she is doing is right. Her marriage to Antonio, because it is clearly not a judicious marriage, is a display of passion unbecoming in a woman and inexcusable in a duchess.

It is not only the Duchess' brothers who find her behaviour shocking. The voice of the people first proclaims the Duchess a "strumpet" (III, i, 30) and then, when the fact that she and Antonio have been married all along is revealed, it expresses wonder at her choice of a social inferior. Even Cariola, her loyal attendant and sympathetic confidante, sees her love of Antonio as "a fearefull madness" (I, i, 578). These reactions indicate the social norm, in the world of *The Duchess of Malfi*, in attitudes towards sexual love—a norm of cynicism and fear that is concretely embodied in the mutually opportunistic sexual relationship between the Cardinal and Julia. Bosola, Ferdinand's hired spy and assassin, is so infected by cynicism that it is not until he has murdered the Duchess that he finally ceases to fight off the recognition that she was neither a lecher nor a silly female, but a strong and loving woman.

Thus, the brothers' misinterpretation and condemnation of the Duchess' desires and her egalitarianism is supported by general opinion. Their determination to punish her is supported in more concrete ways by the highest authorities of church and state, who emply legal means to assist the brothers in their persecution of her. Although the Pope remains an off-stage figure, it is clear that his blessing goes with the avengers (at least to a point), for he is responsible for the seizure of the Duchess' land and then for the lovers' banishment from the state of Ancona, where they have begged asylum. Here, as in *The White Devil*, the avengers use both legal and illegal means to achieve their end, and they are supported both by traditional morality and established power. The extent of their power is dramatically symbolized, just before the catastrophe, in the scene in which the Cardinal's assumption of military status makes explicit the union of religious authority with worldly power.[3]

In this respect, the role of the brothers in *The Duchess of Malfi* is vastly different from that of such traditional revenge figures as Hieronimo, Hamlet, and Vendice, all of whom are forced into political opposition in order to carry out a personal vendetta. In *The Duchess of Malfi*, the roles of avenger and victim are reversed. The avengers are supported by the highest authorities, while the victims find themselves alone and helpless before the forces combined against them. This is even more the case here than in *The White Devil*, where the forces are more evenly matched in terms of worldly power. Thus, while the category of *revenge play* is a useful critical tool, it can be misleading when applied too rigidly to *The Duchess of Malfi*, for it tends to obscure the social implications of the play's central conflict. It is perhaps for that reason that some critics have attempted to explain the motivation of the brothers in terms of broad symbols of natural evil, failing to see that such a formulation does not take into account an outstanding fact about the Duchess' position—her powerlessness to combat the superior forces which oppress her. If the evil the brothers represent is natural, it is nonetheless distinctly connected by Webster with social power and traditional morality.

The motivation of the Arragonian brothers has always presented a challenge to critics. Some have attempted to justify Webster by turning the apparent lack of proper motivation from a fault into a dramatic virtue. Thus J. R. Mulryne, typically, states that "the threat offered to [the lovers'] relationship by Ferdinand or Bosola is of a deliberately unspecific nature. It is imaged throughout in terms of a restless and malignant quiet."[4] And Bogard sees the function of these characters as largely symbolic of a general destructive element in humanity and in nature.[5] Certainly, on one level of symbolism, the brothers are connected with forces of natural destruction. Much of the imagery of the play functions as a link between these characters and such forces. In particular, the brothers are repeatedly seen in terms of images of parasitism. Bosola refers to both of them, in an imaginary dialogue with Antonio, as "these most cruel biters, that have got / Some of thy blood already" (V, ii, 376-377). And the dying Duchess is obsessed with the parasitism of her brothers:

> I have so much obedience, in my blood,
> I wish it in ther veines to do them good. (IV, ii, 168-169)

>   Farwell Cariola,
> In my last will, I have not much to give—
> A many hungry guests have fed upon me. (IV, ii, 202-204)

> Go tell my brothers, when I am laid out,
> They then may feede in quiet. (IV, ii, 243-244)

But this broad level of symbolism is not the only one operative in the play, and the "natural evil" formulation is misleading insofar as it tends to obscure the less abstract meanings. Webster did not have to blur specific motivation in order to imply symbolic function. Rather, the Cardinal and Ferdinand, as some critics have noted, are presented as distinct characters with sharply contrasting personalities.[6] While they are both social parasites, their parasitism takes different forms, reflecting diverse motives. By examining them separately, we shall come to see that the Duchess threatens the existence of each of them in a different way, and that Webster connects their personal motives with their symbolic functions as aspects of a society that is repressive of individuals who have the courage to postulate their own ethical values.

The parasitism of the Cardinal consists in feeding on others in order to maintain and strengthen his worldly position. It is he, not Ferdinand, who is primarily concerned with the dishonour inherent in the meanness of the Duchess' match. The essential difference between the brothers is revealed as they both attempt to advise their sister on the question of remarriage:

> FERDINAND: You are a Widowe:
>   You know already what man is: and therefore
>   Let not youth... high promotion, eloquence—
> CARDINAL: No, nor anything without the addition, *Honor*,
>   Sway your high blood.
> FERDINAND: Marry? they are most luxurious
>   Will wed twice.
> CARDINAL: O fie! (I, i, 320-327)

It is clear that although the Duchess feels the brothers are in accord, they are actually stating two different points of view. To Ferdinand, any remarriage would be undesirable because only a lascivious woman could want a second husband. To the Cardinal, it is vital that the Duchess subordinate passion to the more worldly consideration of honour. That is, the Cardinal is less concerned about his sister's sex life than he is about maintaining the power and good name of the family.

The difference between the brothers is borne out in their own lives. Ferdinand has no lover, while his clerical brother, characteristically, satisfies his needs without taking risks. That is, he keeps a mistress, Julia, but he does not make the mistake of trusting or loving her. This is a perfect expression of his attitude towards life, of the ideological parasitism that underlies all his actions. Along the same lines, he allows Ferdinand to make the compact with Bosola, safeguarding himself by keeping his role in the murder as secret as possible. And just as he has no compunctions about murdering his mistress when she threatens his safety, he does not hesitate to condemn Bosola to death once the latter has outlived his usefulness.

The Cardinal's Machiavellian restraint is reinforced by hypocrisy. Thus, he condemns the Duchess for what he at first imagines is extra-marital passion, when he himself has violated his vows to God in taking a mistress. And he counsels Bosola to become "honest" (I, i, 41), although he himself is responsible for corrupting Bosola in the first place. This is more than a cultivated ability to lie. It is a habit of hypocrisy that is so engrained that the Cardinal himself is half taken in by his own pretences. Because he has successfully masqueraded as a lord of the church for so long, he almost believes, at times, that he is a religious man. Webster makes effective satire of this in the speech in which the Cardinal tells Bosola how to go about finding Antonio:

> Follow him [Delio] to Masse—may be *Antonio*
> Although he do account religion
> But a Schoole-name, for fashion of the world,
> May accompany him—or else go enquire out
> *Delio's* Confessor, and see if you can bribe
> Him to reveale it. (V, ii, 135-140)

The Cardinal is too impressed by his external role to perceive the incongruity between his tone of moral superiority towards Antonio and his own intention to violate the confessional.

The Cardinal's preoccupation with externals and the habitual hypocrisy this leads to determine his reactions to his sister. When Ferdinand tells him that their sister is a "strumpet," the Cardinal's first reaction is to exclaim, "Speake lower." It is only when Ferdinand replies that her behaviour has already been well publicized that the Cardinal begins to lament the tainting of his family's royal blood (II, v, 6-33). In other words, his family's blood would be less tainted if nobody knew about it. To the Cardinal, his sister's greatest sin lies in her refusal to let considerations of status and reputation take precedence over her passions. His sense of honour is not the deep passion we find depicted in the plays of the French classicists, but a mere concern with keeping up appearances.

The final revelation of the Cardinal's primary concern with externals occurs as he faces death, the favourite Websterian test of character. Bosola, who has seen the Duchess grow more finely human in her death, contemns the Cardinal's undignified collapse:

> Now it seemes thy Greatnes was onely outward:
> For thou fall'st faster of thy selfe, then calamitie
> Can drive thee; I'll not wast longer time. (V, v, 56-58)[7]

Webster's insistence on dignity in the face of death only seems severe if it is taken literally. As Rupert Brooke says, the Websterian test of death is a convention: an assumption, for dramatic purposes, "that men are, in the second of death, most essentially and significantly themselves."[8] I believe that underlying this convention is the late medieval image of Death the Leveller, a personage who, like the modern "equalizer," eradicates all the advantages of the rich and powerful here on earth. In accepting the convention, we accept Bosola's perception that the Cardinal's plea for mercy reveals the superficiality of his greatness, the lack of any real sense of personal honour. Because his whole life has been directed towards the establishment and maintenance of his worldly position, the Cardinal has never come to grips with his own soul.

The Cardinal's symbolic function is a simple outgrowth of the dominant aspects of his character. He takes on symbolic proportions as the spokesman for the social ideal of passionlessness, of the subordination of human feeling to worldly goals. On this level, he cannot tolerate the continued existence of the Duchess because the established power that he represents cannot tolerate any challenge to its hypocritical morality. For it is on this moral code that the power of the establishment rests, on the repression of its own most human impulses.[9] The Duchess' emotional freedom constitutes an act of rebellion against the ideology of her class which threatens to disrupt its power—by demolishing the fiction of honour upon which it bases its claim to superiority, by undermining the Machiavellian techniques which have served it so well, and by replacing its members with a multitude of deserving Antonios. In other words, the Duchess' commitment to nature involves an endorsement of the principle that all people are equal in nature. In the strict hierarchical world of *The Duchess of Malfi*, such a commitment cannot go unpunished.

Ferdinand's role in the play complements the Cardinal's. Whereas the Cardinal stands for authority, with its pragmatic,

The Duchess of Malfi: *The Roots of Judgment* 85

politically derived ideology of repression, Ferdinand represents the inner drives that give that ideology force and implementation. The Cardinal stands for the society that demands the sacrifice of its free spirits. Ferdinand is the judge who takes pleasure in pronouncing the verdict. Webster's portrait of Ferdinand moves outward from Antonio's description of his behaviour as chief justice of his dukedom:

> He speakes with others Tongues, and heares mens suites,
> With others Eares: will seem to sleepe o'th bench
> Onely to intrap offenders, in their answeres;
> Doombes men to death, by information,
> Rewards, by heare-say.

Delio, for whose benefit Antonio is imparting this information, responds:

> Then the Law to him
> Is like a fowle blacke cob-web, to a Spider—
> He makes it his dwelling, and a prison
> To entangle those shall feede him. (I, i, 175-183)

Delio's highly evocative image compresses the picture of Ferdinand that gradually takes detailed form in the course of the play. Especially vital is the idea that Ferdinand makes the law his "dwelling," for it is Ferdinand's conception of himself as an embodiment of law that dominates his behaviour towards the lovers and defines his symbolic role in the play. Ferdinand is not merely a remiss judge. He is one who uses the law in order to satisfy his particular form of parasitism.

Ferdinand's use of the law is defined by his association throughout the play with images of great and devastating natural forces. The Cardinal asks him: "Why doe you make your selfe / So wild a Tempest?" And Ferdinand replies:

> Would I could be one,
> That I might tosse her pallace 'bout her eares,
> Roote up her goodly forrests, blast her meades,
> And lay her generall territory as wast,
> As she hath done her honors. (II, v, 23-27)

The function of such imagery is not only to connect Ferdinand with natural evil, but also to imply that Ferdinand becomes associated with evil through pride. Like Shelley's Cenci, Ferdinand identifies with the destructive forces of nature insofar as they manifest God in his punishing mood. He desires to be transformed into a tempest so that he can possess God's power to implement his judgments. Ferdinand's megalomania is exposed to Bosola when he says:

> He that can compasse me, and know my drifts,
> May say he hath put a girdle 'bout the world,
> And sounded all her quick-sands.

To which, Bosola:

>   you
> Are your owne Chronicle too much: and grosly
> Flatter your selfe. (III, i, 104-106; 110-112)

    Ferdinand's assumption of the functions of the deity is further revealed by the way he goes about punishing the Duchess. For the most part, he remains in the background, ordaining the Duchess' fate without revealing his own hand in it. When he does appear to her, it is unexpectedly, as in the bedchamber scene, or shrouded by darkness, as in Act IV, scene i. Throughout the fourth act, he is concerned with manipulating the external environment in order to affect her emotional and moral state. In all this, he is imitating Calvin's tyrannical deity, the commander of destinies, whose basic nature is inscrutable to humanity, but whose will is inexorable and not to be questioned.[10]

    Ferdinand, then, represents the urge to play God with another person—to judge and punish with the force and objectivity of the whirlwind. Ostensibly, his motive for persecuting the Duchess is moral outrage stemming from a superior moral sensitivity. Unlike his cynical brother, Ferdinand seems to believe in his ideal of chastity. On the other hand, we are almost immediately aware that Ferdinand is driven by something other than moral rectitude, that his actual motives have to do with purely personal needs. What these needs are is made fairly clear by the end of the play.

    Early in the play we discover that Ferdinand, like Francisco, is choleric.[11] The Cardinal, to whom any strong emotion is reprehensible, chastises Ferdinand for the boundlessness of the latter's anger towards his sister:

> How idlely shewes this rage!—which carries you,
> As men convai'd by witches, through the ayre,
> On violent whirle-winds!
> ....
>   there is not in nature
> A thing, that makes man so deform'd, so beastly,
> As doth intemperate anger. (II, v, 65-67; 74-76)

While the Cardinal's Aristotelian regard for temperance makes him no less a murderer than his brother, the images he uses to adorn his little lecture do help to characterize Ferdinand. Especially effective is his association of Ferdinand's rage with diabolical possession, for it isolates, by contrast, Ferdinand's own sense of the righteousness of his wrath. Ferdinand may justify his desire to punish the lovers on the grounds that he represents a superior morality, but, from the start, Webster would have us examine this moral passion to see how it is interrelated with diabolical, deformed emotions.

It is the very excessiveness of Ferdinand's reaction that makes us question its origin. His original desire to punish the Duchess for fornication is explicable. When the knowledge of her marriage fails to impress him, we realize that his rage possesses a life of its own. The nature of the punishments he contrives reinforces this impression, for he is not satisfied with hurting, or even killing the lovers. He must consume them utterly, body and soul. Thus, he ingeniously envisions having their bodies "burn't in a coale-pit, with the ventage stop'd, / That their curs'd smoake might not ascend to Heaven" (II, v, 88-89). The punishment he finally does inflict on the Duchess is physically less sensational, but to the same purpose. He is not content with having her killed. He must first, as he confides to Bosola, do everything he can "to bring her to despaire" (IV, i, 140). To explain the overwhelming disproportion between the Duchess' transgressions and Ferdinand's fury by asserting, as some critics have, that Renaissance people cared more about honour than we do[12] is to reduce both the character and the play to absurdity. Honour, for Ferdinand, is merely one rationalization he uses to satisfy himself that he is doing God's work. Once he has murdered the Duchess, he no longer even remembers what the pretext was.

On one level, the explanation for Ferdinand's behaviour echoes the characterization of Francisco in *The White Devil*. Ferdinand can be seen as revelling in the emotion of anger for its own sake, because it provides an outlet for pent-up aggression. To some extent, Webster prepares us, from the very beginning, for Ferdinand's outburst of fury. As he compliments Antonio on his prowess at the tilt, Ferdinand reveals his own impatience with war games and his yearning for the real thing:

> Give him the Jewell: when shall we leave this sportive-action, and
>   fall to action indeed? (I, i, 93-94)

As the scene continues, Ferdinand goes on to argue that soldiering is an appropriate occupation for a prince, thus expressing a longing for combat which closely resembles Francisco's impatience with "the misery of peace" (V, i, 115).

In fact, all three murderers, Ferdinand, the Cardinal, and even the hired Bosola, seem to find in war a satisfying expression of their personalities. When the Cardinal is called upon, late in the play, to resume his earlier military function, we have the feeling that he will be well suited to the role. As a cardinal, he has exhibited no inclination towards spirituality; we know that he is capable of destruction. Bosola, too, has had an earlier career as a soldier. Probably the only complimentary reference to Bosola's past is Antonio's statement that, as a soldier, Bosola was "very valiant" (I, i, 77).

The three men responsible for the destruction of the Duchess thus share a military virtue which, when it finds no outlet in war, expresses itself in less heroic ways. But it is only in the case of Ferdinand that we sense a stifled passion to destroy. The Cardinal's capacity for destruction is constant, but it is passionaless, almost mechanical, coming into play when the occasion arises. With Bosola, personal frustration is evident, but his need for action, if competitive, is not strictly combative. The rest of Antonio's speech on the subject of Bosola's past heroism is pertinent:

> This foule mellancholly
> Will poyson all his goodness, for (i'le tell you)
> If too immoderate sleepe be truly sayd
> To be an inward rust unto the soule;
> It then doth follow want of action
> Breeds all blacke male-contents, and their close rearing
> (Like mothes in cloath) doe hurt for want of wearing.
> (lines 77-83)

Bosola, like Ferdinand, needs action, but it need not be destructive action. It is when society denies him an honourable competitive function that he channels his energies into the evil role that is offered to him.

Ferdinand's longing for action is much more defined. From the first, we are aware of a general psychological malaise, a grim restlessness that threatens to erupt into aggression. In the first scene, Antonio describes Ferdinand as "a most perverse, and turbulent Nature," and he casts a sinister light on Ferdinand's apparent good humour when he says, "What appears in him mirth, is meerely outside" (lines 169-170). Later in the play, Antonio characterizes Ferdinand in a particularly suggestive metaphor:

> Those houses, that are haunted, are most still
> Till the divell be up. (III, i, 26-27)

While Ferdinand apparently participates in the normal, peaceful activities of life, he is merely waiting for the opportunity to release his restless, repressed appetite for destruction. When he appears calm and quiet, it is only because his particular devil is temporarily at rest.

The force of the image of the spider and the web becomes apparent ("He makes [the law] his dwelling, and a prison / To entangle those shall feede him"). Ferdinand's form of parasitism is psychological. By dwelling within the law, he can find release for his destructive urge in punishing the transgressions of others. His behaviour towards his sister, although it takes place outside Ferdinand's court, follows the general pattern of his behaviour as judge. The Duchess becomes a victim, one of those that "feed" Ferdinand's perverse appetite, when her violation of sexual laws makes her fair game. By the time Ferdinand discovers that the Duchess is actually married, he has given himself over so completely to the passion of moral indignation that he cannot reconsider and turn back. Modifying his pretext, he surrenders entirely to the disintegration of his character.

In *The White Devil*, we saw that what first appeared to be a traditional moral position on the part of Francisco and Monticelso was ultimately revealed to be the expression of an urge to destroy. The pattern repeats itself in *The Duchess of Malfi*. Ferdinand's first reaction to his sister's imagined sexual crime is so traditional that an audience might sympathize with his anger and shame, while regretting his rashness. When the revelation of her marriage fails to appease him, all justification for his reaction vanishes, and the initial moral indignation itself becomes suspect. Here, the parallel between the two plays ends, for in *The Duchess of Malfi* Webster attempts a deeper examination of moral judgment by creating a character whose passion to judge and whose conviction of moral superiority distinguish him from the avengers in the earlier play. Ferdinand's moral sense is not simply an excuse for venting aggression, as is Francisco's; for whereas Francisco does not finally care whether or not he is acting justly ("What harmes it Justice?" [V, iii, 278]), Ferdinand must feel that he is acting in the name of right and law, and it is this sense of moral justification that accounts for the intensity of his fury. The profundity of Webster's analysis of Ferdinand lies in its exposure of the psychological origins and manifestations of a twisted, destructive moral sensitivity.

The core of Ferdinand's character—the conflict that generates his actions and ultimately drives him mad—is the opposition within him between megalomania and self-hatred. We have already observed Ferdinand's tendency to associate himself with the grand forces of nature and the inscrutability of God. At the very moment of his death, when repentance might be expected to make him humble and afraid, he boasts that he will "vault credit, and affect high pleasures, / Beyond death" (V, v, 86-87). On the other hand, Ferdinand repeatedly reveals a suppressed but fierce self-loathing, and sometimes vacillates wildly between the two, as in the following dialogue:

> MALATESTE: Why doth your Lordship love this solitarines?

> FERDINAND: Eagles commonly fly alone: They are Crowes, Dawes, and Starlings that flocke together: Looke, what's that, followes me?
>
> MALATESTE: Nothing (my Lord).
>
> FERDINAND: Yes:
>
> MALATESTE: 'Tis your shadow.
>
> FERDINAND: Stay it, let it not haunt me.
>
> MALATESTE: Impossible; if you move, and the Sun shine:
>
> FERDINAND: I will throtle it. (V, ii, 30-37)

The passage is too poignant to be read in the farcical spirit that dominates the rest of the scene. The "shadow" that haunts Ferdinand is the same devil in the haunted house of an earlier image. It is the same inescapable propensity for evil, rising to the surface of Ferdinand's consciousness, and filling him with a desire to inflict pain upon himself.

The ultimate manifestation of Ferdinand's self-hatred is the lycanthropy that afflicts him in the final act of the play. Bogard's analysis of Ferdinand's illness, in emphasizing its satirical implications, misses its more important relation to Ferdinand's personality:

> When Ferdinand goes mad, the image [of human beastliness] becomes actuality. The beast in man appears in its grimmest, most horrible manifestation. Ferdinand *is* an animal. The metaphor is interpreted literally, and presented in a way unknown to the formal satirists, as reality that underlay the cause of evil in the outward form of man.[13]

The interpretation is too literal, for after all it is always Ferdinand himself who insists that he is a wolf. He appears that way to himself, not to those around him. The subjective nature of Ferdinand's disease is emphasized by his insistence that while a wolf's skin is hairy "on the out-side," his own is hairy "on the In-side" (V, ii, 18-19). This is Ferdinand's way of expressing his sense of guilt, because he is still too arrogant to express it in humility and repentance, as is apparent when he tries to shift the burden of the Duchess' death to Bosola. However he may attempt to justify himself and maintain his ego, his sense of inner evil keeps rising to the surface. Thus, his lycanthropy is an unconscious confession of guilt. And when he challenges the doctor to "rip up his flesh" (V, ii, 20) to see whether or not it really is hairy inside, he is not merely trying to make a point. In his own way, he is expressing a desire to be purged and destroyed.

Ferdinand's lycanthropy occurs after he has killed the Duchess, when his self-hatred is at its peak. Even before the murder, though, his egomania is startlingly mingled with self-loathing. The Cardinal is shocked when one of Ferdinand's first reactions to the report of his sister's sinful behaviour is to associate her evil with evil in himself and in his brother:

> I could kill her now,
> In you, or in my selfe, for I do thinke
> It is some sinne in us, Heaven doth revenge
> By her. (II, v, 82-85)

The lines are central to our understanding of Ferdinand's reaction to his sister, for they reveal the strange bond that Ferdinand feels exists between them. His own repressed sense of guilt, fostered by a conception of God as essentially severe and vengeful, immediately rises to the surface as he hears of his sister's transgression. But his initial impulse to pronounce judgment on himself quickly abates, for he is incapable, as we have seen, of admitting to evil in himself. Instead, he transfers all his self-hatred to her and, taking upon himself the role of the God he fears, proceeds to punish himself through her.[14] This is the inevitable neurotic solution for the split within him between self-love and self-hatred, for in playing the deity and destroying her, he gives expression to both impulses at once.

Like all neurotic solutions, Ferdinand's only succeeds in intensifying the original problem. The split within him between a harsh morality and his inner drives widens as he projects it outward into action, and he eventually loses all contact with reality. In Freudian terms, Ferdinand has transformed himself into an embodiment of his own superego, while his sister represents, for him, his own basic drives. The Duchess lends herself to this schematization, for she has chosen to live according to her desires, without dread either of herself or of the consequences. In sharp contrast to her brother, she trusts her own impulses and values what she feels is natural. Her passion is justifiable to her because it is the expression of a natural order which she feels is essentially beneficent. She expresses this when she compares sexuality in nature with socially controlled human sexuality:

> The Birds, that live i'th field
> On the wilde benefit of Nature, live
> Happier than we; for they may choose their Mates,
> And carroll their sweet pleasures to the Spring. (III, v, 25-28)

Attempts to control the natural sexual impulses of human beings, whether through ideology or institutions, seem pointless, artificial, and even destructive to the Duchess. She mocks the ideal of chastity by relegating it to the world of inanimate objects:

> Sir, be confident,
> What is't distracts you? This is flesh, and blood, (Sir,)
> 'Tis not the figure cut in Allabaster,
> Kneeles at my husbands tombe. (I, i, 518-521)

And she challenges the power of the church to sanctify marriage. In Act I, when the lovers are expressing their vows to one another, she makes it clear that, to her, marriage is created freely by individuals, and not by the pressure of a legal contract:

> What can the Church force more?
> ....
> How can the Church build faster?
> We now are man, and wife, and 'tis the Church
> That must but eccho this. (I, i, 558; 562-564)

Perhaps the best, most subtle, expression of the Duchess' feeling that the sexual ideals fostered by the church are anti-human is her comparison of Antonio's lifeless parting kiss with that which she has seen "an holy Anchorite / Give to a dead mans skull" (III, v, 104-105).

Ferdinand, on the other hand, repeatedly expresses a fear of what is natural in human beings. During his first confrontation with the Duchess, he compares pursuit of desire with the motion of "the irregular Crab, / Which though't goes backward, thinkes that it goes right, / Because it goes its owne way" (I, i, 355-357). Again and again, he associates human passion with beasts of nature: Antonio is counselled to live among dogs and monkeys (III, ii, 121-123); the Duchess' children are referred to as "cubbs" (IV, i, 40) and "young Wolffes" (IV, ii, 275). The imagery is reductionist. There is a vast difference between the Duchess' choice of the songbird to symbolize natural passion and Ferdinand's choice of the crab. Ferdinand's choice of such images always implies that when people yield to passion they are forfeiting their special status as human beings and *descending* to the level of the animals.

Thus, Ferdinand's condemnation of the Duchess is a particular form of his distrust of nature. Burdened by an exaggerated Christian sense of humanity's basic depravity, he is driven to condemn and destroy, in himself and others, the spontaneous expression of natural desire. The harsh god he has chosen for himself demands the sacrifice of human feeling, and it is Ferdinand's mission to see that his god's will prevails. The great irony of the play is that what Ferdinand's mission against sin really accomplishes is the caging of a nightingale, while his own natural impulses are twisted and depraved by the very control he seeks to apply. Totally out of contact with reality, Ferdinand convinces himself that he is fighting his sister's bestiality, when he is actually giving vent to his own. For in the end, it is Ferdinand himself who, denying the animal in human beings, is transformed into a wolf. The release that he has never allowed himself is finally achieved in an orgy of destruction.[15]

Ferdinand's self-deception is accomplished by what modern psychologists call *projection*. The corruption that he experiences within himself is projected onto humanity in general and, with particular vehemence, onto his sister:

> FERDINAND: talke to me somewhat, quickly,
> Or my imagination will carry me
> To see her, in the shameful act of sinne.
>
> CARDINAL: With whom?
>
> FERDINAND: Happily, with some strong-thigh'd Bargeman;
> Or one o'th' wood-yard, that can quoit the sledge,
> Or tosse the barre, or else some lovely Squire
> That carries coles up, to her privy lodgings.
>
> (II, v, 53-60)

Ferdinand's own stifled libidinousness, or what he calls his "imagination," interferes so completely with his perception of his sister that the true nature of her passion never occurs to him. He can only visualize it (and visualize it he must) in terms of his own preoccupation with the flesh. He is convinced that she has carried out in reality the licentious behaviour that haunts his imagination, and for that he cannot forgive her. In his mind, she has broken a compact among human beings, ordained by God, to go through life with as little pleasure as possible. The envy her transgression arouses has no outlet but destruction.

Ferdinand's hatred of the Duchess becomes entirely explicable once we recognize the overpowering envy that her behaviour arouses. Although Ferdinand's envy has nothing to do with money or power, it is no less potent a motivating force than Macbeth's envy of his king. If, as many critics have suggested, Ferdinand is also burdened by specifically incestuous desires, then the intentsity of his outrage becomes even more understandable. And there is every reason to accept the theory that incest is a part of Ferdinand's complicated motivation. His preoccupation with his sister's body would be hard to explain in any other way. The very nature of Ferdinand's personality almost requires the addition of this factor, for, if Ferdinand suffers from inordinate self-love, it is logical that the sexual object he fastens on should be of his own flesh and blood. All of this is quite clearly and succinctly expressed when Ferdinand exclaims:

> Damne her, that body of hers,
> While that my blood ran pure in't, was more worth
> Then that which thou wouldst comfort, (call'd a soule).
>
> (IV, i, 146-148)

Suddenly dropping the pretext of concern for his sister's moral and spiritual condition, Ferdinand reveals a purely physical involvement with her, not only because she is a desirable female, but also because she is a part of himself.

Ferdinand's sexual envy is thus the immediate source of his urge to judge and punish his sister. Webster has here developed an idea which had received brief expression in *The White Devil*, where Flamineo, contemplating Vittoria's approaching trial, comments that she should be judged by cuckolds, because "your cocould is your most terrible tickler of letchery" (III, i, 14-15). Flamineo's insinuation that sexual freedom is a source of irritation only to those who lack it themselves is a key to Webster's more serious presentation of Ferdinand's impulse to judge and punish the Duchess. Incapable himself of spontaneous sexual expression, Ferdinand cannot bear to see it in anyone else. Because society supports his fear of freedom with laws and mores designed to control sexual behaviour, he is able to transform his purely personal reaction into what he feels is a moral position. Thus envy is rationalized as moral judgment.

The challenge to law implicit in Webster's characterizations of Ferdinand and the Duchess is twofold. On one level, there is an attack on laws created to regulate sexual behaviour. As in *The White Devil*, Webster shows that the attempt to apply control to that aspect of existence is not only futile, but also destructive. Passion cannot be suppressed. It can only be forced into different channels. The Duchess is better than her brothers, not because she is more rational, but because she yields herself to the "fearful madness" of love. By doing so, by putting herself in tune with the demands of nature, she escapes the far more fearful madness that Ferdinand's morality leads him to, as well as the ignominiousness that is the poor fruit of the Cardinal's cautious rationality. Again, the test of death is the touchstone. The Duchess, who has not denied her animal nature, is able to rise above torture and the threat of madness and to die with as much nobility as is given to a human being. When Ferdinand is murdered by Bosola, he emerges from madness only long enough to express, once again, vainglory and self-accusation.

Not only is judgment impossible in the face of the indestructibility of passion, but it is also unethical because the judges are, by definition, interested parties. Because they themselves are human, that is, they cannot avoid imposing their own attitudes and needs in considering a case. Antonio touches lightly on this theme when he answers Cariola's question as to the relative merits of wisdom, riches and beauty:

The Duchess of Malfi: The Roots of Judgment

> 'Tis a hard question: This was Paris' case
> And he was blind in't, and there was great cause:
> For how was't possible he could judge right,
> Having three amorous Goddesses in view,
> And they starcke naked? 'twas a Motion
> Were able to be-night the apprehention
> Of the seveerest Counsellor of Europe. (III, ii, 43-49)

The technique here is typically Websterian. Through Antonio's lighthearted banter, the author is commenting on the serious action of the play. The importance of the comment is that it has the effect of generalizing the particular action. Ferdinand's presumption in attempting to judge his sister's sexual behaviour is made a particular instance of the general impossibility of impartial judgment where sex is involved.

But this challenge to law is subsumed under another, more fundamental attack. For the innate goodness of the Duchess stands as an overwhelming argument against the very basis of law as social necessity. Montaigne, confessing that his own virtues all stemmed, not from rational control, but rather from instinctive aversions to most forms of vice, posed the question whether "to be wholly good we must be so by some occult, natural, and universal property, without law, without reason, without example."[16] Webster's play might almost be a direct answer to the question, for the goodness of the Duchess is entirely natural. She does not achieve virtue by controlling her desires, but by yielding to them. Nor does she show any propensity to judge others according to preconceived standards of behaviour. Both she and Antonio demonstrate an almost incredible willingness to be reconciled to her brothers, a willingness that Webster emphasizes as a foil to Ferdinand's need to condemn.

The implication is totally anarchistic. Whereas the Duchess represents impulsive goodness, Ferdinand is a dramatic incarnation of the attempt to impose rigid principles upon life. His failure to create anything but evil implies the failure of law in a chaotic world. Devotion to abstract ideals can only lead to the destruction of whatever good humanity manages to create freely. Through his characterization of Ferdinand, Webster sheds sinister light on the aphorism, *fiat Justitia, pereat mundus*. Under the guise of lofty morality, people destroy not only life, but beauty and goodness as well.

The responsibility is not entirely Ferdinand's, for he depends upon the support of the Cardinal's authority, both worldly and spiritual. Spiritually, the Cardinal's ideology provides the basis for Ferdinand's rationalization. Materially, the Cardinal's influence on the Pope reduces the lovers to a state of helplessness and makes it impossible for them to escape their persecutor. In general symbolic terms, the brothers together represent what Irving Ribner calls "the death world" which is opposed to the "principle of life" represented by the Duchess.[17] In social terms, with Ferdinand standing for the judge and the Cardinal representing the established power served by the judge, the "death world" becomes particularized as a society so corrupt that it can only maintain itself by strict repression of individual creativity. The parasitism of a law which, as the Second Madman says, "will eate to the bone" (IV, ii, 97) reflects the parasitism of rulers who dread the essential egalitarianism and irrational abundance of nature unconfined by law.

The significance of *The Duchess of Malfi* is anarchistic, but not, as Clifford Leeech has said, chaotic,[18] for a clear positive statement does emerge. Goodness, Webster shows us, is possible in the world, but it cannot be created by force or rational control. Rather, it must be freely created by individuals who have the courage to give themselves fully to life. The Duchess is not the only example of such freely chosen goodness. The point is clearly made through Antonio, who says:

> Were there nor heaven, nor hell,
> I should be honest: I have long serv'd vertue,
> And nee'r tane wages of her. (I, i, 503-505)

People are not made virtuous by threats of damnation or promises of either earthly or otherworldly favour. They are good because they love goodness. That is what Bosola finally learns. Before his conversion, Bosola has been trapped by a conviction that he might as well be evil as good, since there is no just authority to reward and punish ("miserable age, where onely the reward of doing well, is the doing of it!" [I, i, 33-47]). This is the particular form of parasitism of which he is guilty. He passively accepts the society that his betters have created for him and only seeks to find something for himself within that framework: "Could I be one of their flattring Panders, I would hang on their eares like a horse-leach, till I were full, and then droppe off" (I, i, 53-55). The example of the Duchess teaches him that goodness is desirable for itself, and that his failure to choose goodness has stemmed from cowardice. In ridding himself of fear, he finally raises himself out of the "deepe pit of darknesse" in which "(womanish, and fearefull) mankind live" (V, v, 125-126). The coupling of "womanish" and "fearefull" here, where it so utterly contradicts the action of the play, is a particularly poignant example of the recurrent gap in Webster between conservative statement and radical demonstration.

Notes to Chapter Four

1 *The Crisis of the Aristocracy* (Oxford: Oxford University Press, 1967), p. 284.
2 Ibid., p. 285.
3 It may be necessary to point out that the brothers' power over the Duchess is neither a reflection of continental lawlessness nor a vastly exaggerated picture of the power of the king of England. The king of England could imprison anyone indefinitely, without showing cause (see Catherine Bowen, *The Lion and the Throne* [Boston: Little, Brown, 1957], pp. 479-480). That this power was used is illustrated by the case of Arabella Stuart, which bears a suggestive resemblance to the story of the Duchess. Because she was a potential claimant to the throne, Arabella Stuart was a constant object of suspicion to both Elizabeth and James. She was imprisoned by Elizabeth for hearing a proposal of marriage. James was evidently less watchful, for during his reign she managed to get married secretly. However, when the marriage was discovered, she was imprisoned again and, after an attempted escape, committed to the tower, where she finally died, insane, in 1615 (David Jardine, *Criminal Trials* [London: M. A. Nattali, 1847], vol. I, p. 399). It seems clear that the power of Ferdinand and the Cardinal directly reflects the power of a tyrant during a period in England when the king was considered to be above the law.
4 "*The White Devil* and *The Duchess of Malfi*," in *Jacobean Theatre*, Stratford-upon-Avon Studies I, ed. John Russell Brown and Bernard Harris (London: Arnold, 1960), p. 220. This essay makes perceptive comparisons between the two plays, especially with respect to overall mood and tone.
5 Travis Bogard, *The Tragic Satire of John Webster* (Berkeley: University of California Press, 1957), p. 51.
6 Robert Ornstein's comparison of Ferdinand's "fever of egoism" with the Cardinal's "emotional lifelessness" anticipates aspects of the analysis presented here (*The Moral Vision of Jacobean Tragedy* [Madison, Wisc.: University of Wisconsin Press, 1960], pp. 146-147).
7 Webster uses similar words to describe superficial greatness in his prose character of "An Intruder into favour": "He is small wine that will not last: and when hee is falling, hee goes of himselfe faster then misery can drive him" (*Works*, vol. IV, p. 30).
8 *John Webster and the Elizabethan Drama* (New York: John Lane, 1916), pp. 107-108.
9 Cf. Robert Griffin, who says that the "dialectic" of the play "polarizes around the opposition between the natural and the unnatural, the fruitful and the sterile, the impulse and the calculated response" (*John Webster: Politics and Tragedy*, Salzburg Studies in English Literature [Salzburg: Institut für Englische Sprache und Literatur, Universität Salzburg, 1972], p. 109).
10 In "Religion and John Webster," Dominic Baker-Smith looks for reflections in Webster of the religious pessimism and "stress on the arbitrary will of God" that he feels reached a climax in the early seventeenth century (*John Webster*, ed. Brian Morris [London: Ernest Benn, 1970], p. 211). I find less evidence of a hidden God in Webster's own cosmology than in that of Ferdinand, a reflection that Baker-Smith fails to notice. Since Webster is certainly critical of this character, it is logical to infer criticism of his theology.
11 This has been pointed out by D. C. Gunby, in "*The Duchess of Malfi*: A Theological Approach," in Brian Morris, ed., *John Webster*, p. 182.
12 See, for example, Lucas, vol. II, pp. 23-24; Thomas Parrott and Robert Ball, *A Short View of Elizabethan Drama* (New York: Scribners, 1943), pp. 230-231;

and Muriel Bradbrook, *John Webster: Citizen and Dramatist* (New York: Columbia University Press, 1980), p. 157.
13 Bogard, *The Tragic Satire of John Webster*, pp. 136-137.
14 Ferdinand's effort to expunge his own guilt by punishing his sister has been discussed by James L. Calderwood in "*The Duchess of Malfi*: Styles of Ceremony," reprinted in *Twentieth Century Interpretations of The Duchess of Malfi*, ed. Norman Rabkin (New Jersey: Prentice-Hall, 1968).
15 Here my analysis is diametrically opposed to that of Calderwood, who seems to see something positive in Ferdinand's conversion of "an essentially private vengeance into the appearance of public justice. Ferdinand's role is obviously synthetic," he says, "an attempt to dignify incestuous frustrations that urge him to retaliation. Yet by restraining his desire for immediate vengeance, and, more important, by transforming it and his sexual desires as well into elements of a formal process, he makes a gesture of sublimation which, even though synthetic, suggests a confirmation of order" ("*The Duchess of Malfi*," p. 82). Calderwood is not the only critic who has gone to great lengths to find in Webster an affirmation of the values of order and degree; but he is probably the only one who has found such an affirmation in the sublimations of a murderous psychopath. Calderwood's determination to find within the play the "internal scale to measure depravity" that other critics have found wanting in Webster (p. 74) distorts what is in other respects an especially perceptive analysis.

A more recent and more elaborate effort to show that *The Duchess of Malfi* expresses an endorsement of the "values of community, order, degree, and justice in the face of the radical individualism that threatens those values" has been made by Joyce Peterson in *Curs'd Example, The Duchess of Malfi and Commonweal Tragedy* (Columbia, Missouri: University of Missouri Press, 1978). Peterson sees *The Duchess of Malfi* as an example of a sub-genre she calls "commonweal tragedy," a type of didactic tragedy evolved from the political moralities, whose purpose is to teach both rulers and ruled to subordinate their individualism to "the institutions that man has erected against his own potential for evil" (p. 35). In *The Duchess of Malfi* we see a ruler "circumvent, overturn, or pervert one after another of the norms, traditions, conventions, and institutions that are intended to insure... order" (p. 107), the ruler in question being the Duchess herself, who is thus seen as a very faulty ruler, albeit a charming individual.

One might object that the Duchess' own violations of order are minuscule compared with those of her more powerful brothers, which makes it hard to see her as the "curs'd example" of the play. There are other serious weaknesses in the argument. Peterson's case largely rests on an acceptance of the sub-genre she has invented. Here she makes the mistake of attributing to the play (as well as to other tragedies included in this genre, such as *Lear* and *Macbeth*) rather too much of the moral play quality she sees as its inheritance. Thus her reading tends to make the play into a Brechtian *lehrstück*, in which the conflict between order and desire is more ironic than tragic. This seems to me to cut too much of the meat out of the play. Secondly, although there is a great deal of talk about "norms, traditions, conventions, and institutions" in Peterson's book, there is no clear indication of what these are in the world of the play and who may be said to uphold them. In fact, the Duchess' marriage to Antonio might be regarded as just the sort of wedding of public and private good that is needed to provide the unpoisoned fount that the Duchess' world lacks. The norms that the Duchess opposes or circumvents to achieve this marriage are those upheld by Ferdinand, the Cardinal, and the Pope. If Peterson is saying that the

Duchess should have supported the values of a decadent ruling class because any order is better than any change, I must object that that does not amount to much of a tragic statement. Nor (and I suppose this is more to her point) is it particularly moral.

16 *The Complete Essays*, ed. and trans. Donald Frame (Garden City, N.Y.: Doubleday, 1960), vol. II, p. 104.
17 *Jacobean Tragedy, The Quest for Moral Order* (New York: Barnes and Noble, 1962), pp. 106-107.
18 Clifford Leech, *John Webster: A Critical Study* (London: Hogarth Press, 1951), p. 65.

Chapter Five

The Duchess of Malfi, the Royal Prerogative, and the Puritan Conscience

Webster's challenge to the rationalistic, hierarchic view of humanity that was a keystone of orthodox Renaissance philosophy is even more trenchant in *The Duchess of Malfi* than it had been in *The White Devil*. As I have pointed out, the "reason" the Cardinal talks about is only a tool of statecraft. And Ferdinand's assumption that people are better than other animals—or that they should be—makes him a destructive force, whereas his sister's passionate pursuit of her own fulfilment is graced by an essential humility and gentleness. In effect, Webster has reversed the traditional hierarchy so that the rational faculty lies lower in the scale of values than the sensory and emotive faculties that people possess in common with other creatures. The devastating effects of the myth of reason are explored simultaneously on two related planes: the human microcosm and the macrocosm of political society.

The idea that people alone among the creatures of the universe had been endowed with reason had always had hierarchical political corollaries. From Plato on, the conception of the human being as a creature whose "inferior" faculties (sensory, emotive) are controlled by the superior faculty of reason implied a social stratification in which the thinkers rule over the doers. In a well-ordered state, as in a well-ordered personality, everything is in its proper place in the hierarchy, performing its appropriate function. Since the best society is one in which reason reigns supreme, ideal rulers are the people who have most completely subordinated their other faculties to their reason. It would be as absurd for passionate individuals (or workers) to rule the state as it would be for the human heart (or hand) to rule the human head.

In the tradition of Aquinas and Hooker, this classical concept was supported by a further analogy to God as the supreme intellectual force, ruling the universe through immutable laws of "Eternal Reason." The "operations of nature," says Aquinas, "are seen to proceed in an orderly manner even as the operations of a wise man."[1] Good rulers are analogous to God in that their dominating intelligence creates order and harmony in their realm just as the eternal intelligence has created order and harmony throughout the universe.

For Aquinas and Hooker, this implied the rule of law. Just as God could never violate the immutable laws of reason and nature that he had created, good rulers would never disobey the positive law that had been made in the image of the divine law.[2] In its original and orthodox form, the comparison between the king and God did not imply that the king was free to exercise absolute power according to his whims. In the seventeenth century, however, the traditional analogies became useful to those who, by shifting the emphases, could incorporate them into a justification of absolutism. In the writings of Richelieu and James, the traditional association of reason with the ruling class becomes a total identification of law with the king. People should be reasonable, but in fact most are not. Therefore, it is the function of the king to impose law and reason upon his subjects. Reason can only reign supreme if the sovereign power is absolute:

> Common sense leads each one of us to understand that man, having been endowed with reason, should do nothing except that which is reasonable, since otherwise he would be acting contrary to his nature, and by consequence contrary to Him Who is its Creator. It further teaches us that the more a man is great and conspicuous, the more he ought to be conscious of this principle and the less he ought to abuse the rational process which constitutes his being, because the ascendancy he has over other men requires him to preserve that part of his nature and his purpose which was specifically given to him by Him Who Chose him for elevation.

To this point in the passage Richelieu is faithfully echoing the orthodox commonplaces of natural law philosophy. This is the "given" part of the argument, easily available to the "common sense" of the reader. What he is really aiming at is revealed in the next few lines:

> This precept is the source of another, which teaches us that since we should never want the accomplishment of anything not reasonable and just, neither should we ever want the ac-

complishment of anything without having it carried out and our commands followed by complete obedience, because otherwise reason would not really reign sovereign.³

It is a short step further to James' assertion that "that which concerns the mystery of the King's power is not lawful to be disputed."⁴

We can now grasp the full significance of the Duchess' impatience with outward form. It is relevant that she is reprehensible, according to traditional concepts of order, on both political and sexual grounds, for Webster has her stand for total antagonism to the supposedly natural system of hierarchies that, with considerable historical justification, he has come to associate with tyranny. Thus, she violates her subordinate position as a woman by wooing Antonio; she rejects the idea that her position as a ruler necessitates stricter repression of her animal nature; and she disregards the class structure of her society in marrying her social inferior. Her rebellion on the macrocosmic (social) level is enmeshed with her rebellion on the microcosmic (personal) level. And the "wilderness" that she deliberately enters is the chaotic, undefined abundance of life once the artificial limitations imposed by a hierarchical ideology have been discarded.

The Duchess of Malfi does not believe in a universal harmony resting upon obedience, order, and rational limitation. Rather, she acts on the assumption that personal harmony with the universe depends upon the acceptance of the real laws of human nature, which, when the vain pretension to reason has been abandoned, appear to be much the same as those governing the rest of creation. If the Duchess is wrong, it is only in her failure to perceive that her isolated act cannot stand against all of society. As Calderwood puts it, she "displays a disrespect for external realities which is... dangerously naive."⁵ This she learns as her earlier optimism gives way to a recognition of the vulnerability of her family. But in cosmic terms she is vindicated. Her harmony with nature leads to a harmony within herself that is not shaken by torment. And the echo that Webster sets up between the Duchess' affirmation that she is the Duchess of Malfi still and Bosola's affirmation that the stars shine still perhaps suggests a unity of personality with universal law—a triumph over the mutability that normally governs the sublunary world—which defeats the traditionalists on their own grounds.

The Duchess is Webster's highest tribute to human nature. Among the challengers of natural law philosophy, there were those, like Luther and Machiavelli, who found human nature to be essentially bad. Haydn makes the very good point that, after centuries of theological conditioning, it was inevitable that a naturalistic view of human beings would, to most people, mean a downgrading of humanity.[6] The naturalistic image would be juxtaposed with the traditional ideal image and people would react either by violently rejecting the former as a heretical slander or by reluctantly accepting it as a harsh reality. It is remarkable, then, that there were those who, finding people to be irrational, did not consider this a cause for lament. Montaigne is at one with Machiavelli in rejecting the concepts of the "guiding role of reason, the hierarchical composition of the soul, the traditional linking of happiness and virtue under right reason." But he differs in that he "still proclaims (with qualifications) the essential goodness of man's nature."[7] For Montaigne, however, this goodness does not reside in the development of a faculty that distinguishes human beings from animals; on the contrary, their goodness lies precisely in the instinctive qualities that they share with other creatures. In the *Apology*, as I pointed out earlier, Montaigne bitterly attacks reason as an interference in the smooth functioning of the universal laws of nature. Animals, he says, are kind to their young, ignorant of the art of war, and, in many cases, faithful to their mates, whereas human beings, with their supposed reason, are incapable of these natural virtues.[8] In the *Essays*, this negative emphasis tends to give way to a positive one, an affirmation of the potential of human beings for true integration with natural goodness once they are liberated from the bonds of rationalistic philosophy.

Webster, retracing Montaigne's route, moves from the iconoclasm of *The White Devil* to the affirmation of *The Duchess of Malfi*. Haydn writes of Montaigne's Nature:

> She is the indifferent mother of an infinite diversity and mutability, and her works are all equally good, all the children of her fertility in a world innocent of comprehensive systematizing and universal regulative principles of degree, vocation, etc. She is, if you will, Venus Genetrix, mother of instincts and senses, of biological motivation and uninhibited fertility.[9]

It is to this nature, rather than to the ghostly ideal of the philosophers, that people must conform their own behaviour, and in *The Duchess of Malfi* Webster creates such a human being, an intellectual creature who is possessed of the simple virtue and dignity that, in the *Apology*, Montaigne had reserved for animals. In creating this character, whose natural element is peace and love, and whose last thoughts, as she is about to die a violent death, have to do with cough medicine for her children, Webster seems to be asserting that it is possible for human beings to escape the curse of reason. In making her a member of the ruling class, he suggests the extension of this ideal to the level of the macrocosm.

It is odd that Webster critics have not made much of the very striking fact that both of his great tragedies have women as heroes.[10] Shakespeare did not write a single tragedy in which the hero is a woman (Cleopatra shares the honours with Antony). Nor do Webster's heroines conform to the type of long-suffering female that was becoming increasingly popular with patrons of the private theatres. In fact Webster's heroines conform to no type, which is in itself a challenge to an audience accustomed to seeing stage females as saints or sinners.

Other challenges are implicit in these characterizations. In the introduction, I mentioned what I conceive to be the most important fact about Webster's heroines: that they combine assertiveness with what was taken to be femininity. Without in any way implying that there *is* such a thing as femininity, I would like to suggest that for Webster and his audience, femininity had to do with an affinity with nature. The notions of fertility as essential to a woman's role, of the Earth as feminine, of women as creatures of passion and impulse rather than reason—these were parts of the mentality of the period. For that very reason, women were not suitable heroes: the hero of a tragedy must possess (even if he fails to use it) the highest of human faculties, which is reason. That Webster chose to centre his tragedies around women is one of the most significant manifestations of his rejection of the hierarchic ideology of his time.[11] What Webster's protagonists possess in the highest degree is not the ability to reason, but the impulse to live in harmony with nature.

The psychological opposite of the Duchess is represented, as we have seen, by her brothers. Perhaps the most intellectually innovative aspect of *The Duchess of Malfi* is its close examination of the psychological implications of traditional hierarchical thought. The final evidence of the superiority of the Duchess' concept of natural law—and the major irony of the play—is the degeneration of Ferdinand to a subhuman level as he suffers from lycanthropy. But the fact that Ferdinand is dangerously out of harmony with the real laws of nature has been symbolically evident all along, for it is he, not the Duchess, who is associated throughout the play with the storms and earthquakes that traditionally symbolized disruption of the universal order. For all her violation of social order, the Duchess is incapable of cursing the world "to its first Chaos" (IV, i, 119), whereas Ferdinand's very existence calls forth the corresponding tempests and whirlwinds that reflect, on a cosmic level, his inner disquiet.[12]

On the individual psychological level, then, the myth of reason is a barrier to true self-knowledge and self-fulfilment. On the political level, those who act in the name of reason and order are brutal and tyrannical. The Cardinal, like Richelieu, finds it convenient to use the word "reason" when what he is talking about is reason of state. Ferdinand is more complex, because, whereas the Cardinal's ideology is purely secular, Ferdinand's hierarchical convictions are fortified by a very literal rendering of the traditional analogy between ruler and God. In this respect, Ferdinand bears an intriguing resemblance to James I, the crux of whose political philosophy was an image of the union of judge, king, and God in one personality. The people, said James, must acknowledge the king to be "a Judge set by God, over them, having power to judge them, but to be judged onely by God."[13] And he told his son that God had made the king a "little *God*, to sit on his Throne, and rule over other men."[14] One could find no better words to describe Ferdinand's image of himself, an image that I have already discussed from a less political point of view. In his characterization of Ferdinand, Webster has fleshed out the doctrine of divine right, connecting the political theory with its psychological counterpart in self-worship. He had not far to go. James' speech to Parliament in 1609 would have been sufficient in itself to provide the raw materials for the portrait of Ferdinand:

> Kings are justly called Gods, for that they exercise a manner or resemblance of Divine power upon earth... they make and unmake their subjects: they have power of raising, and casting downe; of life, and of death.... They have power to exalt low things, and abase high things, and make of their subjects like men at the Chesse; a pawne to take a Bishop or a knight.[15]

It is a similar breathtaking egotism that we sense in Ferdinand as he goes about destroying the Duchess in his god-like way, an egotism that finds satisfaction in the possession of absolute power over another life.

Although Ferdinand worships a hidden God, it would be a mistake to conclude that Webster is implying in this a criticism of Puritanism, for strict Calvinism was only one stream in a very various movement. And in his view of the relationship between the individual and the state-church establishment, Webster had much in common with the Puritans. The secular power of the church, manifest in the structure of its hierarchy and in the continued power of the ecclesiastical courts, was a major issue to Jacobean Puritans. In opposition to clerical control of matters of faith and morality, the Puritans stressed the personal nature of religion and denied the right of the church courts to punish deviations. A corollary of the conviction that religion cannot be imposed by law was a rejection of penance and a corresponding emphasis on the penitence of individuals who felt they had violated their covenant with God.[16] A similar emphasis on the primacy of the individual covenant led to a rejection of the anti-divorce position of the established church. Many Puritans seem to have felt, as Milton was to put it, that "it is not the outward continuing of marriage that keeps whole that covenant."[17] Although remarriage after divorce was forbidden by law, Puritan ministers repeatedly performed such marriages.[18]

This set of interconnected ideas is echoed in both *The White Devil* and *The Duchess of Malfi*. The treatment of marriage in both plays might be summed up by the Puritan thesis that "to command love and *sympathy*, to forbid dislike against the guiltles instinct of nature, is not within the province of any law to reach."[19] This is a major theme—perhaps *the* major theme—of both plays. Another major theme is the perniciousness of the alliance of state and church. In *The White Devil* the secular power of the church is attacked in Webster's portrayal of the Cardinal as judge and avenger. In *The Duchess of Malfi*, where the fusion of church and state is symbolically represented by the fraternal relationship of the Cardinal and Ferdinand, clerical control of personal morality is shown in the most devastating light. Both plays plainly demonstrate that the secular power of the church, far from making the state holy, only facilitates tyranny.

But the most striking echo of Puritan doctrine in *The Duchess of Malfi* is the dramatized opposition between penance and penitence incorporated in the conflict between Ferdinand and the Duchess. Ferdinand's desire to inflict penance on his sister's "delicate" body does not stem from a real desire to make her penitent, but from his own perverse needs. She, on the other hand, converses with God in her own way, in spite of her casualness about the outward forms of religion. In this respect (as in the partnership-marriage of the Duchess and Antonio), *The Duchess of Malfi* comes much closer to Puritan ideology than does *The White Devil*; for while the earlier play shares Puritan criticisms, *The Duchess of Malfi* expresses, in the character of its heroine, the Puritan ideal of the individual conscience. Talking about Clarissa Harlowe, Christopher Hill says:

> Clarissa's attitude is a logical application of the Protestant theory of justification by faith, with its emphasis on the inner intention of the believer rather than on his external actions. Purity of motive, chastity of mind, is more important than formal rectitude of behaviour.[20]

I believe that the Duchess embodies this doctrine with a fervour and a heroic grandeur that was no longer possible in the time of Richardson. Confident in her own election, impatient with ritual and superstition, humble when alone in the presence of God, and strenuously devoted to the Puritan ideal of marriage, the Duchess is a perfect Puritan heroine.

We can begin to sense the power of this play in its own time. Major causes of declining deference towards the aristocracy in pre-revolutionary England were, in Stone's words,

> the pervasive influence of the rise of individualism, the Calvinist belief in a spiritual hierarchy of the Elect, and the Puritan exaltation of the private conscience, which affected attitudes towards hierarchy and obedience in secular society.[21]

The spiritual hierarchy of which the Duchess is a part is pitted against the hierarchy of power represented by her brothers. As their earthly power crumbles, the Duchess' spiritual strength prevails. Nor is this an otherworldly message, for Bosola is fired by her example to fight for what is right in this world.[22]

But if *The White Devil* and *The Duchess of Malfi* express a revolutionary individualism akin to the Puritan emphasis on the individual conscience, they do not share Puritan faith in the potential regenerative power of a purified common law. Whereas the Puritan party in Webster's time looked to the common law as the basis of resistance to established power, both *The White Devil* and *The Duchess of Malfi* depict the futility of appealing to any law when law is synonymous with power. Vittoria appeals to the law upon her trial—and the demands she makes anticipate legal reforms that were to take place during the revolutionary period—but it is useless to appeal to law in Monticelso's court. In *The White Devil*, destruction of the individual is a tragic inevitability.

In *The Duchess of Malfi*, too, the only kind of law that exists is the law that Bacon was talking about when he admitted that there is a "kind of force which pretends law, and a kind of law which savours of force rather than equity."[23] In a fit of remorse, Ferdinand denounces Bosola for having executed the Duchess without legal warrant:

> FERDINAND: By what authority did'st thou execute
> This bloody sentence?
> BOSOLA: By yours—
> FERDINAND: Mine? was I her Judge?
> Did any ceremoniall forme of Law,
> Doombe her to not-Being? did a compleat Jury
> Deliver her conviction up i'th' court?
> (IV, ii, 320-325)

On the face of it, Ferdinand's statement would seem to imply that there is some difference between law and force in the world of

The Duchess of Malfi. In reality, this difference is as shadowy and elusive as it was in the real world of Jacobean England. The realities of the Jacobean legal system—or lack of system—are reflected in the world of *The Duchess of Malfi.* Ferdinand may momentarily regret his disdain of the forms of common law, but the fact is that he lives in a world in which such disdain is possible for those in power. As the ruler of his little kingdom, and a judge, he wields the legal machinery of the state. That he is unaccustomed to concern himself about whether or not he is acting according to the rules of law is revealed when he ends his little speech about the ceremonies of law by threatening to judge and execute Bosola as peremptorily as he had the Duchess. In essence, Ferdinand, like James I, believes himself to be above the law. And in a very real sense, he is.

In such a world of lions and foxes, the Duchess cannot survive. The beauty she embodies is a real potential for humanity (Antonio says that she "lights the time to come" [I, i, 213]), but she is destroyed by a world in which goodness appears to be incompatible with power. And yet there is a strong suggestion at the end of the play that goodness could—and should—be stronger than it is. For the world has changed, albeit in small ways, as a result of the life and death of the Duchess. A piece of the hierarchy has crumbled away, revealing its internal weaknesses. And one man has learned that it is necessary to act according to the dictates of conscience, for there is no greater defeat than a life spent in cynical obedience to a corrupt master.

Criticism has been very divergent on the question of Bosola's role in the play. While some have seen in the fifth act a conversion that implies some sort of hope for the future, others have contended that Bosola does little or nothing to dispel the sense of a "meaningless universe"[24] that we are left with at the end of the play. Clifford Leech, for example, concludes that "hope cannot go very deep" at the end of the play because Bosola is such a sorry excuse for a hero:

> For the dominant strain in the play's ending, the key is in the presentation of Bosola. In this last act we have seen him drawn into sympathy with Antonio and his dead wife, yet slaying an innocent servant without compunction, mistakenly killing Antonio, complaining always of being neglected. As an instrument of justice he is pitifully imperfect, while he had shown address as tormentor and executioner.[25]

In a recent variant of this view, Jacqueline Pearson argues that as the focus shifts at the end of the play from the Duchess to Bosola and Antonio, the generic focus "shifts from tragedy to inversions

The Duchess of Malfi, *Prerogative, and Conscience* 109

and parodies of tragedy." According to Pearson, Webster's aim is to "define tragedy objectively and to place the tragic affirmation of a heroic individual in the perspective of an anti-heroic society."[26]

While I agree with critics who refuse to orchestrate Bosola's fifth act changes into a heroic symphony, I would also contend that it is precisely because Bosola has not suddenly, miraculously metamorphosed into a tragic hero that we can believe in his change. And because we are able to believe that his change is not just a literary convention—that it could really occur in life—the play should not leave us despairing.

Webster seems to be saying that, although the Duchess embodies an ideal, it is the Bosolas of the world, "pitifully imperfect" as they are, who determine to what extent such ideals affect events. That Bosola is crucial is such a disquieting point that Webster devotes an entire act of the play to impressing it upon the audience. Leech's dissatisfaction with Bosola as "an instrument of justice" is understandable. Fortinbras would make a cleaner job of it. Not only is Bosola ethically imperfect, capable of total coldness in the face of human suffering, and almost incurably opportunistic, but he is also (I know no better word for it) creepy. I think it is this—the decay he seems to exude like bad breath—that makes it so hard for us to accept him as the avenger of the Duchess.

And yet the Duchess herself sees so much goodness in Bosola that she makes the fatal error of trusting him in what I conceive to be the moment of climax and *peripety* in the play. The Duchess' tragic flaw (to use another old-fashioned term) has been, all along, that she is too trusting.[27] At a moment when she crucially needs friends, Bosola delivers a lengthy defence of Antonio, whom the Duchess has pretended to find guilty of dishonest management. There is nothing in it for Bosola. Opportunist that he is, his move would be to support her denunciation, hoping to raise himself in her eyes. But he does the opposite. He commits himself totally to the position that she is wrong, that Antonio is incapable of dishonesty. The Duchess concludes that Bosola is a good man and she fatally entrusts him with her secrets: that she is married to Antonio and that they are about to flee. Bosola lengthily expresses his amazement that virtue (Antonio) has been so recognized and rewarded by authority (the Duchess). As the scene ends, with the Duchess employing Bosola to help her and her family, we wonder what Bosola will do. I think we really know.

Bosola will return to his boss and report what he knows. He detests himself for it. His defence of Antonio, his praise of the Duchess for marrying Antonio, are sincere; but he cannot act upon his ethical premises because basically Bosola is a slave, with the mind and will of a slave who simultaneously detests and grovels before his master.

A controlling image of the play, stated in the very first scene, is a comparison between a virtuous court and a clean water-source, as opposed to a defiled court, or fountain, contaminating everything as it descends. The play bears out the image: the Duchess is a pure source; Ferdinand, the more powerful stream, carries infection. Bosola, a mass of contradictory impulses, is infected by the force of Ferdinand's disease. Called upon to utilize his worst impulses, he complies, although the love of goodness is always there, in one form or another. I do not believe that he is really much of a tormentor. As I read the fourth act, I see Bosola as curious, probing, testing the Duchess' apparently boundless gift of sanity. He is Ferdinand's tool, with all that that implies, and as such he cannot help but act out Ferdinand's wishes. Yet he pleads with Ferdinand to end the torture. He would like to see the Duchess fail because that would justify his cynicism. But he would like to see her win because he loves her.

It is the nature of tragedy that, if the characters had known at the outset what they know at the end, the tragedy would never have happened. If the Duchess had not trusted Bosola, she and her family might have escaped. If Bosola had had the courage to cease being Ferdinand's cesspool, her trust would have been justified. When Bosola finally reverses the course of the stream, something very important has taken place. In giving us Bosola rather than, say, Antonio as avenger, Webster makes the profoundly disquieting suggestion that it is up to just such bumbling sinners as ourselves to resist the infection of corrupt authority.

Notes to Chapter Five

1 Hiram Haydn, *The Counter-Renaissance* (New York: Scribners, 1950), p. 132.
2 Ibid., p. 133.
3 *The Political Testament of Cardinal Richelieu*, ed. and trans. Henry Bertram Hill (Madison, Wisc.: University of Wisconsin Press, 1961), pp. 71-72.
4 See above, Chapter 3, p. 103.
5 James L. Calderwood, "*The Duchess of Malfi*: Styles of Ceremony," in Norman Rabkin, ed., *Twentieth Century Interpretations of the Duchess of Malfi* (Englewood Cliffs, N.J.: Prentice-Hall, 1968), p. 79.
6 Haydn, *The Counter-Renaissance*, p. 382.
7 Ibid., p. 405.
8 *The Complete Essays of Montaigne*, ed. and trans. Donald Frame (Garden City, N.Y.: Doubleday, 1960), pp. 130-160.
9 Haydn, *The Counter-Renaissance*, p. 465.
10 Muriel Bradbrook takes note of Webster's general concern with women's problems (*John Webster: Citizen and Dramatist* [New York: Columbia University

Press, 1980], pp. 119, 142, 430, and elsewhere), but by and large it has been in more general works on Elizabethan and Jacobean drama that Webster's sympathy with women has been noted (see above, introduction, note 31). Simon Shepherd does not deal with *The White Devil*, but he does note that the fact that the Duchess is in the centre of her play distinguishes *The Duchess of Malfi* from other plays ca. 1612 that have active and sexual female characters (*Amazons and Warrior Women* [New York: St. Martin's Press, 1981], pp. 116-118).

11 There has been an unfortunate tendency in some feminist criticism of Shakespeare to accept without protest the Bard's refusal to put women at the centre of his tragedies. Thus Linda Bamber is content to find women at the centre of comedies: "The feminine other . . . is Shakespeare's natural ally in the mode of festive comedy. Precisely because she is Other, precisely because her inner life is obscure to her author, she seems gifted with precisely the qualities that make for comedy: a continuous, reliable identity, self-acceptance, a talent for ordinary pleasures" (*Comic Women, Tragic Men: A Study of Gender and Genre in Shakespeare* [Standford: Stanford University Press, 1982], p. 41). A similar line of thought is pursued by Paula S. Berggren in "The Woman's Part: Female Sexuality as Power in Shakespeare's Plays" (in *The Woman's Part: Feminist Criticism of Shakespeare*, ed. Carolyn Lenz, et al. [Urbana: University of Illinois Press, 1980]). Berggren says: "The comic world requires childbearers to perpetuate the race, to ensure community and continuity; the tragic world, which abhors such reassurance, consequently shrinks from a female protagonist. Such women as exist in tragedy must make their mark by rejecting their womanliness, by sublime sacrifice, or as midwives to the passion of the hero" (pp. 18-19). Berggren does refer to *The Duchess of Malfi* in a footnote, but her generalizations still stand.

The Duchess, of course, possesses in abundance "the qualities that make for comedy" according to these critics. Webster's play demonstrates that these qualities can also make for tragedy. Shakespeare did not write *The Duchess of Malfi* because he was more committed than Webster to the rationalist ideology, with its built-in hierarchical and sexist implications.

Shakespeare is an imposing figure, of course, but we must resist what a recent critic has referred to as "the domination of the patriarchal Bard" if it leads us to entertain seriously a view of women as good for laughs. (See Kathleen McLuskie, "The patriarchal bard: feminist criticism and Shakespeare: *King Lear* and *Measure for Measure*," in Jonathan Dollimore and Alan Sinfield, eds., *Political Shakespeare: New Essays in Cultural Materialism* [Ithaca: Cornell University Press, 1985]).

12 On tempests, etc., see E. M. W. Tillyard, *The Elizabethan World Picture* (New York: Macmillan, 1944), p. 86.
13 *The Political Works of James I*, ed. Charles McIlwain (Cambridge: Harvard University Press, 1918), p. xliii.
14 Ibid., p. xxxv.
15 "A Speech to the Lords and Commons of the Parliament at Whitehall," in *Political Works*, p. 308.
16 Christopher Hill, *The Century of Revolution, 1603-1714* (London: Nelson, 1961), pp. 79-80.
17 *The Doctrine and Discipline of Divorce*, in *Complete Prose Works*, gen. ed., Don Wolfe (New Haven: Yale University Press, 1963), vol. II, p. 258.
18 Ernest Sirluck, ed., vol. II of Milton, *Complete Prose Works*, p. 146. The relations between Puritan ideology with respect to marriage and women's roles, on the one hand, and the English Renaissance drama, on the other, is one of the

prime concerns of Juliet Dusinberre in *Shakespeare and the Nature of Women* (London: Macmillan, 1975).
19 *Doctrine and Discipline*, p. 345.
20 Christopher Hill, *Puritanism and Revolution* (London: Secker and Warburg, 1958), p. 385.
21 Lawrence Stone, *The Crisis of the Aristocracy* (Oxford: Oxford University Press, 1967), p. 351.
22 It is illuminating to consider the Duchess in the light of Simon Shepherd's discussion of Spencer's Britomart, the type of his *warrior woman* (*Amazons and Warrior Women* [New York: St. Martin's Press, 1981]): "Britomart's lover is the knight who represents justice; she herself represents chastity. True justice can only be saved and re-established when chastity defeats its opposite, lust" (p. 5); "It is in pursuit not only of her own destiny but of her historical obligation to Britain that Britomart fights her way towards Artegall" (p. 27); "The true warrior woman will challenge men to greater bravery and their true militancy" (p. 28). Shepherd makes us aware that Webster was working within a tradition that associated female virtue with political rejuvenation.
23 Quoted by William Holdsworth, *A History of English Law* (London: Methuen, 1922), vol. V, p. 249.
24 Normand Berlin, "*The Duchess of Malfi*: Act V and Genre," *Genre* 3 (1970), p. 360).
25 Clifford Leech, *Webster: The Duchess of Malfi* (London: Arnold, 1963), p. 27.
26 *Tragedy and Tragicomedy in the Plays of John Webster* (Manchester: Manchester University Press, 1980), pp. 89-95. Her chapter on *The Duchess of Malfi* essentially restates the position expressed by Berlin in the article cited above.
27 Compare Leonora Leet Brodwin: "Her tragic error lies not in choosing to love but in overestimating the ability of a hostile world to accept her vision of moral health" (*Elizabethan Love Tragedy* 1587-1625 [New York: New York University Press, 1971], p. 286). My perception of this play coincides with Brodwin's at several points, especially where she says that the "Duchess' 'fearful madnes' lies in her desire to fulfill both the claims of her greatness and of her femininity" (p. 284).

Chapter Six

The Devil's Law Case

> The Inconvenience of an Arbitrary is intollerable, and therefore a certaine Lawe, though accompanied with some mischeife, is preferrable before itt. But it is not possible for any humane thing to be wholly perfect.
> Lord Chief Justice Matthew Hale

After 350 years of almost total neglect, *The Devil's Law Case* has recently become the object of considerable critical attention, much of it bent upon demonstrating that the attention is merited by hitherto unperceived aesthetic and ethical values. Especially interesting is Jacqueline Pearson's book, *Tragedy and Tragicomedy in the Plays of John Webster*, which links generic features of the play with similar qualities in the tragedies. But for all that her analysis is perceptive and her argument ingenious, I cannot accept her conclusion that *The Devil's Law Case* is one of Webster's "four perfectly structured plays," an assessment that crests the recent wave of critical enthusiasm.[1] My own interest in the play has to do with its treatment of the themes I have been tracing in the tragedies. But I also hope to show that what I see as the play's considerable aesthetic weaknesses are intrinsically bound up with the way those themes are handled here.

In *The Devil's Law Case* and *Appius and Virginia*, Webster reverses his anarchistic position and asserts the priority of social order. In both plays, he manifests a more positive attitude towards the function of law in society by attempting to outline the qualities of a fair trial. His very satire on specific aspects of law in these plays is part of this attempt to project a valid system of law, rather than an attack upon the fundamental assumption that law is a social good. This shift in Webster's view of law coincides with a shift in his view of nature. In his treatment of the theme of the unnatural parent, which is central to both plays, he expresses a general disillusionment with nature as a moral and beneficent force in relation to humanity. As Webster becomes more pessimistic about nature, he turns to law to replace it, or at least to control it.

And yet Webster's most characteristic qualities of mind remain the same. He still scoffs at the orthodox image of human beings as rational, and of the law as a divine appeal to that rationality. More than ever, he rejects the idea that those in power are ordained by God and that judges mete out divine justice on earth. On what, then, is social order to be founded? The ideology of absolute power as a necessary imposition upon the chaos of human nature is no less repugnant to Webster now that it was when he wrote the two great tragedies. The other alternative available to Webster and his contemporaries, as I pointed out earlier, was faith in the common law as source of social order. In the two plays we are about to consider, we shall find a detailed expression of the positive social values of a revised and strengthened system of common law. At the same time, we shall see Webster groping towards a more fundamental rationale for an ideology of order.

Both *The Devil's Law Case* and *Appius and Virginia* are marred by a lack of aesthetic coherence that reflects an underlying failure to resolve the philosophical problems they raise. This is more conspicuously true of *The Devil's Law Case*, probably the earlier of the two plays, which seems to represent Webster in the grip of disillusionment and philosophical uncertainty. Lucas' description of the mood of *The Devil's Law Case* is apt:

> Between *The Duchess of Malfi* and *The Devil's Law Case* lies a gulf... it is in a changed mood that we find Webster here— resigned to live, and to take life as the bitter comedy it may become to the head, when the heart has begun to harden and not to care.[2]

Modern criticism balks at Lucas' old-fashioned freedom to empathize with the man Webster, but by and large it also finds bitter comedy, if not resignation, in this play. Unable here to sustain a vital opposition to standard mores and laws, Webster is equally unable to embrace them with full emotional and intellectual conviction. His vindication of law in the play seems less an affirmation than a concession, the result of exhaustion or necessity rather than conviction. It is tempting to imagine that when Webster came into his patrimony as a result of his father's death in 1615, he suddenly found himself obliged to turn from philosophical speculation about humanity and nature to practical considerations of how to run things.[3] Whether or not that is the case, the sententious statement, put into the mouth of an idealized judge, that "bad Suits, and not the Law, bred the Lawes shame" (IV, i, 77) strikes us as a lame answer to the questionings of the earlier plays. And a similar weakness manifests itself in characterization, plot, imagery, and, most conspicuously of all, in his choice and use of the tragi-comic genre.

The central action of the play is Leonora's attempt to disinherit her son, Romelio, by falsely proving that he is a bastard. To the judge, Crispiano, her devil's law case is shocking, even assuming that she is telling the truth, for she appears to be violating the law of nature governing maternal impulses:

> Obedience of creatures to the Law of Nature
> Is the stay of the whole world; here that Law is broke,
> For though our Civill law makes difference
> Tween the base, and the ligitimate; compassionat Nature
> Makes them equall, nay, shee many times preferres them.
> (IV, ii, 276-280)

Crispiano's use of the term "law of nature" involves us in a rather complicated problem. It is significant that Hooker, whom Crispiano is echoing here ("See we not plainly that obedience of creatures unto the law of nature is the stay of the whole world?"), was using the word "creatures" in a different sense. In its original context, the line that Webster appropriated has nothing to do with the actions of people, but rather refers to the involuntary "obedience" of stars, oceans and other "mother elements of the world" to the eternal laws that God has set down for their operation.[4] In contrast to these natural forces, human beings, according to Hooker, have the power to choose their own actions: that is, to choose to obey or disobey the laws of nature, which, in the case of human beings, are synonymous with the laws of reason.[5] This distinction between the natural laws governing natural agents and those governing rational creatures is typical of Renaissance natural law philosophy.[6] In terms of that philosophy, Crispiano's statement is meaningless because it judges people in terms that are appropriate only to the world of irrational creatures.

Crispiano's concept of natural law is, then, vastly different from the rationalistic concept of the philosopher he is quoting, but it has a meaning of its own, primitivistic and Websterian. Crispiano is expressing a belief that people are at their best when they are in accord, not with the laws of reason, but rather with the laws of their animal nature. His words are echoed in a play on which Webster may have collaborated, *Anything for a Quiet Life*, in which a parent, this time a father, is denying his sons their patrimony. The elder son chastises his father in terms similar to Crispiano's:

> think how Compassionate
> The creatures of the field that onely live
> On the wilde benefits of *Nature*, are
> Unto their yong ones. (IV, i, 80-83)

The point, in both cases, is that human beings, in denying the instincts that they possess in common with the animals, are corrupting their basic nature. And both these statements, of course, echo the thought and language, if not the attitude, of Ferdinand when he says:

> For though our nationall law distinguish Bastards
> From true legitimate issue: compassionate nature
> Makes them all equal. (DM, IV, i, 42-44)

    We appear, at this point, to have established a relation between *The Devil's Law Case* and the earlier Webster. Crispiano's statement raises a philosophical tension between natural and unnatural behaviour that recalls the Duchess' defiance of her brothers' attempts to restrict her. In resolving this tension in favour of nature, Crispiano is echoing a major theme of both *The White Devil* and *The Duchess of Malfi*. But this time the attitude for which Crispiano is the spokesman is demonstrated to be philosophically worthless; for what Crispiano does not know at this point in the play is that Leonora's violation of the maternal instinct stems precisely from her "obedience" to another law of nature, the sexual impulse. And to this other, apparently more fundamental law of nature the characters in *The Devil's Law Case* exhibit an obedience that seems to preclude the whole question of voluntary behaviour. Because of her love for Contarino, Leonora betrays not only her villainous son, Romelio, but her innocent daughter (Jolenta) as well. Contarino and Ercole are prepared to kill each other, albeit honourably, because of their competition for the love of Jolenta. Julio wishes his father dead so that he may inherit enough money to satisfy his appetite for wenching. Angiolella, the nun, finds that she is unable to fulfill her vow of chastity. Only the judges, Crispiano and Ariosto, seem to feel that there is something in life more important than sex. Crispiano asks:

>   can the fingring Taffaties, or Lawnes,
> Or a painted hand, or a Brest, be like the pleasure
> In taking clyents fees, and piling them
> In several goodly rowes before my Deske? (II, i, 59-62)

But then, Crispiano and Ariosto are both old men.
    Thus, the issue raised by Crispiano's weighty utterance turns out to be somewhat beside the point. There is such a thing as natural law, but it is not the kind of law that can readily be "broke."

Rather, it is capable of overcoming maternal and filial affection, friendship, and obedience to God when those other natural impulses stand in its way. Compared with this inductively derived law, the law Crispiano talks about is ideal, a positive rather than a natural law in the pragmatic sense. And therein lies the fundamental irony of the play, recalling, in its intensity, the sardonic Webster of *The White Devil*. For far from being "the stay of the whole world," the law of nature, as it turns out, is a force capable of undermining the stability of society without compensating for the resulting chaos by any addition of beauty or warmth.

There are a few lines in *The Devil's Law Case* that recall the tragedies in their satire of institutions that curb the free play of natural desire. Angiolella sums up for many of the characters when, at the end of the play, she admits the folly of attempting to resist the natural sexual law:

> But I doe onely wish, that this my shame
> May warne all honest Virgins, not to seeke
> The way to Heaven, that is so wondrous steepe,
> Thorough those vowes they are too fraile to keepe. (V, v, 86-89)

The institution of marriage, when it does not reflect the sexual desires of both parties, is heartily abused by Jolenta's maid:

> Plague of these
> Unsanctified Matches; they make us lothe
> The most naturall desire our grandame *Eve* ever left us.
> (I, ii, 228-230)

Even the libertinism of Julio is lightly defended against the standard Aristotelian attacks of the old men:

> ARIOSTO: Why, I would have you leave your whoring.
>
> JULIO: He comes hotly upon me at first: whoring?
>
> ARIOSTO: O yong quat, incontinence is plagued
> In all the creatures of the world.
>
> JULIO: When did you ever heare, that a Cockesparrow
> Had the French poxe? (II, i, 140-145)

Such statements, however, merely assert, in the manner of Flamineo, the naturalness and necessity of sexual love. They do not in any way imply its goodness or beauty. In fact, sexual desire in this play is singularly unlovely. Rupert Brooke, perceiving this, treated it as a general characteristic of Webster's plays:

> It is typical of Webster that he should smirch with his especial rankness, not only the baser characters of this play, but the lovemaking between his hero and heroine, as he does through Winifred's mouth in the second scene of the play. Like any

Flamineo, she interprets between us and the puppets' dallying, a little disgustingly: 'O sweet-breath'd monkeys, how they grow together!'[7]

It is unfortunate that Brooke generalizes his comment, because his perception that there is something disgusting about the sexual relationships in *The Devil's Law Case* is, by itself, quite accurate. But Webster's treatment of sex in this play is unique in his work. The scene that Brooke refers to cannot be equated with the love scene between Vittoria and Brachiano, if only because it contains no poetry. In contrast to the solemn eroticism of the scene in *The White Devil*, what we have here is the peculiarly uninviting spectacle of the two lovers "dallying" on the stage while the waiting woman makes lascivious remarks. Whereas the earlier plays presented a tension between the cynicism of a Flamineo or a Bosola and the idealism of a Brachiano or a Duchess of Malfi, *The Devil's Law Case* presents no lover's idealism to offset the commentary of the cynical.

In short, love, in *The Devil's Law Case*, does not possess the power to uplift and ennoble. Whereas the Duchess of Malfi was inspired by love to marry beneath her rank and to scorn the outward forms of marriage, the heroine of *The Devil's Law Case* suffers from an annoying preoccupation with making things legal. As for her lover, Contarino, he has a suspicious way of confusing Jolenta with her dowry:

>   I would not publish to the world,
> Nor have it whispered, scarce, what wealthy voyage
> I went about, till I had got the Myne
> In mine owne possession. (I, i, 95-98)

From the context, we know that the metaphor is not irrelevant. And if the seriousness of these lovers' feelings is in question early in the play, it is entirely denied later, when Jolenta suddenly decides that she loves someone else, and Contarino gives in to his fate and marries Jolenta's mother. If Contarino is the hero of this play, he certainly does not fare well by comparison with Brachiano.

If Jolenta and Contarino are denied high seriousness in their passion, the other lovers are even less inspired, except to do evil. Ercole, the most sympathetic of the lot, betrays his friend. Romelio has to be forced, by the court, to marry the woman he has made pregnant. Julio, as I have mentioned, is anxiously awaiting his father's death. And Leonora, far from being humanized or elevated by passion, is impelled to divest herself of maternal feeling. The treatment of Leonora is central to the view of passion expressed in the play. On the one hand, she is seen as a monster, the epitome of the devilish malice of which a woman is capable when possessed by passion. On the other hand, we are made to feel pity for her just because she is so incapable of withstanding the natural force that drives her. When she believes that Contarino is dead, Leonora's distraction reaches the level of a pitiable madness:

> There is no plague i'th world can be compared
> To impossible desire, for they are plagued
> In the desire it selfe
> ....
> oh I shall runne mad,
> For as we love our youngest children best:
> So the last fruit of our affection,
> Where ever we bestow it, is most strong,
> Most violent, most unresistable,
> Since tis indeed our latest Harvest-home,
> Last merryment fore Winter. (III, iii, 269-271; 278-284)

In terms of moral value, Leonora's passion is all one with the love of the hero and heroine. All are helpless victims of an irrational force. If Leonora is driven to extreme malevolence, at least she has the distinction of remaining constant in her love. Far from punishing this monster at the end of the play, Webster takes pity on her and gives her what she has wanted all along.

Leonora's reward and, in fact, all the events of the last scene give final expression to the negative view of passion that permeates the play. As comic resolution, the scene is extraordinary. The generically appropriate coupling does take place, but the atmosphere surrounding these unions is singularly loveless. One betrothal takes place by order of the court. Contarino's vow to Leonora is the surrender of a hunted animal. And the implied future union between Ercole and Jolenta, after all the heroine's protestations of her love for Contarino, is the most absurd touch of all. Nor is any of this treated with the lightness of such a comedy as *A Midsummer Night's Dream*. The characters here are too exhausted by their manoeuvrings to express joy or hope for the future. The coupling is convenient—everyone is taken care of—but it is not happy. Appropriately, there is no wedding feast.[8] For desire is not consummated, but rather it is staved off, worn down, controlled. The spirit that dominates this scene is expressed in a comment on marriage in *Anything for a Quiet Life*: "There is no other remedy for flesh and blood—that will have leave to play whether we will or no, or wander into forbidden pastures" (IV, ii, 78-80).

The tension between natural impulse and law that permeates Webster's plays is thus, for the first time, distinctly resolved in favour of law. Left to go its own way, sexual passion can only create chaos, by destroying social ties and even human life. Natural law is not a good or amoral force, but rather a destructive force that calls for the applications of positive law to control it. That is why the judges play such a decisive role in the plot. Leonora's wild desire for vengeance must be curbed by the law. The sufferings of Angiolella must be relieved by the pronouncement of the court. Contarino and Ercole must be reconciled. And all the entanglements of plot which have been brought about by a combination of greed and passion run amok must be straightened out under the watchful eye of the judge. One is reminded of *Measure for Measure*, except that here it is law and tradition, rather than the unfathomable manipulations of a benevolent despot, that must supply the order that nature, by itself, does not create.

Webster has come a long way from the individualism and philosophical anarchism of his tragedies. But he still has a good distance to go before he can fully reconcile himself to a social ethic. We see his conflict most clearly in his characterization of the main protagonist of the play, Romelio. In the first scene, Contarino observes that Romelio "has very worthy parts, were they not blasted / By insolent vaineglory" (I, i, 124-125). Romelio's outstanding trait is his arrogant faith in himself and all his works. He wilfully sends all his vessels to sea at the same time, defying nature even in naming his ships, which are called *The Stormes Defiance*, *The Scourge of the Sea*, and *The Great Leviathan* (II, iii, 62-64). When his ships fail, he pursues his new scheme with equal bravado and, in fact, with actual bravery. Murder, for the most part, seems to have no reality for him except as a necessary factor in his plans. And the personal risks he undertakes are even less real to him.

It is no surprise to us that Webster's attitude towards Romelio should seem ambivalent, for we have observed the complexity of his point of view in relation to characters like Flamineo, Vittoria, and Bosola, who resemble Romelio in their ambitious and ruthless egotism. But here Webster does not gloss over murder as a sort of byproduct generated by the intense and impersonal operation of a vital human force. Flamino, Vittoria, and Bosola all, in a way, remain a little apart from the consequences of their actions, as if the poet had somehow placed a veil between them and their deeds. In *The Devil's Law Case*, there is no such veil, no aura of mystery. Insofar as he is a murderer, Romelio is made repugnant to the audience. On the other hand, Webster does not condemn the character entirely. Unable to reconcile these contradictions in terms of a complex set of perspectives on the character (as with Vittoria), Webster divides the character according to moral categories, and gives us different Romelios in different scenes.

Thus, we find ourselves attracted to Romelio at the beginning of the play, because he possesses a vitality which sets him apart from the other characters, and which is reinforced by the relatively poetic quality of his speech:

> Oh my Lord, lye not idle;
> The chiefest action for a man of great spirit,
> Is never to be out of action: we should thinke
> The soule was never put into the body,
> Which has so many rare and curious pieces
> Of Mathematicall motion, to stand still. (I, i, 67-72)

Suddenly, in Act III, scene ii, Romelio degenerates into a second-rate Barabas, radiating blood-lust instead of vitality:

> Excellently well habited!—why me thinks,
> That I could play with mine owne shaddow now,
> And be a rare Italienated Jew;
> To have as many severall change of faces,
> As I have seene carv'd upon one Cherrystone;
> To winde about a man like rotten Ivie,
> Eate into him like Quicksilver, poyson a friend
> With pulling but a loose haire from's beard. (lines 1-8)

This is Romelio the murderer. The former Romelio reappears as he faces his mother in court and, oddly, we are made to forget about Romelio the murderer until the end of the scene, at which point we are jolted back to awareness by Ercole's accusation. Romelio's bravery in entering upon the trial by combat once again arouses a sympathetic response. And, as a final touch, Webster has Romelio come up with a quick repentance for the sake of a comic resolution, which has nothing whatever to do with Romelio in either of his aspects.[9]

If Muriel Bradbrook is right, Webster wrote *The Devil's Law Case* "as a vehicle for bravura display of [his actor friend Richard] Perkins's talents," to inaugurate the indoor theatre that the Queen's Men had just acquired.[10] Perkins was noted for his playing of Barabas, and it is quite possible that the composite nature of the role of Romelio has to do with an elaborate set of in-joke ironies about role-playing.[11] The fact that Perkins had also played Flamineo would multiply the prismatic effect. Thus Perkins' virtuosity would have helped to disguise for the original audience what seems too plain to this reader: that in his treatment of Romelio, Webster manifests his inability to reconcile completely the vestiges of his individualism with his increased sensitivity to the problem of social order.

For Romelio the usurer, the headstrong self-seeker, the strong individual concerned with his own fulfilment, is not unattractive. When Romelio's economic individualism leads him to attempt murder, Webster is faced with the fact that he is about to have another sympathetic criminal on his hands, and thus, another relativistic treatment of crime. But Webster seems to have reached a point where he feels compelled to present murder as an absolute crime, even if he cannot quite bring himself to repudiate the arrogant egotism that makes a person capable of such a crime. And so he suddenly undercuts the characterization and effectively transforms Romelio into a total villain, repulsive to the audience because of his delight in the act of murder itself. Webster has not resolved the social and philosophical problem involved, and the inconsistency of the character remains a testimony to the fact. One wonders to what extent Webster himself was aware of this when he wrote, in his prefatory remarks "To The Juditious Reader," "A great part of the grace of this (I confess) lay in action."

Although the denigration of Romelio is fragmentary, it is sufficient to complete the picture of a society too weak and ignoble to exist without law. Brooke's description of "the" world of Webster's plays, although again it lacks the general applicability he gives it, is an almost perfect picture of the world of *The Devil's Law Case*:

> The world called Webster is a peculiar one. It is inhabited by people driven, like animals, and perhaps like men, only by their instincts, but more blindly and ruinously. Life there seems to flow into its forms and shapes with an irregular abnormal and horrible volume.... they kill, love, torture one another blindly and without ceasing. A play of Webster's is full of the feverish and ghastly turmoil of a nest of maggots.[12]

It is difficult to see how the dramatic worlds that contain such figures as Vittoria, the Duchess, or even Ferdinand can be compared with a nest of maggots. In those plays and, as we shall see, in *Appius and Virginia*, the grandeur of individuals defies such a comparison. But the image of humanity projected in *The Devil's Law Case* does correspond to Brooke's description of senseless, feverish, unheroic energy. It is a world without beauty, in which both heroes and villains lack stature—a world which demands a firm authority to repress and organize it.

Webster provides the necessary authority in the figures of Crispiano and Ariosto, both of whom are able to bring justice and order into the lives of the other characters. In giving us two divergent portraits of the just judge, Webster is not merely attempting to give weight to the assertion that justice exists in this world. Rather, he is giving artistic expression to two different concepts of law. In Crispiano, he is projecting the common law ideal of the judge. In Ariosto, he symbolizes the concept of the judge that served as the rationale underlying equity law.

When Sanitonella, a lawyer, hears that Ariosto has been appointed to the bench, he exclaims: "Is hee a Judge? / We must then looke for all Conscience, and now Law" (IIV, ii, 502-503). Sanitonella's statement pinpoints Ariosto's symbolic function in the play, for the equity courts of Webster's time, which included Chancery and Star Chamber, were commonly referred to as courts of "conscience."[13] Webster himself used this terminology as the basis of a quibble in his "Character of a Divellish Usurer," about whom he says, "Hee is a man of no conscience; for... he falles into a cold sweat, if he but looke into the Chauncery" (*Works*, IV, p. 37, lines 22-24). Ariosto's primary allegiance to conscience is evident throughout the play. His reactions are those of a man who, while he worships justice, does not feel himself bound by positive law. This is evident in his refusal to accept Leonora's case and in his continued opposition to her. For Ariosto's opposition is based not on a conviction that Leonora is lying, but rather on a feeling that what she is doing is a violation of human decency: "I take it, you doe very little remember / Either womanhood, or Christianitie" (IV, i, 56-57). That is, Ariosto will not help Leonora to win her suit, even though she appears to be legally in the right, because he values natural and divine law above the laws made by human beings. In this, he is a precise embodiment of the equity court's theoretical function, which was to ameliorate situations in which the peculiar circumstances surrounding a case made it necessary to avoid strict adherence to law in order to fulfill the demands of a higher law.[14]

As an equity judge, Ariosto is ideal, for he is, in himself, an incarnation of justice and order. Early in the play, when Ariosto is still a lawyer, Crispiano tells us that unlike most members of his profession, Ariosto is more interested in justice than in fees, in quick settlements than in lucrative, protracted disputes (II, i, 109-116). When Ariosto is appointed to the bench, Crispiano is hopeful that Ariosto will be able to do what "but few in our place doe — / Goe to their grave uncurst" (IV, ii, 498-499). And Sanitonella, who is rather put out by Ariosto's uncompromising virtue, says:

> Plague on's gowtie fingers,
> Were all of his mind, to entertaine no suits,
> But such they thought were honest, sure our lawyers
> Would not purchase halfe so fast. (IV, i, 79-82)

Ariosto, then, can be trusted to act in accordance with high ideals of justice, even when he is not acting in accordance with the rules. He is honest and merciful enough to function in a court where a great deal is left to his own conscience. The punishments he contrives at the end of the play complete our impression of his humane and scrupulous paternalism. But his acknowledged uniqueness in his profession makes Ariosto insufficient as an answer to the common Jacobean objection to equity that John Selden expressed when he said:

> Equity is a roguish thing. For law we have a measure, know what to trust to. Equity is according to the conscience of him that is chancellor, and as that is larger or narrower, so is equity. 'Tis all one as if they should make the standard for the measure a chancellor's foot.[15]

In order for the equity system to function in reality in accordance with its own ideals, there must be a number of Ariostos to fill its benches. This is not a hypothetical problem restricted to the realm of philosophical speculation. When James I replaced the impeached chancellor, Lord Bacon, with a man who had had no training in the law, it is reported that he justified his action by saying that "he was resolved to have no more lawyers, for they were so nursed in corruption that they could not leave it off."[16] Selden, Coke, and many other common lawyers seem to have had similar doubts about the practicability of equity law given the facts of human nature, only their doubts were not restricted to lawyers.[17]

Webster seems, almost reluctantly, to go along with the opinion of Coke, for he presents Ariosto not only as unique, but also as somewhat unreal in himself. Ariosto's dedication to truth and virtue is so extreme that it is almost an eccentricity—a "humour"—and he himself almost a caricature. In fact, while the portrait of Ariosto is for the most part serious, there are moments when Webster gives way to the comic tendencies inherent in flat characterization, so that Ariosto emerges as a semi-comic angry man, a character strongly resembling Lyly's Diogenes. The very name that Webster has chosen for him is probably meant to imply the character's unreality by evoking associations with the Italian writer of romance who may well be the subject of a reference early in *The Devil's Law Case* to "fantasticks" who "dreame" of "another world i'th Moone" (III, iii, 164-165).

Ariosto is, then, as Crispiano puts it, "the very myracle of a Lawyer" (II, i, 108), and a legal system cannot be built around a miracle. It is for this reason that Webster builds most of the trial scene around the other judge, Crispiano, who differs from Ariosto in that his personal history is not a long tale of selfless idealism. Lucas has objected that Webster is inconsistent in his portrayal of Crispiano as an opportunistic lawyer and a just judge.[18] I do not think so. Crispiano is, in this very respect, a foil to Ariosto, and by means of this more shaded characterization Webster is indicating that a legal system need not be predicated upon the existence of perfectly virtuous men. Crispiano's earlier attachment to his own self-enrichment as opposed to ideals of justice is not, after all, criminal. Crispiano is an ordinary non-malignant opportunist doing what he can for himself within the bounds of the law. That fact that such a man can adapt himself to his new role when he is made a judge is the basis for hope that justice can exist on earth. (Compare the essentially pessimistic implications of the denouement of *Measure for Measure*, where justice depends entirely on the intervention of a *deux ex machina*.) But such a judge had better be circumscribed by rules which somewhat lighten the burden placed on his frail humanity. That is, he must work within the solid kind of framework associated with the tradition of common law.

Leonora's litigation with Romelio provides Webster with an opportunity to be specific about his idea of a properly run court.[19] What is most striking about that court is the extent to which the judge's role is limited. From the modern point of view, Crispiano seems to interfere a great deal, but we have already seen that Jacobean standards were vastly different from our own. When we compare Crispiano's role with that of Monticelso or, as we shall see, with the almost limitless power of Appius in his court, it becomes apparent that Crispiano operates within definite bounds. While he is biased against Leonora because of her breach of natural law, he does not prevent her from bringing witnesses and making a full statement of her case. He asks many questions of Leonora and her witness, but he subjects them to surprisingly little harassment and insult. That is, his close questioning is not aimed at intimidating the plaintiff, but rather at getting at the truth of the matter. It is significant that Crispiano is extremely unwilling to interfere even to this extent, and that he is forced to do so only by Romelio's refusal to hire counsel and prepare a defence. In this respect, Crispiano has little in common with the Chancery judge who, in awarding a verdict favourable to a defendant in spite of the latter's failure to comply with legal technicalities, said: "*Deus est procurator fatuorum* (God acts as attorney to foolish people)."[20] Crispiano is subject to no such tendency to confuse himself with God, and he makes it plain to Romelio that the latter would do better to procure counsel than to trust to innocence and the omniscience of the court.

In all this, Crispiano is manifesting a sense of judicial fallibility that is essential to the way he conducts his court. He feels responsible for the defendant who insists on appearing without prior knowledge of the charges against him, and he strongly suspects that Leonora's case is fraudulent, but he limits his interference to careful attention to the evidence. In the way he goes about this he again manifests a sense of rule and order unusual for his time, for he makes a clear distinction between proof and rhetoric. Refusing to accept the plaintiff's sentimental proposition that there can be no "more lawfull proofe i'th world, / Then the oath of the mother" (IV, ii, 192-193), he constantly urges Leonora's lawyer to get on with his proofs. And he draws a sharp line between "stale declaiming 'gainst the person" and actual evidence, chastising the lawyer for using such "poore malicious eloquence" and finding it strange that men of supposed "gravitie" constantly resort to it (lines 161-167).

Finally Crispiano withdraws voluntarily from the case when he discovers that he has been made a party to it by Leonora, who, failing to recognize him, falsely names him as the man who had allegedly fathered Romelio many years before. As we have seen, there was no rule in Jacobean England to determine the judge's action in such a situation. Again, Webster is projecting a system more strictly geared to a standard of judicial objectivity. As an equity judge in Star Chamber, Crispiano might have had his revenge on Leonora by ordering her to be whipped and fined as a "clamorous and impudent women."[21] But Webster's court, unlike Star Chamber, does not indulge in judicial vindictiveness.

It is clear that Webster's portrait of Crispiano's court is not intended to be a realistic representation of the Jacobean courtroom. There is a constant undertone of satire in the play that serves to remind us of the difference between what is desired and what exists, and the presence of the corrupt lawyer, Contilupo, at the trial itself keeps the contrast alive. But Webster seems to be so far reconciled to the law that he can present this ideal as within the realm of human attainment. By showing us that Crispiano is not an extraordinarily virtuous man, Webster is asserting that an ordinary man can fulfill prescribed social responsibilities if he acts with a sense of duty. If it is clearly established that the judge's function in the court is limited to the intelligent evaluation of evidence and to strict interpretation of the rules of common law; it it is further laid down that a judge should not participate in a case when his animosity is aroused—then something like justice can be achieved.

This optimism, however, is undercut by the fact that it is only an accident of fate the prevents Leonora from winning her case. It is not Crispiano's conduct in the courtroom, but rather his coincidental possession of relevant information (the fact that he did *not* father her child) that defeats the plaintiff's attempt to pervert justice. The ineffectuality of law is again underscored when the court decides that Romelio's trial for murder must take the form of a wager of battle. Since there is no evidence other than the testimony of Romelio on the one side and that of his accuser on the other, the court's only recourse is to revert to the ancient method of letting the two parties fight it out. Here, as in the earlier plays, Webster is stressing the connection between law and force by pinpointing the place where they become indistinguishable. Historically, of course, the wager of battle was rarely used in this period, and it is quite unlikely that a real court would have allowed it in Romelio's case.[22] The episode is unrealistic, but it serves the symbolic purpose of demonstrating that even with such judges as Crispiano and Ariosto, there is no absolute distinction between law and force.

Webster's acceptance of law is thus mitigated by these exhibitions of its weakness. It is further mitigated by something that Webster does not indicate, something that remains unresolved in his attitude and that he does not come to grips with in this play. As we have seen, the question of the ethical validity of *talion*, legalized or otherwise, has been a basic barrier to Webster's acceptance of law. In *The Devil's Law Case*, Webster avoids the problem by digging into the bag of tricks available to writers of tragi-comedy. That is, he makes certain that nobody in the play succeeds in enacting his criminal designs. Contarino and Ercole do not succeed in killing each other; Leonora does not succeed in disinheriting her son; and, most miraculously, Romelio does not succeed in murdering Contarino. There are critics who would discuss this in strictly generic terms, asserting that such miracles are dictated by the need to achieve a comic ending. It is possible that Webster was affected by the popularity of the tragi-comic form.[23] But it is also undeniable that in using the form, Webster gave himself a way out of dealing with the problem that is central to *The White Devil* and *The Duchess of Malfi*, and that reappears, as we shall see, in *Appius and Virginia*. He is able to assert the need for law by portraying human criminality and then to avoid the question of *talion* by refusing to deal with a successful felon. The power of the law to take an eye for an eye is glossed over in the last scene, as we are treated to the wise and merciful decisions of Ariosto, whose punishments are not retributive, but regenerative. It is a pleasant picture of the act of judgment and, in a vague way, it communicates the notion that the law should be geared to the reformation rather than the destruction of wrongdoers. But since we cannot take Romelio's repentance seriously, or even believe in the miraculous recovery of the man he has tried to murder, we inevitably come away unconvinced by Webster's final picture of judicial mildness.

It is this basic dishonesty that is at the root of the aesthetic weakness of the play. Plainly, Webster is allowing himself to have his cake and eat it, so that the dramatic conflict is reducible to heroic postures that are empty, and villainous acts that are as ineffectual as any in the plays of Fletcher. At the heart of all this ineffectuality is the characterization of Romelio, for it is in Romelio that Webster has a potential centre of both heroism and villainy, a figure of sufficient stature to function as a unifying factor for all the complicated grotesqueries of the plot. But, as we have seen, Webster is unable to apply principles of artistic unity to this characterization. To be true to this character, he would have to reconcile fully the contradiction between individualism and law, and, in doing so, he would have to grapple once more with the problem of *talion*, with the paradox of a law which, in destroying evil, also destroys the vital and the heroic. One of the most poignant examples of Webster's dilemma with respect to Romelio is his treatment of this character in the trial scene. On the one hand, Webster gives Romelio lines that are reminiscent of Vittoria's in their complicated combination of hypocrisy, innocence and egotism:

> ROMELIO: My Lord,
> I am so strengthned in my innocence,
> For any the least shaddow of a crime,
> Committed gainst my mother, or the world,
> That shee can charge me with, here doe I make it
> My humble suite, onely this houre and place,
> May give it as full hearing, and as free,
> And unrestrain'd a Sentence.
>
> CRISPIANO: Be not too confident—you have cause to feare.
>
> ROMELIO: Let feare dwell with Earth-quakes,
> Shipwracks at Sea, or Prodegies in heaven,
> I cannot set my self so many fathome
> Beneath the haight of my true heart, as feare.
> (IV, ii, 90-102)

Just as we are beginning to fall under the spell of Romelio's rhetoric, Webster undercuts Romelio's poetry with Ariosto's plain prose: "Very fine words I assure you, if they were / To any purpose (lines 103-104).

The tension and vacillation here give us a perfect insight into the essential weakness of the play. Unable to part completely with heroic ideals, or to reconcile such ideals to a sense of the need for social order, Webster toys with grandeur and drops it, suggests heroism and then defines it as bombast.[24] By the time we reach the last scene, the character of Romelio has undergone so much change that we have ceased, reluctantly, to believe in him at all. Thus, his apparent repentance and the hope for his regeneration that is expressed by Ariosto have no real meaning. They are strictly theoretical, argumentative propositions, with no power as dramatic statements because there is no longer any thread of characterization to attach them to. We shall see that in *Appius and Virginia*

Webster is more forthright and courageous, though still unsuccessful, in grappling with the impediments to a full acceptance of law as a social good.

Notes to Chapter Six

1. Jacqueline Pearson, *Tragedy and Tragicomedy in the Plays of John Webster* (Manchester: Manchester University Press, 1980), p. 1. Almost equally enthusiastic is Peter B. Murray, to whom "the plot is a kind of miracle of ingenuity in its symmetrical and symbolically linked patterns of action, and the theme is coherently and even brilliantly developed through action, character, symbol" (*A Study of John Webster* [The Hague: Mouton, 1969], p. 213). Murray, like D. C. Gunby in "The Devil's Law-Case: An Interpretation" (*MLR* 63 [1968]), finds thematic unity in the play's demonstration of depraved humanity's need for providential intervention. This view is opposed by Lee Bliss, who finds in the play "not the pat Christian exemplum of a tired dramatist and frustrated moralist which several of the play's recent defenders would have us believe," but rather an effective exploration of one of Webster's "most persistent moral concerns: violation of basic human relationships is both cause and symptom of the more general social corruption" ("Destructive Will and Social Chaos in 'The Devil's Law-Case'" [*MLR* 72, 1977], pp. 513, 517). Of two recent editors, one, Elizabeth Brennan, praises the play for its presentation of "problems of situational ethics" (New Mermaids [London: Benn, 1975], p. xx); while the other, Frances A. Shirley, expresses the more traditional view that Webster "here seems unsure of his aim, or even as if he is forcing himself to work at variance with his native bent (Regents Renaissance Drama Series [Lincoln, Nebraska: University of Nebraska Press, 1972], p. xvi).
2. II, 222.
3. See Muriel Bradbrook, *John Webster: Citizen and Dramatist* (New York: Columbia University Press, 1980), p. 166.
4. Richard Hooker, *Of the Laws of Ecclesiastical Polity* (London: Dent, 1907), vol. I, pp. 156-157.
5. Ibid., p. 182.
6. See, for example, Christopher St. German, *The Doctor and the Student* (Cincinnati: R. Clarke, 1874), p. 5. The point is discussed at length in Otto Gierke, *Natural Law and the Theory of Society* (trans. Ernest Barker [Cambridge: Cambridge University Press, 1934]) both in the text and in the translator's introduction. See, especially, p. 49 of the introduction.
7. *John Webster and the Elizabethan Drama* (New York: John Lane, 1916), p. 115.
8. The final scene is praised by Pearson for showing the "convincing imperfection of these new relationships" (p. 112), and by Bliss for refusing "to gloze the difficulty of this apparently simple solution: external forces cannot change the human heart" (p. 523).
9. As far as I know, the only critics who take Romelio's repentance seriously are Murray and Gunby, who see this miraculous conversion as "an act of providential intervention" (Gunby, p. 558).
10. Bradbrook, *John Webster*, pp. 171-172.
11. The importance of role-playing in *The Devil's Law Case* has been noted by Bliss, pp. 515-517.
12. Brooke, *John Webster*, pp. 161-162.

13 William Holdsworth, *A History of English Law* (London: Methuen, 1922), vol. V, pp. 337-338.
14 St. German, *The Doctor and Student*, pp. 44-45.
15 Quoted by Catherine Bowen, *The Lion and the Throne* (Boston: Little, Brown, 1957), p. 360.
16 In a letter by John Chamberlain, quoted by Holdsworth, *A History of English Law*, vol. V, p. 227, note 1.
17 See Sir Frederick Pollock, *The Genius of the Common Law* (New York: Columbia University Press, 1912), p. 79; and Bowen, *The Lion and the Throne*, pp. 144-145. For an interesting discussion of Coke's preference for "artificial reason" (i.e., the common law) over natural reason, see Charles Gray, "Reason, Authority, and Imagination: The Jurisprudence of Sir Edward Coke," in *Culture and Politics from Puritanism to the Enlightenment*, ed. Perez Zagorin (Berkeley: University of California Press, 1980).
18 Lucas, vol. II, p. 331, note to ll. 60ff.
19 Bradbrook tells us that the members of the Inner Temple were opposed to the opening of the new theatre, the Phoenix (p. 170). Is it possible that we partly owe the attention to legal detail in this play to an effort to win them over?
20 Case cited in *The Collected Papers of Paul Vinogradoff* (Oxford: Clarendon, 1928), vol. II, p. 199.
21 See Holdsworth, *A History of English Law*, vol. I, p. 506, note 8.
22 Ibid., pp. 309-310.
23 Bradbrook calls *The Devil's Law Case* a "stylish" play (*John Webster*, p. 172). For the providential critics, of course, the fact that no murderous intents are carried out is, like Romelio's repentance, attributable to heavenly intervention.
24 Pearson notes that "the play ... sets up a system of deflating commentary on the rhetoric of tragedy" (*Tragedy and Tragicomedy*, p. 102).

Chapter Seven

Appius and Virginia

Webster's refusal to get carried away by the heroic potentialities inherent in Romelio has about it an air of self-mockery; in any case, it implies a bitter rejection of the strange humanism of *The White Devil* and *The Duchess of Malfi*. And this rejection, this fading sense of the beauty of unfettered human nature and of the excitement of human striving, is the key to the changed attitude towards law expressed in both *The Devil's Law Case* and *Appius and Virginia*. The moral ambiguity of such characters as Flamineo, Vittoria, and Bosola is impossible in these plays, where evil and good are polarized in the harsher terms of a more conventional morality. Nor is there anything like the sheer beauty of the Duchess of Malfi, for the power of good to perpetuate itself in the world is here presented as dependent upon the ability to combat evil with its own weapons. Even the villains lack the energy and aspirations of Francisco and Ferdinand, so that they no longer imply indirectly the potential power and glory of humanity.

As Webster's image of the dynamic and radiant individual fades, he becomes more concerned with the demands of society. The chaos that has always been a central characteristic of his vision of the world now becomes oppressive because it can no longer be seen as the raw material out of which splendid individuals create their own lives. The Duchess could defeat chaos by asserting, in the moment of extreme agony, the indestructible unity of her personality. In *Appius and Virgina* and *The Devil's Law Case*, the freely expressive personality does not have this power. Unless individuals commit themselves to society, and to socially derived codes and laws, they are helpless before the principle of disintegration that seems to dominate the universe.

In *Appius and Virginia*, this sense of chaos and longing for stability form a melancholy recurrent theme. The very love between Icilius and Virginia, which stands as the antithesis to Appius' destructive lust, and as the positive good for which the sympathetic characters struggle, is seen as subject to decay. In the second scene of the play, the lovers are introduced to us in a brief dialogue that ends, after a momentary flash of gaiety and optimism, on the sad key that permeates the play, as Virginia responds with characteristic realism to Icilius' affectionate words:

> VIRGINIA: It is a flattery (my lord)
> You breathe upon me, and it showes much like
> The borrowed painting which some Ladies use—
> It is not to continue many dayes;
> My wedding garments will outweare this praise.
> NUMITORIUS: Thus Ladies still foretell the funerall
> Of their Lords kindnesse. (lines 18-24)

If doubt is cast upon the permanence of love between men and women, there is even less hope for the stability of trust among men. The soldiers waver in their fidelity to the leader who has sacrificed so much for them. The lawyer who serves Appius is ready to turn against him when it becomes prudent to do so. Even Icilius' friends are reluctant to risk the dangers involved in helping him to oppose Appius, until it becomes apparent that there is no other choice. Betrayal is not, of course, a new theme to Webster. What is new is the element of sadness about it. When Flamineo is betrayed by Brachiano and then by his sister, he is angry with them and with himself. When Appius puts himself into the hands of his servant, asking him, "May I trust thee?," the disparity between Marcus' protestations of fidelity and his actual perfidy becomes a melancholy, ironic comment on cosmic mutability:

> MARCUS: As the firm center to indure the burden
> Of your light foot, as you would trust the poles
> To bear on them this airy cannopy,
> And not to fear their shrinking.
> I am strong, fixt and unshaking. (I, iii, 13-18)

In spite of our desire to see Appius overthrown, we would like to believe that Marcus' metaphysical conceit is an image of reality, that both he and the universe to which he compares himself are as stable as he says. Our underlying conviction that at least one term of the comparison is false is borne out by the end of the play.

The climactic expression of this sense of flux comes in the last scene of the play, in which the pathos becomes so intense that it threatens to wash away the resolution. The scene opens on Appius' bitter words against the populace which has suddenly turned against him:

> The world is chang'd now. All damnations
> Seize on the Hydra-headed multitude,
> That only gape for innovation!
> O who would trust a people? (V, ii, 1-4)

Coming from Appius, who has done everything possible to earn this betrayal, the words sound like a parody of Shakespearian historical drama. But later in the scene, when good men echo Appius' sentiment, we realize that no irony is intended. Virginius is not alone in succumbing momentarily to sympathy with the fallen Appius. Minutius, too, finds himself rendering justice through his tears:

> Although my heart be melting at the fall
> Of men in place and Office, we'l be just
> To punish murderous Acts, and censure Lust. (lines 89-91)

The pity expressed for Appius is a clear violation of dramatic unity. Unlike Richard II, Appius possesses none of the attractive qualities that can make such a shift of sympathy aesthetically acceptable. The longing for stability has culminated in this strange, contradictory half-wish that Appius had retained the support of the populace.

The excess of pathos at the end of the play has been attributed to Heywood on the very good grounds that sentimentality was one of his, not Webster's, bad habits.[1] Whoever is responsible, the important point for us is that the pathos here is only an extreme manifestation of a melancholy strain that runs through the play. And the judges' pity for Appius does have a connection with the general theme of instability. In a way, the wavering of the judges is an example of the most important kind of chaos—the chaos of emotion. If the shock and horror of Virginia's death can fade in her father's consciousness as soon as another strong emotion enters in, then there is little reason for individuals to depend upon themselves, let alone on others. The universal chaos is most frightening when it expresses itself in incomprehensible fluctuations within the individual soul.

It is against this background of cosmic flux that the need emerges for principles to impose upon life. Anarchistic primitivism is no longer a possible solution, for nature is an unreliable guide. This is most clearly expressed in the central action of the play. Appius, the decemvir, impelled by lust, prompts an agent to "prove" in the court over which Appius presides that Virginia is not Virginius' daughter, but this agent's bond-slave. The agent,

Marcus, demands that she be returned to him immediately, and the case, of course, goes his way. Virginius slays his daughter to prevent her enslavement and violation, and later leads a rebellion against Appius and against the institutions that made this perversion of justice possible. In killing his daughter, Virginius chooses to act according to conscious principle (and Virginia's wishes) rather than natural feeling. The debate between Virginius and Icilius about this choice is central to the meaning of *Appius and Virginia*:

> ICILIUS: Old man, thou hast shewed thy self a noble *Roman*,
> But an unnatural Father; thou hast turned
> My Bridal to a Funeral. What divel
> Did arme thy fury with the Lions paw,
> The Dragons taile,
> ....
> And all these by a father
> To be employed upon his innocent child!
>
> VIRGINIUS: Young man, I love thy true description;
> I am happy now, that one beside my selfe
> Doth teach me for this act. Yet were I pleased,
> I cou'd approve the deed most Just and noble;
> And, sure, posterity, which truely renders
> To each man his desert, shal praise me for't.
>
> ICILIUS: Come, 'twas unnatural and damnable.
>
> VIRGINIUS: You need not interrupt me. Here's a fury
> Wil doe it for you! You are a *Roman* Knight.
> What was your oath when you receiv'd your Knighthood?
> A parcel of it is, as I remember,
> Rather to die with honour, then to live
> In servitude. Had my poor girle been ravish'd,
> In her dishonour, and in my sad griefe,
> Your love and pity quickly had ta'ne end.
> Great mens misfortunes thus have ever stood,
> They touch none neerly, but their neerest blood.
> (V, i, 110-132)

The debate is never really resolved. Virginius himself, by his own testimony, is full of self-recrimination for the act that he justifies on ideological grounds. But his argument gains strength from what the play demonstrates about human changeability. When Virginius tells Icilius that the latter would have "quickly" resolved to leave Virginia to her dishonour, Icilius does not protest, and we are reminded of an earlier statement on the mutability of love. Virginius' decision to act according to a defined code instead of relying on his natural feelings and the absolute loyalty of other men is at least logical in terms of what the play as a whole says about human nature.

This, then, is what the play offers as a possible answer to natural chaos. Men must act according to principles of duty and honour, no matter how oppressive of natural feelings those principles are. Appius' life is determined by a single-minded drive to satisfy his desires. To satisfy ambition, he accepts an office for which he is unsuited. To satisfy lust, he not only ruins the life of one woman, but is prepared to starve the whole army as well, leaving Rome open to invasion, in order to destroy Virginius' fortune and make his daughter an undesirable match for Icilius. This latter, this total lack of public conscience, is Appius' greatest crime. Icilius, who is primarily concerned about what happens to Virginia, nonetheless, because he is a good Roman, comments repeatedly on the larger implications of Appius' lust:

> You would bestow me on some Appian Trull,
> And for that dross to cheat me of my Gold;
> For this the Camp pines, and the City smarts.
> All *Rome* fares worse for thy incontinence. (II, iii, 92-95)

And later in the play:

> Better had *Appius* been an upright Judg,
> And yet an evil man, then honest man,
> And yet a dissolute Judg; for all disgrace
> Lights lesse upon the person, then the place. (V, i, 157-160)

In this latter statement, Icilius expresses summarily the major theme of the play, the need to impose externally, socially derived principles upon human behaviour. As Robert Griffin puts it, *Appius and Virginia* "locates personal heroism in self-denial and sacrifice to the community."[2] Appius is evil, not because he has evil desires, but because he does not subordinate his personal feelings to abstract ideas of honour, duty, and justice. There is poetic justice in his ultimate fall from power as a victim of mutability. Virginius, on the other hand, is characterized as an ideal public servant. Throughout the play, there is emphasis on his willingness to sacrifice personal pleasure to the public good. When he is urged by his friends to delay his return to the camp in order to celebrate his daughter's betrothal, he does not hesitate to decide that conditions at the camp necessitate his immediate return:

> I am ingag'd: short farwels now must serve,
> The universal business calls me hence,
> That toucheth a whole people (I, iv, 161-163)

Again, it is the "universal" good that determines his behaviour when he sells his own property in order to feed the soldiers he commands. The intensity of Virginius' sense of social responsibility is revealed in his decision to conceal this fact from the soldiers, leading them to believe that the money comes from Rome. Although he and the soldiers have been insulted and misused, Virginius chooses to pretend that Rome has acted sympathetically, in order that the army may remain loyal, and Rome be protected in spite of itself: "Thus men must slight their wrongs, or else conceal them, / When generall safety wills us not reveale them" (II, ii, 249-250).

Finally Virginius once more sacrifices himself for the general welfare when he consents to lead the rebellion against Appius. "A weak old man, / Weary of life, and covetous of a grave" (IV, ii, 184-185), Virginius is willing to postpone the peace he seeks in order to serve Rome again. Revenge is not what impels him; he would rather leave retribution to the people who still have something to lose if Appius is not destroyed. But the people want Virginius to lead, and he acquiesces in order to ensure the success of their revolt, "in hope," as Virginius says, "to guard you all / From my inhumane sufferings" (IV, ii, 204-205).

Thus, Virginius' sacrifice of his daughter's life is not an isolated act, but rather an extreme expression of his general code of behaviour. If Virginius is able to resist the natural impulse to keep Virginia alive, no matter what, it is because throughout his life he has subordinated such natural impulses to his ethics. Virginius' ability to act in contradiction to his feelings may remain repelling to the audience, as it does to Icilius, but it is clearly demonstrated that the same ability is what makes Virginius a capable, trustworthy leader of society. Nor is it only men in power who need to live by principle. The contrast between Appius and Virginius is reinforced thematically by the contrast between Rome and the camp. For Appius' disregard of the plight of the soldier is typical of the attitude of Rome in general, which has grown so absorbed in self-indulgence that it has abandoned responsibility even for its own safety:

> VIRGINIUS: What Slave would be a soldier to be censured
> By such as ne'er saw danger! To have our pay,
> Our worths and merits ballanc'd in the scale
> Of base moth-eaten peace!
> ....
> They lay their heads
> On their soft pillowes, pore upon their bags,
> Grow fat with laziness and resty ease.
> And us that stand betwixt them and disaster
> They will not spare a *Drachma*. (I, iv, 108-117)

While the city degenerates in a vast orgy of self-seeking, the soldiers remain faithful to their contract even when "nature and necessity" command that they seek their own welfare (II, ii, 12). When starvation finally impels them to rebel, they are rapidly brought back to submission, not by food, but by rhetoric. The same habit of self-discipline and self-denial that underlies Virginius' sacrifice of his daughter's life is what keeps Rome safe from invasion.

Since the action of the play begins with Appius' abuse of judicial power, it is logical that the contrast between Appius and Virginius should culminate in Virginius' displacement of Appius in the judgment seat. Whereas Appius has failed as a judge because of his dedication to self, Virginius has given every indication that he will be suited to the role. A concept of the ideal judge that is shared by all the major characters is enunciated by Appius himself in the first scene of the play, when, addressing his kinsmen, he pretends to commit himself to impartiality:

> Henceforth the face of a Barbarian
> And yours shall be all one, henceforth Ile know you
> But only by your vertue: brother or father
> In dishonest suite shall be to me
> As is the branded slave. Justice should have
> No kindred, friends, nor foes, nor hate, not love—
> As free from passion as the gods above.[3] (I, i, 116-120)

Appius himself has no intention of living up to this ideal, and when we see him in the role of judge he is anything but "free from passion." Virginius, though, appears to possess the self-control necessary to subordinate his personal feelings to the supremely important ideal of justice. The most disconcerting moment in the play occurs when Virginius fails: when, at this crucial point, his habitual dispassion gives way before a disintegrating flood of emotion. We are asked to believe that a man who could harden himself enough to kill a cherished daughter is now incapable of suppressing pity long enough to pronounce sentence on the man whose lust necessitated her death. In terms of characterization, the scene is ruinous. But the philosophical impulse that overrode the authors' sense of character at this point (or the inability of the collaborators to reconcile their differences) saves the play from thematic simplemindedness. Through Virginius' failure, the writers are reminding us of the irrationality of human beings and confessing that ideal justice is unattainable on earth. The black and white contrast between good judge and bad breaks down as, belatedly, the writers raise basic questions about the nature of justice.

The scene contains a good deal of discussion and debate that is not resolved, either through argument or action. The one clear idea that does emerge is that Appius' ideal of justice is as unrealistic as it is hypocritical. No individual, no matter how committed to self-discipline, is as free from passion as the gods. Human justice, in the end, rests upon emotion as much as it rests upon reasonable interpretation of law and precedent. When Virginius begins to talk of mercy, his fellow judges, Numitorius and Minutius, argue with him from the point of view of Appius' ideal:

> NUMITORIUS: *Virginius*, you are too remiss to punish
> Deeds of this nature. You must fashion now
> Your actions to your place, not to your passion—
> Severity to such acts is as necessary
> As pity to the tears of innocence.
> MINUTIUS: He speaks but Law and Justice.
> ....
> Although my heart be melting at the fall
> Of men in place and Office, we'l be just
> To punish murderous Acts, and censure lust.
> (V, ii, 80-91)

The judge must act according to the word of the law, no matter what his personal feelings may be. In terms of Virginius' character, these speeches should be sufficient to recall him to a sense of his "place," for they merely reiterate the ideal of behaviour that he, as opposed to Appius, has really lived by. But it is no such reasonable consideration that finally moves Virginius to pronounce sentence of death. Icilius, who throughout the play has expressed a more impetuous, passionate approach to life, does not rely upon arguments, but instead concocts a scene that is calculated to renew the strength of Virginius' hatred. It is not an abstract idea of justice, but the sight of Virginia's corpse that drives away Virginius' pity for Appius. When Virginius finally judges Appius, he is acting as much from personal passion as Appius ever did when he sat on the bench.

Thus, after all the emphasis on discipline, duty, justice, and dispassion, the play ends on a confession of the fragility of these values. When justice is achieved, it is the passionate justice of rebellion and revenge. It is not even entirely clear that "justice" is a moral good. Again, the writers express philosophical doubt by means of an unresolved debate between Icilius and Virginius. This time, the debate occurs over the question of the efficacy of punishment. Appius, in his last attempt to save his life, appeals to Virginius to be merciful rather than just:

> If in mine eminence I was stern to thee;
> Shunning my rigor, likewise shun my fall.
> And being mild where I shewed cruelty,
> Establish still thy greatness. (V, ii, 58-61)

Seeing that Virginius has been moved by Appius' argument, Icilius attempts to reduce to absurdity this impulse to forgive:

> Thinks not *Virginius*,
> If he should pardon Appius this black deed,
> And set him once more in the Ivory Chair,
> He would be wary to avoid the like,
> Become a new man, a more upright judge,
> And deserve better of the Common Weal? (lines 71-76)

But Virginius is evidently impervious to Icilius' irony, for he responds, " 'Tis like he would." It is at this point that Icilius, despairing of argument, decides to fetch Virginia's corpse.

In the end, of course, Virginius decides for justice over mercy, and Appius himself approves the sentence, regretting that he himself has not been so "noble" a "Justicer" (line 123). But Appius' approval notwithstanding, the argument that people are capable of reformation has not been answered, and the very fact that Appius praises Virginius' behaviour as judge lends weight to that argument. The whole philosophical foundation of the play seems to shake and crumble during this scene, as the writers undermine the very concepts that the play has established.

To reduce all this to a coherent whole would be to create unity where it does not exist. The fact is that the play does manifest philosophical confusion, and that it suffers aesthetically because of it, in terms of inconsistency of character and mood as well as a general talkiness which, at moments, turns an epic tragedy into a *débat*. We cannot help sensing that the writers are not entirely convinced of the values that, for the most part, they seem to embrace. The undercurrent of chaos, which is, to them, the one sure fact of existence, keeps threatening to undermine all the structures they can build to control it. In spite of all the emphasis on the Roman virtues, passion still emerges as the dominant fact of human existence, and the retaliatory basis of the law remains a human approximation rather than a divine principle.

It is the question of *talion* that most seriously undercuts the ideological basis of the play. After all, "justice" is finally done, even though Virginius has proven that even a good judge can falter in his dedication to the word of the law. But if the word of the law itself comes into question, if there is doubt about the moral validity of what society calls "justice," then there is neither human virtue nor abstract principle to rely upon in the conduct of human affairs, and the human attempt to create order is just a shot in the dark. To some extent, this is what happens in *Appius and Virginia*. Nor is the final scene entirely disconnected from the rest of the play in manifesting such doubt. Earlier in the play, during Virginia's trial,

Icilius makes a comment which recalls Webster's earlier attitudes towards the abstraction of justice, and which points forward to the confusion of the last scene. Appius, in an attempt to discredit Icilius as a witness, offers to present a "character" of him for the benefit of the court. Unlike Monticelso, he does not get the chance, for Icilius interrupts him, saying:

> Do, but do it with Justice,
> Clear thy self first, O *Appius*, ere thou judg
> Our imperfections rashly, for we wot
> The Office of Justice is perverted quite
> When one thief hangs another. (IV, i, 272-276)

The apparent conventionality of the remark somewhat obscures the dynamite it contains, and we might never consider it more than casually were it not that the dynamite goes off in the last scene. For what the statement implies is that people must clear themselves of all guilt before they can claim the right to judge others. And it follows, since no person is free of guilt, that all human justice is more or less a matter of one thief judging another. There is another implication, too, that is spelled out in the last scene. That is that people who are most aware of their own failings and most free of real guilt are least likely to be the ones to cast the first stone. Whereas the evil Appius has gained the reputation of a hanging judge, Virginius, with his consciousness of his own human faults, so little relishes his power to punish that he can barely muster enough hostility to pass sentence.

This is the most important meaning of what happens in the last scene. Appius is right when he connects his "rigour" as a judge with his moral failure in that role. He has been stern because of an inadequate consciousness of his own guilt. And Virginius is so sensitive to that point that he carries it to its logical conclusion and discovers that, on the level of pure ideals, he cannot claim the right to punish Appius. In short, Virginius discovers that there is no abstract justification for punishment. That is why the punishment finally proceeds from passion rather than principle. People judge others not because the principle of justice demands it, or because Divine Reason prompts them, but rather because passion impels them to. That is the point the writers make when they break down the artifice of calm, rational, judicial procedure in the last scene and transform a trial into an act of revenge. Webster has not forgotten that there is no essential difference between revenge and *talion*.

And yet, although his attitude towards law has not changed in this essential way, Webster has come to feel that law is necessary. And, with all its faults, law becomes acceptable when it can be made into an instrument for good by people who desire the good of all society. This is the essence of Webster's approach to law here. He no longer postulates the glorious, powerful or morally radiant individual as an answer to the evil entrenched in a society. The suffering of the Duchess and the revenge-atonement of a Bosola were sufficient to purge the society created and ruled by the Arragonian brothers. To rid Rome of Appius and the tyranny for which he stands, all those who are dedicated to the welfare of Rome must join together and, not only depose the tyrant, but create a new society as well. If law has been an instrument of oppression, it must now be made a force for good. Individuals, acting alone and willfully, cannot cope with socially entrenched evil. They must make themselves part of an organism, and in doing that, they must accept the rule of law.

To put it succinctly, the social ideal that has replaced Webster's radical individualism demands reconciliation with the pragmatically derived realities of power. At first, Virginius makes the mistake of depending too entirely on his own virtue, and if he is in any way guilty of his daughter's death, it is because he vainly attempts to fight Appius' cynicism with ideals. Because he feels that the institution of the law is morally impure, he refuses to taint the truth of his case by hiring an advocate:

> Truth needs no Advocate, the unjust Cause
> Buyes up the tongues that travel with applause
> In these your thronged Courts. I want not any,
> And count him the most wretched that needs many. (IV, i, 66-69)

The self-destructiveness of his position becomes apparent as he paradoxically confesses reliance on his enemy, Appius, to compensate for his own unfamiliarity with the Law:

> I have no skill i'th'weapon, good my Lord;
> I mean, I am not travell'd in your Lawes.
> My suit is therefore by your special goodness
> They be not wrested against me. (lines 75-78)

By the end of the scene, Virginius has recognized the folly of counting on Appius' sense of fair-play and his own innocence:

> Good men too much trusting their innocence
> Do not betake them to that just defence
> Which Gods and Nature gave them; but even wink
> In the black tempest, and so fondly sink. (lines 310-313)

Virginius has become aware of the full significance of his earlier reference to the law as a "weapon." He realizes that while the weapon is repugnant to him, he cannot hope to win the fight unless he learns how to use it. Through Virginius, Webster is reiterating the point that Crispiano tried to impress upon Romelio in *The Devil's Law Case*: people must accept the fact that law is not an ideal, but rather a mode of social conflict. And in such a conflict people are obliged to defend themselves by the available means.

Thus the answer to Appius' corrupt and tyrannical reign as chief judge of Rome must not be a rebellion against all law and order, but rather the creation of a better, though still imperfect system. By means of both positive and negative examples, the writers indicate the kind of system people should strive to establish. The most important feature of this system is the circumscribed role allotted to the judge. In Appius' court, everything works for the judge and against the defendant. The judge is permitted to intimidate witnesses, belittle their testimony by slandering their character, and even prevent them from speaking altogether. He is able to prevent Icilius from introducing evidence. Even more important, he is able to determine the outcome of the trial by timing it to take place before Virginia's "friends / Can be assembled, ere her self can study / Her answer or scarce know her cause of summons / To descant on the matter" (II, iii, 225-228).

In all these details, Appius' court is the exact opposite of Crispiano's, in which, as we have seen, the defendant was urged to familiarize himself with the charges, hire counsel, and take time to prepare a defence. *The Devil's Law Case* and *Appius and Virginia* are thus similar in their common emphasis upon the need for a strengthening of the defendant's status. But *Appius and Virginia* goes further in that it makes a direct connection between judicial paternalism and tyranny. In *The Devil's Law Case*, the characterization of Ariosto tends to perpetuate, vaguely, the ideal of perfect justice. In *Appius and Virginia*, it is clearly demonstrated that the ideal of the perfect judge must be abandoned in favour of a workable conception which allows for human failure and partiality. Appius, skilled in the idealist rhetoric surrounding Renaissance law, refers to judges as "Gods on earth" (V, ii, 141) and rationalizes the judge's paternal role by demanding, "Who stands for father of the Innocent, / If not the judge?" (III, ii, 313-314). But his own example clearly demonstrates that these ideals have nothing to do with real human behaviour, and later on, Virginius shows us that even a good judge is something less than a god on earth.

To construct a workable system of law, these ideals must be thrown out, for, in practice, they are merely a rationalization for tyranny. This side of the coin is exposed by Icilius, who views Appius' assumption of God's role in a more cynical light:

> Will no man view these papers? What not one?
> *Jove* thou hast found a Rival upon earth,
> His nod strikes all men dumb. (IV, i, 280-282)

And again:

> Attend! A petty Lawyer t'other day,
> Glad of a fee, but, cal'd to eminent place,
> Even to his betters, now the word's Attend.
> This gowned office, what a breadth it bears!
> How many tempests waite upon his frowne! (II, ii, 26-30)

The mythology surrounding the figure of the judge and symbolized by his awe-inspiring robe serves no better purpose than to delude people into confusing the ideal with the reality, the dream of god-like justice wiht the mere mortal who, at best, is striving to work towards that ideal. At worst, the myth provides a cover beneath which the unscrupulous individual can tyrannize at will.

It is significant that Virginius' dramatic opposition to Appius' tyranny reaches its apex as he puts himself in the hands of a jury consisting of the whole army. Appius' judgment of Virginius' slaying of his daughter is clear, and it is up to the army either to go along with that judgment or to overrule it: "You are my Sentencers:... / Sentence my Fact with a free general tongue" (IV, ii, 159-161). The rebellion and the purification of the state are thus linked with a transfer of the power of judgment from a single individual who presumably possesses special qualifications to a large number of ordinary people. In one sweeping gesture, Virginius has undermined the institution of the Decemviri together with all the claptrap that has supported it. The justice of the soldiers' decree makes it abundantly clear that, given human failings, it is better to trust to numbers than to deify an individual.

While this people's court is not institutionalized in the new society, the structure that is established goes far to carry out a less mythified conception of the judge. Even the trial of Appius, though it is characterized by the peremptoriness of a revolutionary tribunal, manifests a more democratic spirit, for Virginius' fellow judges, unlike those who shared the bench with Appius, are not overawed by the chief judge. On the contrary, they express their disagreement without inhibition. And, although Appius does not have much to say for himself, he is allowed to say it at length, and to a judge who is humble enough to listen.

But the most important expression of the changed conception of the judge in the new society is the fact that judges are now to be chosen by "the peoples suffrage" (V, ii, 189). The replacement of an earlier system of appointment by a system of election is all-important, not only because it makes the judge responsible to the whole society, but also because it does away with the mystery surrounding the judge's calling. If the people elect Icilius and Virginius to the bench, it is because in leading the rebellion these two men have demonstrated that they possess certain strictly human qualities that the people admire. By broadening the basis of justice, the new government is calling attention to the humbleness of its roots.

On the whole, *Appius and Virginia* embodies a more satisfying treatment of law than *The Devil's Law Case*. The problem of the relation between judgment and human emotions is not resolved, nor is the moral objection to *talion* thoroughly dealt with. But both problems are at least stated, and the statements are not without dramatic interest. More important, *Appius and Virginia* expresses a trenchant attack upon the paternalistic image of the judge, an attack that is important both in its contemporary significance and in its dramatic value. The contemporary significance, which will be discussed in detail in the final chapter, becomes apparent when we consider that even Coke, who was no friend to tyranny, justified the denial of counsel to a defendant in a criminal trial on the grounds of the very same idealistic notion that Webster is here opposing. "The court ought to be instead of counsel for the prisoner," he said, "to see that nothing be urged against him contrary to law and right."[4] There is no better example of the way in which the paternalistic image of the judge was used as an argument against strengthening the position of the defendant. The philosophical strength of *Appius and Virginia* lies in its clear demonstration of what happens when a society constructs its legal system on the basis of such a delusion.

Much of the play's dramatic strength derives from the same source. Probably the only consistent source of dramatic tension in *Appius and Virginia* is the dichotomy between the god-like dedication to justice ascribed to Appius by the people of Rome and his actual villainy. The gradual breakdown of this image, as individuals and, finally, masses of people become able to liberate themselves from the paternalistic illusion, is the fundamental dramatic movement of the play. Its climax occurs when Virginius suddenly recognizes, after the first trial, that he has been betrayed by this illusion of perfect justice. From that point on, Virginius' recognition spreads with increasing rapidity to the rest of the society until it culminates in revolution. (Compare, again, *Measure for Measure*, where the Duke does whatever he can to *maintain* the paternalistic illusion by glossing over Angelo's perfidy.) In spite of its inconsistencies, and the flatness of its characters, *Appius and Virginia* remains an engrossing play because of the successful exploitation of the dramatic value inherent in this theme. Produced epic-theatre style, with the tragic elements subordinated to a historical sweep (much as one might produce *Mother Courage*, for example), the play would, I believe, prove stageworthy.

But what of Virginia in all this? Is she, as Simon Shepherd states, a "silent, barely characterized figure, with only one or two flashes of female toughness"?[5] Does she function only as victim and reminder of the male characters' neglect of their duty to oppose tyranny?

Certainly Virginia is a minor character in spite of her crucial function in the plot. That is because her experience is seen as an instance of suffering under tyranny, rather than as the centre of a pathos-oriented rape story. Still, although she is subsumed by the epic mode, Virginia is a defined character. A motherless young woman, indulged by her loving and surprisingly maternal father—who, though a soldier, fondly recalls singing her to sleep—Virginia moves about the city unchaperoned, clearly accustomed to being on her own and trusted. It is Virginia who first sees through Appius and who tries, in vain, to get her uncle to take some action, since her father is off fighting a war. And it is she who decides that she will not live as a slave. In short, Virginia is presented as intelligent, realistic, active, and brave. Because she is not a superstar like Vittoria or the Duchess, it is especially terrible that her world demands her sacrifice.

Webster's reconciliation with law is more convincing in *Appius and Virginia* than in *The Devil's Law Case*, because in *Appius and Virginia* it does not rest upon dramatized visions of perfect judges and perfect justice. The hope for social regeneration expressed at the end of *Appius and Virginia* does not imply a hope for a perfect legal system. Little can be done to prevent another Marcus from claiming another Virginia by producing "firme proofs, notes probable, sound Witnesses" (II, iii, 210); for, as Virginius and Numitorius point out, "Who cannot counterfeit a dead man's hand? / Or hire some villains to swear forgeries?" (IV, i, 239-240). Nor can anything be done to make all lawyers scrupulous. The cynical advocate who represented Marcus is not touched by the ruin of those he served, and we may assume that he, or others like him, who deal in "formal glosses" and "cunning showes" (IV, i, 166) will continue to ply their trade under the new administration. Obedience to the rules of law, no matter how wisely those rules are made, can never guarantee the justice of the outcome. But in the very recognition that a trial must remain a dubious combat lies the possibility that people can make it a real combat rather than a refined instrument for the oppression of the weak.

Notes to Chapter Seven

1 For a discussion of the authorship question, see Peter B. Murray, *A Study of John Webster* (The Hague: Mouton, 1969), Chapter 13 and Appendix IV and Fernand Lagarde, *John Webster* (Toulouse: Publications de la Faculté des Lettres et Sciences Humaines, 1968), pp. 288-300. Those who have studied the matter have generally attributed the last two scenes of the play to Heywood. However, so respectable a scholar as G. E. Bentley thinks Heywood had nothing to do with the play at all (*The Jacobean and Caroline Stage* [Oxford: Clarendon, 1941-68], vol. V, p. 1247). Although I am inclined to agree with Murray, Lucas, and others who see a collaborator's hand here, the tests used to determine authorship do not seem to me conclusive. Furthermore, a collaboration always involves some degree of subtle interaction, not to be revealed even if the authorship of every line were established. In my discussion of *Appius and Virginia* I have chosen to ignore the question of who wrote which scenes and to assume Webster's artistic responsibility for the play as a whole. This is not intended to contradict Murray's contention that the differences between Webster and Heywood account for some of the play's inconsistencies. But it would be well to consider other possible explanations. For example, it may be that most of the weeping over the fall of great men towards the end of the play represents nothing but the efforts of prudent writers to get a subversive play past the censor. Given the present state of scholarship, any discussion of this play must be tentative.
2 *John Webster: Politics and Tragedy*, Salzburg Studies in English Literature (Salzburg: Institut für Englische Sprache und Literatur, Universität Salzburg, 1972), p. 34. Given the emphasis on this theme it is difficult to understand Murray's statement that "the action has no coherent theme" (p. 252).
3 One wonders whether Webster is commenting ironically here upon a speech made by Coke that closely parallels Appius' declaration (see Catherine Bowen, *The Lion and the Throne* [Boston: Little, Brown, 1957], pp. 286-287).
4 Quoted by William Holdsworth, *A History of English Law* (London: Methuen, 1922), vol. V, p. 192.
5 *Amazons and Warrior Women* (New York: St. Martin's Press, 1981), p. 198.

Chapter Eight

Conclusion: The Rule of Law

> "What is it that you chiefly aim at in this war?" the troops were asked in *The Souldiers Catechism* of 1644; and the reply was, after reforming religion and bringing the enemies of Church and state to justice: "At the regulating of our courts of justice,which have been made the seats of iniquity and unrighteousness."
> Christopher Hill, *Intellectual Origins of the English Revolution*, p. 260

We have traced a split between the two great tragedies on the one hand and *The Devil's Law Case* and *Appius and Virginia* on the other. Our tentative chronology suggests that Webster moved away from an earlier radical and anarchistic individualism to make a protagonist of society in the later plays. I want to stress again that the order in which the plays were written is not crucial to this analysis. Since the plays represent two sides of a dialectic, they can be seen as expressing different moods of a writer who was struggling to work out deeply felt contradictions. The plays do not suggest any particular line of development—we cannot say that one play absorbs and resolves the contradictions of any other play. It may well be that *The Devil's Law Case* is best approached as Webster's comic inversion of his own tragic poetry, a kind of antimasque or satyr play made up of the anti-heroic impulses he largely suppressed when he was writing tragedy. In that case, the play would not represent a new development in the writer so much as an alternative mood, a mood of cynicism that he would have correctly associated with the tragi-comic genre. As for *Appius and Virginia*, although there are reasons (as we shall see) for dating it in the 1620s, we cannot be sure that it was not written as early as 1603.

Indeed, the earlier period produced a succession of plays about tyranny, one of which, *The Famous History of Sir Thomas Wyat*, is among the earliest plays Webster is known to have had a share in writing. So although it is convenient to refer to earlier and later plays, I ask the reader to bear in mind that the internal logic of the plays reveals a dialectical, not a chronological, relationship.

As we have seen, the two great tragedies are centred on the destruction of powerful individuals. In the other plays we have discussed, it is the fate of the society as a whole that is at stake. In *The Devil's Law Case*, Webster seems to be almost consciously rejecting his earlier position. The creation of Romelio is tantamount to a rejection of radical individualism. And the portrait of Leonora is a refutation of the naturalistic primitivism that had inspired the creation of the Duchess, for instead of being ennobled by her natural affections, Leonora is divested of maternal impulse and transformed into a fury. She is Venus Genetrix gone haywire, a living demonstration that the simple animal virtues are not available to human beings. In such a world, order becomes desirable, even if the modalities of order are necessarily imperfect. Webster has finally reached the Hobbesian position that social peace is a worthwhile human goal.

But Webster never contradicts his earlier conviction that social peace cannot be imposed forcibly from without by an absolute ruling power with ambitions and drives of its own. What, then, is to be the agency of order, if reason is not to be looked for either in princes or commoners? In *The Devil's Law Case*, Webster attempts to endorse the Puritan party's idealization of common law as the means of simultaneously ordering social relations and safeguarding the liberties of the individual. It is the two-fold function of law as conceived by Pym when he said that "if you take away the *Law*, all things will fall into a *confusion*.... The *Law* is the *Boundarie*, the *Measure* betwixt the *Kings Prerogative*, and the *Peoples* Liberty."[1] The rationale for Law in *The Devil's Law Case* is secular and relativist, rather than religious and absolute. Law is not a reflection of Divine Reason, but it represents humanity's most successful attempt to be reasonable. Coke expresses the position clearly:

> The laws, that by long experience and practice of many successions of grave, learned and wise men, have grown to perfection, are grounded no doubt upon greater and more absolute reason than the singular and private opinion or conceit of the wisest man that liveth in the world can find out or attain unto. Therefore the law shall stand for reason.[2]

The implications of the position are communal and, for the time, democratic.

Conclusion: The Rule of Law   149

When Pym made the speech quoted above, in 1641, he was expressing the ideology that had served his party throughout the Jacobean and Caroline periods. By the very next year, the Parliamentarians had found it necessary to reverse their position and assert that fundamental political goals are more important than particular laws.[3] As Henry Parker put it in 1643, laws "may be imployed either to the benefit or prejudice of any Nation.... Nothing has done us more harme of late, then this opinion of adhering to Law only for our preservation."[4] The revolution had suddenly brought into sharp focus the truth that had so long been avoided: the recognition that law can be used to serve the aims of whoever happens to be in power. One weakness of *The Devil's Law Case* is that it too evades the problem of the political authority behind the law, presenting the court as a free-floating member detached from the rest of the body politic. The judges and the ruler who appoints them have no personal interest in the decisions of the court; they only desire to see that justice is done. This idealistic picture of law as a neutral institution mediating among the individuals of society is as anticlimactic in the context of Webster's work as the latter part of *Measure for Measure* is unsatisfactory as an answer to the questions about justice raised in the earlier part of that play. One senses Webster's own uneasiness throughout *The Devil's Law Case*.

In *Appius and Virginia*, Webster abandons the pre-revolutionary position that social order is dependent upon obedience to positive law, and moves, ahead of his time, to the revolutionary position that "the people's safety is the supreme law, taking precedence over all other laws."[5] In *Appius and Virginia*, the agency of order is the people. The rule of law implied at the end of the play has been demanded by the society, rather than imposed upon it. It is not an isolated sovereign who brings law to the people, but, on the contrary, it is the people who demand law from him. The image of self-absorbed, anti-social individuals that dominates Webster's earlier plays is here pushed into the background, embodied in the shadowy portrait of the citizens of Rome. Among the major characters, the conflict is precisely between those, like Appius, who are not committed to society and those, like Virginius, who are. The victory goes to Virginius, because he expresses the will of the people.

Appius is a judge in the tradition of Ferdinand, a pretender to divinity, a supposed father to the innocent and stern censurer of the guilty, with power to destroy those who would question his uprightness. Under his administration, law is as clearly an oppressor's weapon as it had been in the earlier plays. But here, for once, Webster poses the possible alternative of a law which is expressive of the sovereign will, not of a tyrant, but of the people. It was a dangerous and revolutionary idea. As late as 1642, as Sirluck points out, it was a "revolutionary assertion" to declare that Parliament is the basis of government.[6] To locate the source of power in the people as a whole remained revolutionary throughout the civil war period. In 1647, Overton called upon the army to defend the rights of the people against Parliament. In response to the objection that the army was not the formal representative of the people, Overton declared:

> The Body naturall must never be without a mean to save it selfe, and therefore ... any person or persons ... may warrantably rise up in the ... behalf of the people, to preserve them from imminent ruine.[7]

The situation in *Appius and Virginia* is strangely prophetic of the struggles of the late 1640s, and in his sympathetic portrayal of insurrection, Webster anticipates the most radical exponents of the social-contract theory.

Superficially, it is paradoxical that Webster's acceptance of social order as a worthwhile goal involves a simultaneous endorsement of revolution. But this paradox, of course, is the crux of the social-contract theory. Law is not a separate and neutral mechanism. Rather, it is an aspect of the contract made between ruler and people. When the contract is violated—when law is used for the sole benefit of the ruler—the people are released from their obligation to obey. It is this theory that underlies the arguments of Overton and Lilburne in the 1640s. The tyranny of Parliament has served to

> dissolve the legall frame and constitution of the civill policy and government of the Kingdome, by suffering will and lust, but not lawe to rule and governe us, and so reduce us into the originall Law of nature, for every man to preserve and defend himself the best he can.[8]

Once the rule of law ceases, violence becomes necessary:

> For it is clearly evident, there is now no power executed in England, but a power of force, a just and morall act done by a troop of Horse, being as good law as now I can see executed by any Judge in England.[9]

Webster's reconciliation to law in *Appius and Virginia* is thus a revolutionary position. In shifting his focus from the individual to the society, Webster has come to envision resistance to oppressive power as something more potent than the acts of isolated individuals—the passive resistance of the Duchess; the spirited equivocation of Vittoria. In *Appius and Virginia*, resistance is a

Conclusion: The Rule of Law

social act, made possible by the voluntary submission of individuals like Virginius to the general will.

But in retrospect, we can see that the germ of this statement is contained in the tragedies. In *The White Devil*, the passive suffering of Isabella is made pathetic, but not noble; and although we sympathize with the individualistic rebellion of Vittoria and Flamineo, we are left with an overwhelming sense of the futility of their isolated acts of defiance. *The Duchess of Malfi* is a subtle, intensely moving examination of passive resistance. Because we are made to endure with the Duchess the prolonged agonies of the fourth act, and because we have to go on existing in a fifth-act world made gloomy by her absence, we leave the theatre asking ourselves the inevitable question: why was her death necessary? The answer is complex, as it must be in tragedy, but part of it is that both she and Bosola act too late. Her idealistic sense that her innocence will carry her safely through the dangers she dimly perceives yields too late to an understanding that she must act to protect herself and her family. In a sense, she has made the mistake of trying to separate her inner and outer worlds—to keep her little escape world of personal happiness apart from the dangers and intrigues of the larger world of public life. In so doing, she has left this private world unprotected. The tragic complexity lies in the fact that it is precisely through the Duchess' martyrdom that Bosola finally learns that obedience to an evil authority brings no rewards and that trust is possible between human beings.

Thus we can trace the theme of resistance as forming another constant in Webster's work. The political importance of the theme becomes clear when we compare Webster's *Appius and Virginia* with the hybrid morality play written on the same theme in the 1560s by one R. B. In this play, as in five other hybrid plays of the same period, the theme, as David Bevington puts it, is that "only God could dispose of an evil yet legitimately established monarch."[10] Individuals must resist the command of a tyrant (it is interesting that in four of these plays tyranny is associated with sexual aggression), but resistance must take the form of passive disobedience rather than active opposition. Bevington's description of the earlier Appius play stresses this point:

> Virginia and her parents are models of passive obedience and chaste affection.... Confronted with Judge Appius' 'filthy lust', suborning of witnesses, and other abuses of his power of office, Virginia's family never considers an act of reprisal (unlike Livy's heroic plebeians, who openly threaten the decemvirs with armed rebellion).... As in *Cambises*, their passive obedience means not catering to Appius' whim but a willingness to die for the ideals of chastity and duty.[11]

When Appius is punished at the end of the play, it is not by human agents, but by the allegorical figures of Justice and Revenge. Bevington comments perceptively on the thematic significance of this allegorical retribution:

> True justice cannot be bent to the practice of tyranny. Yet insofar as Appius possesses all the machinery of justice for whatever use he wishes, the dilemma remains unresolved. What human hands would dare touch the king and elect Virginius in his stead? The hybrid morality, by bringing in abstractions at this point, only intensifies the puzzlement of those who would know how a tyrant can actually be deposed without human rebellion.[12]

It was probably even more dangerous in Jacobean England than it had been during Elizabeth's reign to portray the human hands that would dare to touch a king, or even his agent. To disguise the king as a Roman and plead historical accuracy would not necessarily provide adequate cover, as Jonson learned when he found himself in trouble over his historical play *Sejanus*.[13] And yet in *Appius and Virginia*, not only does Webster present a rebellion against legitimate authority and a democratization of the legal system, but also, in making Icilius question the necessity of Virginia's martyrdom, he implies a criticism of the doctrine of obedience (or, if you will, Christian stoicism).

The play must also have been offensive to the authorities in another respect. The episode of the starvation of the army by Appius, with its consequences, is not to be found in Webster's sources. But it was a subject of importance in Webster's time, especially during the early 1620s, when English troops were being left to starve to death on the continent as the result of a confused and corrupt foreign policy.[14] Webster's sympathy with Virginius and his troops strongly implies a commitment to the radical Protestant position that England must take a stand with the Protestant powers of Europe against Spain and Catholicism—a position that was being undermined by the wheeling and dealing of Buckingham, whose contradictory moves were paid for in soldiers' lives. It is likely that in the character of Appius many of Webster's audience saw Buckingham himself, the overbearing upstart using his vast power to enrich himself at the state's expense, notorious for the sexual transgressions that tickled his monarch's fancy.[15] It may also be that in Virginius they saw Sir Henry Vere, "the most famous and best loved commander of the day,"[16] whose expedition to the Netherlands in the cause of Protestantism was thwarted by Buckingham's opposition.

What the censor made of this play had long been one of my unanswered questions about Webster until recent scholarship

Conclusion: The Rule of Law

suggested a line of speculation. In her book on Middleton, Margot Heinemann discusses Jacobean censorship generally and postulates that there was a relaxation of censorship in 1624 for the licensing of *A Game at Chess*, Middleton's outrageously anti-Spanish play. The fact that at that moment in history licensing was in the hands of the Herbert family is germane to her argument, for the Herberts tended to support Puritan aims within the limits of political discretion.[17] Even more suggestive is the material presented in the chapter of her book entitled "Drama and Opposition, 1619-40." There we find that the years 1622-1624 produced a handful of plays whose subversive content managed to survive censorship. These plays contained criticism of foreign policy, "of incompetent favourites disastrously appointed to high posts," of clerical corruption, and of "undue reverence for rank." Particularly interesting in connection with *Appius and Virginia* is Massinger's *The Bondman*, in which the city of Syracuse, like Webster's Rome, is presented as "corrupted by favouritism and soft living" to the point where military obligations are scorned and neglected. Heinemann points out that Massinger's play clearly implies a critique of the government's failure to adopt a militant anti-Spanish foreign policy.[18]

In the light of this flurry of activity on the part of the playwrights and a corresponding inactivity on the part of the censor, it becomes possible to see *Appius and Virginia* as Webster's response to a particular historical moment, when the existence of a crisis made action an imminent possibility. The increasingly outspoken and vehement popular criticism of James' foreign policy in the early 1620s led to outbursts of manic defiance—attacks upon the Spanish ambassador, bonfires in the streets to celebrate the failure of Prince Charles' wooing of the Infanta. In such an atmosphere, with the king and Parliament in open and extreme antagonism,[19] a popular playwright with political impulses might well change his mode of writing. This appears to be the case with *Appius and Virginia*, where an earlier concern with philosophical subtleties and tragic (and tragi-comic) ironies gives way to an investigation of the bases for political action.[20] It is to be noted that in this same period (1624) Webster wrote the work in which Bradbrook finds, for once, "an openly political statement."[21] This is his city pageant, *Monuments of Honour*, in which Webster symbolized the perfect ruler, not in the person of either James or Charles, but in that of the dead Prince Henry. Perhaps it is not too fanciful to imagine that it was what Virginius calls "the universal business . . . that . . . toucheth a whole people" that impelled Webster to shift his focus from the individual to the society, and his genre from tragedy to chronicle and city pageant.

At the very beginning of his career as a playwright, Webster had participated in theatrical celebration of another political crisis (surrounding the accession of James) by collaborating with Dekker on *The Famous History of Sir Thomas Wyat*.[22] In this early play, one already finds certain Websterian hallmarks: a Machiavellian bishop who doubles as the play's corrupt and vindictive judge; a central trial scene in which specific rules of procedure are exposed as prejudicial to the defendant; a heroine whose public role prevents her from fulfilling her personal desires. Particularly interesting is the fact that *Sir Thomas Wyat* states the theme of resistance in a way that anticipates *The Duchess of Malfi* and *Appius and Virginia*. Wyat is a good man who acts on principle for the sake of the commonweal. Early in the play he champions the incumbent Queen Mary against the supporters of Lady Jane Grey, the doctrine of legitimacy overriding his Protestantism. Mary's determination to marry Philip of Spain forces Wyat to reverse his position, but it is too late to mount a successful rebellion and he dies in the effort. The play is overtly (often crudely) anti-Spanish. And the implication seems clear that over-much obeisance to legal authority may prove destructive to the commonweal as well as personally suicidal. As we have seen, much the same point is made in *The Duchess of Malfi*, where the obeisance (by Bosola) stems from cynicism rather than, as in Wyat's case, from lack of political sophistication. In *Appius and Virginia*, even more clearly than in *Sir Thomas Wyat* or *The Duchess of Malfi*, undue reverence for legitimate authority, whether through awe, cowardice, cynicism, or political naiveté, is shown to be dangerous both to individuals and to the commonweal.

Thus, if our dating of *Appius and Virginia* is correct, it becomes possible to see Webster's political position as fundamentally consistent from the beginning to the end of his career as a writer, although his work orients itself towards political action only at times of crisis. One more aspect of this position should be mentioned, because it figures so largely in both chronicle plays, and that is the treatment of the city called London in the earlier play and (more circumspectly) Rome in the later. In *Sir Thomas Wyat*, the rebellion fails because the city goes back on its promise to rally to Wyat's cause. The implications of this betrayal are spelled out in Wyat's last words: "Had London kept its word, Wyat had stood, / But now King Philip enters through my blood." In the later play, the city eventually goes over to the army, just in time to prevent a general slaughter. The betrothal of Icilius, the citizen, to Virginia, the general's daughter, has issued in this union of city and camp against a decadent ruling class. Though both plays carry a warning

Conclusion: The Rule of Law   155

to the city of London to protect itself against a pro-Spanish government, the later play implies that rebellion will occur even without the support of the city. Can it be that Webster played some small part in preparing for the alliance of citizens and soldiers that was so crucial in the 1640s?

Notes to Chapter Eight

1 Quoted by Ernest Sirluck in John Milton, *Complete Prose Works* (New Haven: Yale University Press, 1963), vol. II, pp. 14-15.
2 Quoted by Catherine Bowen, *The Lion and the Throne* (Boston: Little, Brown, 1957), pp. 144-145.
3 See Sirluck, vol. II, pp. 13ff.
4 *The Contra-Replicant*, quoted by Sirluck, vol. II. pp. 38-39.
5 See Perez Zagorin, *A History of Political Thought in the English Revolution* (London: Routledge and Paul, 1954), p. 6.
6 Sirluck, p. 21.
7 Quoted by Zagorin, p. 24.
8 Ibid., p. 15.
9 Ibid., p. 16.
10 *Tudor Drama and Politics* (Cambridge, Mass.: Harvard University Press, 1968), p. 157.
11 Ibid., p. 161.
12 Ibid., p. 162.
13 Margot Heinemann, *Puritanism and Theatre* (Cambridge: Cambridge University Press, 1980), pp. 39-40. She also gives an instance in which such a ploy seems to have worked, during the early 1620s (pp. 218-219).
14 See Lucas, vol. III, pp. 125-126; and Bradbrook, *John Webster*, p. 179.
15 See Lawrence Stone, *The Crisis of the Aristocracy* (Oxford: Oxford University Press, 1967), p. 299.
16 Bradbrook, *John Webster*, p. 179. She talks about Vere in connection with the play but does not suggest an actual identification with Virginius.
17 Heinemann, *Puritanism and Theatre*, Chapter 10.
18 Ibid., pp. 200-218.
19 Godfrey Davies, *The Early Stuarts, 1603-1660* (Oxford: Clarendon, 1949), pp. 22-27; Barry Coward, *The Stuart Age* (London: Longman, 1980), pp. 132-136.
20 Although my analysis of the play coincides with Griffin's on some major issues, it is diametrically opposed on the question of political implications. Griffin says: "A new group comes into power and the political realignment which accompanies this transition brings into being a new set of 'reigning fictions' to lend it legitimacy.... The final play is a celebration of the new order" (pp. 165-166). I would attribute the changed vision of *Appius and Virginia*, not to some hypothetical "new order," but rather to Webster's participation in a movement to overthrow the old one.
21 Bradbrook, *John Webster*, p. 180.
22 The play, published in 1607 with the two authors' names on the title-page, appears to have been a reworking of an earlier play created by the joint effort of a whole stable of writers, among them Dekker and Webster. See Bradbrook, *John Webster*, pp. 99-102.

Works Cited

Acts of the Privy Council of England, 1613-14. London, 1912.
Alexander, Franz and Hugo Staub. *The Criminal, the Judge, and the Public.* Rev. ed. Glencoe, Ill.: Free Press, 1956.
Allen, John William. *English Political Thought.* 2nd ed. London: Methuen, 1961.
Archer, Peter. *The Queen's Courts.* 2nd ed. Middlesex: Penguin Books, 1963.
Bacon, Francis. *Essays, Advancement of Learning, New Atlantis, and other Pieces.* Ed. Richard Jones. New York: Odyssey Press, 1937.
———. *The Works of Francis Bacon.* 15 vols. Ed. James Spelling, Robert Ellis, Douglas Heath. London: Longmans, 1857-74.
Baker-Smith, Dominic. "Religion and John Webster." In *John Webster.* Ed. Brian Morris. London: Ernest Benn, 1970.
Bamber, Linda. *Comic Women, Tragic Men: A Study of Gender and Genre in Shakespeare.* Stanford: Stanford University Press, 1982.
Becker, Carl. *The Heavenly City of the Eighteenth-Century Philosophers.* New Haven: Yale University Press, 1959.
Bentley, Gerald E. *The Jacobean and Caroline Stage.* 7 vols. Oxford: Clarendon, 1941-68.
Berggren, Paula. "The Woman's Part: Female Sexuality as Power in Shakespeare's Plays." In *The Woman's Part: Feminist Criticism in Shakespeare.* Ed. Carolyn Lenz, Gayle Green, and Carol Neely. Urbana: University of Illinois Press, 1980.
Berlin, Normand. "*The Duchess of Malfi*: Act V and Genre." *Genre* 3 (1970).
Berry, Ralph. *The Art of John Webster.* Oxford: Clarendon Press, 1972.
Bevington, David. *Tudor Drama and Politics.* Cambridge, Mass.: Harvard University Press, 1968.
Bliss, Lee. "Destructive Will and Social Chaos in 'The Devil's Law-Case'." *MLR* V, 72, no. 3 (1977).
———. *The World's Perspective: John Webster and the Jacobean Drama.* New Brunswick, N.J.: Rutgers University Press, 1983.
Bodin, Jean. *Six Books of the Commonwealth.* Ed. and trans. M. J. Tooley. Oxford: Blackwell, 1955.
Bodtke, Richard. *Tragedy and the Jacobean Temper: The Major Plays of John Webster.* Salzburg Studies in English Literature. Salzburg: Institut für Englische Sprache und Literatur, Universität Salzburg, 1972.

Works Cited

Bogard, Travis. *The Tragic Satire of John Webster*. Berkeley: University of California Press, 1955.

Boklund, Gunnar. *The Sources of the White Devil*. Uppsala, Sweden: Lundequistska Bokhandeln, 1957.

Bowen, Catherine. *The Lion and the Throne: The Life and Times of Sir Edward Coke*. Boston: Little, Brown, 1957.

Bowers, Fredson. *Elizabethan Revenge Tragedy*. Gloucester, Mass.: P. Smith, 1959.

Bradbrook, Muriel. *John Webster: Citizen and Dramatist*. New York: Columbia University Press, 1980.

Brennan, Elizabeth. "'An Understanding Auditory': An Audience for John Webster." In *John Webster*. Ed. Brian Morris. London: Ernest Benn, 1970.

Brodwin, Leonora Leet. *Elizabethan Love Tragedy, 1587-1625*. New York: New York University Press, 1971.

Brooke, Rupert. *John Webster and the Elizabethan Drama*. New York: John Lane, 1916.

Bush, Douglas. *The Renaissance and English Humanism*. Toronto: University of Toronto Press, 1939.

Calderwood, James L. "*The Duchess of Malfi*: Styles of Ceremony." In *Twentieth Century Interpretations of the Duchess of Malfi*. Ed. Norman Rabkin. Englewood Cliffs, N.J.: Prentice-Hall, 1968.

Calendar of State Press, domestic series, 1603-10. London, 1857.

The Complete Newgate Calendar. 5 vols. Ed. John Rayner and L. T. Crook. London: The Navarre Society, 1926.

Coward, Barry. *The Stuart Age: A History of England 1603-1714*. London: Longmans, 1980.

Dallby, Anders. *The Anatomy of Evil: A Study of John Webster's* The White Devil. Lund: Gleerup, 1974.

Danby, John. *Shakespeare's Doctrine of Nature: A Study of* King Lear. London: Faber and Faber, 1949.

Davies, Godfrey. *The Early Stuarts, 1603-1660*. Oxford: Clarendon Press, 1949.

Dekker, Thomas. *The Belman of London*. In *The Guls Hornbook and the Belman of London*. London: J. M. Dent, 1928.

Dent, R. W. *John Webster's Borrowing*. Berkeley: University of California Press, 1960.

Dollimore, Jonathan. *Radical Tragedy: Religion, Ideology and Power in the Drama of Shakespeare and his Contemporaries*. Brighton, Sussex: Harvester Press, 1984.

Donne, John. *The Poems of John Donne*. Ed. Sir Herbert Grierson. London: Oxford University Press, 1933.

Doran, Madeleine. *Endeavors of Art: A Study of Form in Elizabethan Drama*. Madison, Wisc.: University of Wisconsin Press, 1954.

Dusinberre, Juliet. *Shakespeare and the Nature of Women*. London: Macmillan, 1975.

French, Marilyn. *Shakespeare's Division of Experience*. New York: Summit Books, 1981.

Fulbrook, Mary. *Piety and Politics: Religion and the Rise of Absolutism in England, Württemberg and Prussia*. Cambridge: Cambridge University Press, 1983.

Gierke, Otto. *Natural Law and the Theory of Society*. 2 vols. Trans. Ernest Barker. Cambridge: Cambridge University Press, 1934.
Gill, Roma. "'Quaintly Done': A Reading of *The White Devil*." *Essays and Studies*, NS 19 (1966).
Gooch, George. *English Democratic Ideas in the Seventeenth Century*. 2nd ed. Cambridge: Cambridge University Press, 1927.
Goodman, William. *The Social History of Great Britain during the Reigns of the Stuarts*. 2 vols. New York: W. H. Graham, 1847.
Goldman, Michael. "Characterizing Coriolanus." *Shakespeare Survey* 34 (1981).
Gray, Charles. "Reason, Authority, and Imagination: The Jurisprudence of Sir Edward Coke." In *Culture and Politics from Puritanism to the Enlightenment*. Ed. Perez Zagorin. Berkeley: University of California Press, 1980.
Greenblatt, Stephen, ed. *The Power of Forms in the English Renaissance*. Norman, Oklahoma: Pilgrim Books, 1982.
——— . *Renaissance Self-Fashioning from More to Shakespeare*. Chicago: University of Chicago Press, 1980.
Greene, Robert. *A Quip for an Upstart Courtier*. In *The Harleian Miscellany*, vol. 2. London: Dutton, 1808-11.
——— . *A Notable Discovery of Coosnage*. London: John Lane, The Bodley Head, 1923.
Griffin, Robert. *John Webster: Politics and Tragedy*. Salzburg Studies in English Literature. Salzburg: Institut für Englische Sprache und Literatur, Universität Salzburg, 1972.
Gunby, David. "The Devil's Law Case: An Interpretation." *MLR* 63 (1968).
——— . "*The Duchess of Malfi*: A Theological Approach." In *John Webster*. Ed. Brian Morris. London: Ernest Benn, 1970.
Haydn, Hiram. *The Counter-Renaissance*. New York: Scribners, 1950.
Heinemann, Margot. *Puritanism and Theatre: Thomas Middleton and Opposition Drama under the Early Stuarts*. Cambridge: Cambridge University Press, 1980.
Hellenga, Robert. "Elizabethan Dramatic Conventions and Elizabethan Reality." *Renaissance Drama* NS 12 (1981).
Hill, Christopher. *The Century of Revolution, 1603-1714*. London: Nelson, 1961.
——— . *The Good Old Cause: The English Revolution of 1640-60*. London: Lawrence & Wishart, 1949.
——— . *Intellectual Origins of the English Revolution*. London: Oxford University Press, 1972.
——— . *Puritanism and Revolution: Studies in Interpretation of the English Revolution of the 17th Century*. London: Secker and Warburg, 1958.
Holdsworth, Sir William. *A History of English Law*. 12 vols. 3rd ed. London: Methuen, 1922.
Hooker, Richard. *Of the Laws of Ecclesiastical Polity*. 2 vols. London: J. M. Dent, 1907.
Hoopes, Robert. *Right Reason in the English Renaissance*. Cambridge, Mass.: Harvard University Press, 1962.
James, I. *The Political Works of James I*. Ed. Charles McIlwain. Cambridge: Harvard University Press, 1918.

Works Cited

Jardine, David. *Criminal Trials*. 2 vols. London: M. A. Nattali, 1847.
Jenks, Edward. *A Short History of English Law*. 2nd ed. Boston: Little, Brown, 1922.
Kahn, Coppélia. "Coming of Age in Verona." In *The Woman's Part: Feminist Criticism of Shakespeare*. Ed. Carolyn Lenz, Gayle Greene, and Carol Neely. Urbana: University of Illinois Press, 1980.
Kettle, Arnold. *An Introduction to the English Novel*. 2 vols. London: Hutchinson, 1951.
Leech, Clifford. *John Webster: a Critical Study*. London: Hogarth Press, 1951.
──────. *Webster: The Duchess of Malfi*. London: Arnold, 1963.
Lenz, Carolyn, Gayle Greene, and Carol Neely, eds. *The Woman's Part: Feminist Criticism of Shakespeare*. Urbana: University of Illinois Press, 1980.
Lever, J. W. *The Tragedy of State*. London: Methuen, 1971.
Machiavelli, Niccolò. *The Prince and the Discourses*. Ed. Max Lerner. New York: Modern Library, 1940.
Maclean, Ian. *The Renaissance Notion of Woman*. Cambridge: Cambridge University Press, 1980.
McLuskie, Kathleen. "The Patriarchal Bard: Feminist Criticism and Shakespeare: *King Lear* and *Measure for Measure*." In *Political Shakespeare: New Essays in Cultural Materialism*. Ed. Jonathan Dollimore and Alan Sinfield. Ithaca: Cornell University Press, 1985.
Manchée, William Henry. *The Westminster City Fathers*. London: John Lane, 1924.
Marshall, Heddley H. *Natural Justice*. London: Sweet & Maxwell, 1959.
Middlesex County Records. 4 vols. Ed. John C. Jeaffreson. London: Middlesex County Record Society, 1886-92.
Milton, John. *Complete Prose Works*. 3 vols. Gen. ed. Don Wolfe. New Haven: Yale University Press, 1963 (vol. 2, ed. Ernest Sirluck).
Montaigne, Michel de. *The Complete Essays of Montaigne*. 3 vols. Ed. and trans. Donald Frame. Garden City, N.Y.: Doubleday, 1960.
Moore, Don. *John Webster and His Critics, 1617-1964*. Baton Rouge: Louisiana State University Press, 1966.
Moretti, Franco. "'A Huge Eclipse': Tragic Form and the Deconsecration of Sovereignty." In *The Power of Forms in the English Renaissance*. Ed. Stephen Greenblatt. Norman, Oklahoma: Pilgrim Books, 1982.
Morris, Brian, ed. *John Webster*. London: Ernest Benn, 1970.
Mulryne, James R. "*The White Devil* and *The Duchess of Malfi*." In *Jacobean Theatre*. Stratford-upon-Avon Studies I. Ed. John Russell Brown and Bernard Harris. London: Arnold, 1960.
Murray, Peter B. *A Study of John Webster*. The Hague: Mouton, 1969.
Orstein, Robert. *The Moral Vision of Jacobean Tragedy*. Madison: University of Wisconsin Press, 1960.
Osborne, Bertram. *Justices of the Peace, 1361-1848*. Dorset: Sedgehill Press, 1960.
Parrott, Thomas and Robert Ball. *A Short View of Elizabethan Drama*. New York: Scribners, 1943.
Pascal, Blaise. *Pensées et opuscules*. Ed. Léon Brunschvicg. Paris: Hachette, 1904-14.

Pearson, Jacqueline. *Tragedy and Tragicomedy in the Plays of John Webster*. Manchester: Manchester University Press, 1980.
Peterson, Joyce. *Curs'd Example: the Duchess of Malfi and Commonweal Tragedy*. Columbia: University of Missouri Press, 1978.
Pollock, Sir Frederick. *The Genius of the Common Law*. New York: Columbia University Press, 1912.
Pound, Roscoe. *An Introduction to the Philosophy of Law*. Rev. ed. New Haven: Yale University Press, 1954.
Quarter Sessions Records of Chester, 1559-1790. Cheshire, 1940.
Reiwald, Paul. *Society and its Criminals*. Ed. and trans. T. E. James. New York: International Universities Press, 1950.
Ribner, Irving. *Jacobean Tragedy: the Quest for Moral Order*. New York: Barnes & Noble, 1962.
Richelieu, Cardinal. *The Political Testament of Cardinal Richelieu*. Ed. and trans. Henry Bertram Hill. Madison: University of Wisconsin Press, 1961.
St. German, Christopher. *The Doctor and Student*. Rev. and cor. William Muchall. Cincinnati: R. Clarke, 1874.
Sharpe, J. A. *Crime in Seventeenth Century England: A County Study*. Cambridge: Cambridge University Press, 1983.
Shepherd, Simon. *Amazons and Warrior Women: Varieties of Feminism in Seventeen Century Drama*. New York: St. Martin's Press, 1981.
Spencer, Theodore. *Shakespeare and the Nature of Man*. New York: Macmillan, 1942.
Stephen, Sir James F. *A History of the Criminal Law of England*. 3 vols. London: Macmillan, 1883.
Stilling, Roger. *Love and Death in Renaissance Tragedy*. Baton Rouge: Louisiana State University Press, 1976.
Stoll, Elmer. *John Webster*. Boston: Alfred Mudge, 1905.
Stone, Lawrence. *The Crisis of the Aristocracy*. Oxford: Oxford University Press, 1967.
Thomson, Peter. "Webster and the Actor." In *John Webster*. Ed. Brian Morris. London: Ernest Benn, 1970.
Tillyard, E. M. W. *The Elizabethan World Picture*. New York: Macmillan, 1961.
Traill, Henry Duff, ed. *Social England*. 6 vols. London: Cassell, 1894-98.
Ure, Peter. "Character and Role from *Richard III* to *Hamlet*." Stratford-upon-Avon Studies V. Ed. John Russell Brown and Bernard Harris. London: Arnold, 1963.
Vinogradoff, Paul. *The Collected Papers of Paul Vinogradoff*. 2 vols. Oxford: Clarendon, 1928.
Webster, John. *The Complete Works of John Webster*. 4 vols. Ed. F. L. Lucas. London: Chatto and Windus, 1927.
——— . *The Devil's Law-Case*. Ed. Elizabeth Brennan. New Mermaid Series. London: Ernest Benn, 1975.
——— . *The Devil's Law-Case*. Ed. Frances A. Shirley. Regents Renaissance Drama Series. Lincoln: University of Nebraska Press, 1972.
——— . *The White Devil*. Ed. Elizabeth Brennan. The New Mermaids. London: Ernest Benn, 1966.
——— . *The White Devil*. Ed. John Russell Brown. Cambridge: Harvard University Press, 1960.

———. *The White Devil*. Ed. Clive Hart. Edinburgh: Oliver and Boyd, 1970.
———. *The White Devil*. Ed. James R. Mulryne. Regents Renaissance Drama Series. Lincoln: University of Nebraska Press, 1969.
———. *The White Devil*. Ed. Anthony Trott. London, 1966.
Whitman, Robert. *Beyond Melancholy: John Webster and The Tragedy of Darness*. Salzburg Studies in English Literature. Salzburg: Institut für Englische Sprache und Literatur, Universität Salzburg, 1973.
Wrightson, Keith. *English Society, 1580-1680*. Hutchison Social History of England. London: Hutchinson, 1982.
Zagorin, Perez. *A History of Political Thought in the English Revolution*. London: Routledge and Paul, 1954.
———. *Rebels and Rulers, 1500-1660*. Cambridge: Cambridge University Press, 1982.

Index

absolutism, 71, 74-75, 101-102, 105, 114, 148
Acts of the Privy Council, 46
aggression, 38-39, 40n. 13, 87-89
Althusius, 65
anarchism, 9-10, 11, 75, 96-96, 113, 120, 133, 147
anger, 35-39, 41n. 37, 59, 86
Angiolella, 116, 117, 120
anti-authoritarianism, 12-13, 43
Antonio, 17, 80, 81, 84, 88, 94-95, 96, 108, 109, 110
Appius, 125, 132-33, 134, 135, 136, 137, 138, 139, 140, 141, 142, 143, 144, 145, 149, 152
Appius and Virginia (by R. B.), 151-52
Aquinas, Thomas, 31, 64-65, 101
Ariosto, 116, 117, 122-24, 127, 128, 142
Aristotle, 65, 68
the Army, 136-37, 143, 152, 154-55
astronomy, 4
authority: disintegration of, 4-5; repressive, 9-10; unjust, 58-60, 84-85, 122, 151; reverence for, 154

Bacon, Sir Francis, 6, 8, 9, 30-31, 33, 34, 65, 68, 107, 124
Baker-Smith, Dominic, 97n. 10
Becker, Carl, 66
Bamber, Linda, 111n. 11
Bentley, Gerald E., 20nn. 20, 21, 146n. 1
Berggren, Paula, 111n. 11

Berry, Ralph, 20n. 23, 40n. 12, 61n. 38
Bevington, David, 151-52
Bliss, Lee, 20n. 27, 40n. 10, 129nn. 1, 8, 11
Bodin, Jean, 70
Bodtke, Richard, 18n. 11, 76n. 27
Bogard, Travis, 2, 81, 90
Bosola, 13, 80, 81, 83, 84, 85, 86, 87, 88, 96, 102, 107, 108-10, 118, 120, 131, 141, 151, 154
Bowen, Catherine, 35, 55
Bowers, Fredson, 38
Brachiano, 14-15, 17, 22, 23, 25-27, 28, 29, 30-31, 32, 36, 37, 39, 52-53, 59, 72, 73, 75, 118
Bradbrook, Muriel, 7, 9, 19nn. 15, 19, 73, 110n. 10, 121, 130n. 19, 153, 155nn. 14, 16
Brecht, Bertolt, 3, 98n. 15, (*Mother Courage*), 144
Brennan, Elizabeth, 58, 62n. 39, 129n. 1
Britomart, 112n. 22
Brodwin, Leonora, 112n. 27
Brooke, Rupert, 1, 84, 117-18, 122
Brown, John Russell, 54
Burton, Robert, 4
Bush, Douglas, 66

Calderwood, J. L., 98nn. 14, 15, 102
Calvinism, 6, 71, 86, 105, 107
Camillo, 14-15, 22-23, 25-26, 28, 29, 36, 37, 53

Index

the Cardinal, 7, 80, 81-85, 86, 87, 88, 91, 94, 95, 96, 97nn. 3, 6, 98n. 15, 100, 104, 105, 106
Cariola, 80, 94
Catholicism, 7, 67-68, 152
Cavaliers, 5
censorship, 153
chaos, 70, 73-75, 95-96, 102, 104, 117, 119, 131-35, 139
Chapman, George, 6, 8
characterization: Monticelso, Francisco, Lodovico, 37-38, 41n. 38; Flamineo and social forces, 50-52, 61n. 34; Vittoria, 58, 63n. 50; in Webster's plays, 61n. 38; in *WD* and *DM*, 79; Ferdinand and the Cardinal, 81-94; the Duchess, 103; of women, 104, 111n. 11; Bosola, 108-10; Romelio, 120-22, 128; Virginius, 135-39; Virginia, 145. *See also* individual characters
the Church, 1, 3, 7, 9, 29, 51, 52, 64, 80-81, 83, 92, 95-96, 105, 106, 153
Cicero, 65
class, 11, 16, 22-24, 50-52, 75, 100-101, 102
Coke, Sir Edward, 35, 45-46, 53, 71-72, 124, 144, 146n. 3, 148
Colet, John, 67
Contarino, 116, 118, 119, 120, 127
Contilupo, 126
Cornelia, 14, 22, 27, 32, 36, 50, 52
corruption, 1-2, 8, 51, 96, 110, 142, 153. *See also* law
Counter-Renaissance, 12, 66-67, 75
the Court, 1, 2, 7, 8, 23-25, 50-52, 61n. 34, 110
courts: ecclesiastical, 6, 40n. 10, 45, 46, 47, 53-54, 105; chancery, 125; Leet, 46; Privy Council, 46; Star Chamber, 123, 126
Crispiano, 115-16, 122, 123, 124-26, 141-42
Cromwell, Oliver, 11

the Crown, 24, 43-48, 59, 97n. 3, 101-102, 105, 108, 149

Dallby, Anders, 62n. 39, 63nn. 50, 57
Danby, John, 66
death, 4, 23, 25, 84, 94, 96
Dekker, Thomas, 9, 60n. 14, 154
Delio, 85
democracy, 13, 16, 71, 80, 84, 96, 102, 143-44, 148-50, 152
Dent, R. W., 20n. 27
Deveureux, Robert (second Earl of Essex), 39n. 5, 45, 48, 55, 56, 59
didacticism, 12-16
divine right, 105, 114
Dollimore, Jonathan, 19n. 16, 61n. 34
Donne, John, 4, 8, 9, 24
Doran, Madeleine, 33
the Duchess, 4, 10, 11, 17, 80, 82, 83, 84, 86, 89, 91-94, 95-96, 98n. 15, 100, 102-104, 106-107, 108-10, 118, 131, 141, 148, 150, 151
Dusinberre, Juliet, 20n. 28
duty, 30, 135-37, 138

Elyot, Sir Thomas, 65, 70
English Revolution, 3, 5-6, 11, 48-49, 71, 74, 148-49, 150, 155
equality (and inequality), 11, 46-48, 49-52, 84
Ercole, 116, 118, 119, 120, 127
the Establishment, 9, 16-17, 52, 54, 78, 80-81, 84-85, 95-96, 108. *See also* the Church; the State

the family, 1, 16-17, 51, 64, 65-66, 70, 73, 79-80, 82-83, 114, 115-17, 134, 145
Ferdinand, 11, 15-16, 80, 81-82, 84-94, 95, 96, 97nn. 3, 6, 10, 98nn. 14, 15, 100, 104, 105, 106, 107, 108, 110, 116, 131, 149
Flamineo, 13, 14-15, 22, 23-25, 26,

31, 32, 35, 38, 49-52, 58, 59, 63n. 50, 72, 73, 75, 78, 79, 94, 118, 120, 121, 131, 132, 151
foreign policy, 7, 8, 152-53, 154
Francisco, 14, 22, 28-30, 31, 36-37, 38, 41n. 38, 49, 72, 79, 87, 89, 131
French, Marilyn, 40n. 17
Fulbrook, Mary, 19n. 14

gambling, 23-24
Gill, Roma, 25, 62n. 39
Gorky, Maxim, 3
Greene, Robert, 46, 47
Griffin, Robert, 19n. 19, 41n. 19, 61n. 34, 63n. 60, 97n. 9, 135, 155n. 20
Grotius, Hugo, 65
Gunby, D. C., 18n. 6, 129nn. 1, 9

Hastings, Lady Margaret, 79-80
Haydn, Hiram, 12, 66-67, 102-103
Hayward, John, 67
Heinemann, Margot, 19n. 15, 153, 155n. 13
Henry, Prince of Wales, 153
Herbert, George, 8
Heywood, Thomas, 10, 20n. 21, 133, 146n. 1
Hieronimo, 81
Hill, Christopher, 3, 6, 21n. 29, 24, 45, 106
Hobbes, Thomas, 24, 70-71, 74-75, 148
Hollis, Sir John, 44
honour, 10, 27, 82-84, 87, 134-35
Hooker, Richard, 31, 64-65, 69, 70, 72, 75, 101, 115
Hoopes, Robert, 68
Howard, Frances, 48

Icilius, 132, 134-35, 136, 138-39, 140, 142-43, 152, 154
iconoclasm, 2-3, 11, 12-16, 20n. 24, 64, 72, 75, 103, 114
ideology, 1-17, 18n. 9, 19n. 16, 25, 27-28, 29-33, 43-44, 48-50, 52, 64-75, 84-85, 91-92, 94-96, 98n. 15, 100-108, 114-17, 119-20, 127-29, 131, 133, 134-35, 137-45, 147-52, 154

incest, 93-94
individualism and order, 7-10, 11-12, 73-75, 96, 98n. 15, 102, 104, 105-107, 113-14, 120-22, 128, 131-37, 141-42, 147-48, 150-51, 153
injustice, 46, 49, 51-52, 57-60. *See also* justice
intellectual history, 4-6
irony, 14-16, 28, 30, 32, 40n. 12, 92, 104, 117, 132, 153
Isabella, 14, 17, 22, 27, 28, 30, 37, 38, 151

Jacobean society: art, 1-22, 48-49, 153; ideas, 3, 6-7, 10-11, 48-49, 71-72, 107, 148-49; struggle for change, 3, 5-7, 10-11, 16, 48-49, 155n. 20; intellectual atmosphere, 3-9, 10-11, 12-13, 16; economics, 7-8, 22-25, 50; social conditions, 7-8, 24-25; politics, 7-8; legal system, 48-49
Jacobean stage, 5, 6-7, 8-9, 121
James I, 7, 24, 43, 48, 70-71, 97n. 3, 101, 105, 108, 124, 152, 153, 154
Jolenta, 116, 118, 119
Jonson, Ben, 6, 8, 152
Julia, 80, 83
Julio, 116, 117, 118
justice, 33-34, 35-39, 49-52, 57, 59-60, 70, 112n. 22, 122-23, 125, 126, 135, 137-39, 140, 142-44, 145, 149. *See also* injustice

Kahn, Coppélia, 40n. 13
Kettle, Arnold, 16

Lagarde, Fernand, 20n. 20
Lamb, Charles, 1
law: benefit of clergy, 46-47; common law, 45, 53, 54, 107, 108, 114, 122, 124-26, 130n. 17, 148; contemporary criticism of, 11, 48, 59; corruption of, 11, 47-48, 49, 124, 145; criminal, 34-35, 44-45, 46-48, 59-60, 127, 138-40; the Crown and, 43-48, 59, 97n. 3, 101,

Index

105, 108, 149; the defendant, 44-47; 53-60, 125, 141, 142-44, 154; divine, 65-68, 101, 114, 123, 140; divorce, 40n. 10, 106; equity, 48, 54, 122-24; importance of, in Webster's plays, 10-12; ineffectuality of, 27, 32, 94-96, 106, 126-27; inequality of, 11, 46-48, 49-52; the judge, 10-11, 33-34, 35-39, 43-46, 52-60, 78, 85-96, 105, 108, 120, 122-27, 133, 135, 137-41, 142-45, 149, 154; judgment and emotions in, 35-39, 59-60, 94-95, 126, 133, 137-39, 140, 144; the jury, 44, 53-54, 143; vs. nature, 26-33, 70-71, 73-75, 78, 94-96, 113-14, 119-20, 122; paternalism of, 11, 43-46, 48, 52, 54, 59, 123, 142-44, 149; penal code, 34-35, 48, 49; philosophy of, 27-28, 32-36, 39, 43-48, 49, 64-75, 94-96, 101-108, 114-17, 119-20, 122-29, 137-45, 148-50, 154; positive, 64-69, 101, 119-20, 123, 149; and power, 11, 43-60, 70-72, 74-75, 80-81, 84-85, 95-96, 101-102, 105, 106, 107-108, 114, 141, 145, 149-50; precedent, 45; procedure, 35-36, 44-46, 52-60, 125-26, 142-45, 154; and revolution, 148-50; wager of battle (trial by combat), 34, 121, 126-27. *See also* courts
law of nature. *See* natural law
lawyers, 123, 124, 126, 132, 141, 145
Leech, Clifford, 50, 108-109
Leonora, 115, 116, 118-19, 120, 123, 125, 126, 127, 148
Lever, J. W., 19n. 16, 61n. 34
Lilburne, John, 150
literary history, 5-7
Lodovico, 36, 37-38, 49, 51, 73
London, 7, 154-55
Lucas, F. L., 114, 124, 146n. 1
Luther, Martin (and Lutheranism), 12, 66, 68, 102

Machiavelli, Niccolò (and machiavellian), 12, 66, 69-70, 71, 72, 84, 102-103
MacLean, Ian, 21n. 30
Marcello, 14, 23, 32, 52, 79
Marcus, 132, 133, 145
Marlowe, Christopher, 6, (*The Jew of Malta*), 121
marriage, 16-17, 22-23, 25-27, 29, 40n. 10, 64, 79-80, 82, 92, 106-107, 117, 118, 119, 132
Marston, John, 8
Martin Marprelate, 6
Marvell, Andrew, 5
Massinger, Philip, (*The Bondman*), 153
McLuskie, Kathleen, 111n. 11
Middleton, Thomas, 6, 8, 153
Milton, John, 5, 106
Minutius, 133, 138
Montaigne, Michel de, 6, 12, 25, 27, 32, 33, 66, 68-69, 72, 74-75, 76n. 27, 95, 103
Monticelso (Cardinal), 14, 27, 28-30, 31, 32, 35-37, 45, 49, 52-60, 72, 74, 89, 106, 125
morality, 1-3, 12-14, 22, 27, 28-33, 36-38, 51-52, 54, 57-58, 62n. 39, 63n. 50, 64-65, 72, 75, 78-79, 81, 83-87, 89-96, 106-108, 131, 140, 141
Moretti, Franco, 18n. 9, 75
Mulryne, J. R., 63n. 57, 81
Murray, Peter B., 18n. 6, 62n. 39, 129nn. 1, 9, 146n. 1
mutability, 75, 102, 103, 132-35

natural law, 33, 64-71, 72-75, 101-104, 115-17, 119-20, 123, 125, 150
naturalism, 103, 115-17, 133, 148
nature (and natural), 22-23, 25-33, 64-70, 72-75, 78-79, 81, 84, 85, 91-96, 97n. 9, 101-104, 106, 113-14, 115-17, 119-20, 133, 134-35, 136
nihilism, 2-5, 75
nominalism, 12-13
Numitorius, 138

order. *See* individualism and order

Ornstein, Robert, 12, 97n. 6
Overbury, Sir Thomas, 44, 47
Overton, Richard, 150

parasitism, 79, 81-83, 85, 88-89, 96
Parker, Henry, 149
parliamentarianism, 5, 6, 11, 71, 148-49, 150
Pascal, Blaise, 67-68
Peacham, Sir Henry, 49
Pearson, Jacqueline, 108-109, 113, 129n. 8, 130n. 24
Perkins, Richard, 121
Peterson, Joyce, 98n. 15
Plato, 100
political philosophy, 14, 19n. 19, 64-66, 69-72, 73-75, 100-102, 104-105, 108, 110, 114, 135-37, 141, 143-44, 148-55
Pound, Roscoe, 70
power, 11, 16-17, 32, 43-60, 70-72, 73-75, 80-81, 84-85, 96-96, 101-102, 104-105, 106, 107-108, 114, 141, 150
principles vs. personal feelings, 131-39, 140, 144
Prynne, William, 6
punishment, 32-33, 37-39, 59-60, 86-96, 123, 127-28, 138-40. *See also* law: penal code
Puritanism, 5-6, 16, 105-107, 148, 152-53
Pym, John, 6, 148-49

Raleigh, Sir Walter, 24, 35, 48, 53, 55, 56, 57, 59, 70
rationalism (and rationalist philosophy), 12-13, 27-33, 33-34, 35-36, 39, 64-70, 72-75, 94-96, 100-105, 111n. 11, 114, 115-17, 137, 140, 148
reason, 13, 27-33, 35-36, 39, 45, 64-70, 72-75, 94-96, 100-105, 115, 148; law of, 27-33, 64-70, 72-75, 101-105, 115; right, 33, 39, 68, 103; of state, 74-75, 100, 105
rebellion, 9-10, 25, 75, 84, 134, 138, 142. *See also* revolution; resistance

Reiwald, Paul, 58
religion, 2-3, 62n. 39; and Ferdinand, 85-87, 89, 91-93, 97n. 10, 105-107. *See also* Calvinism; Catholicism; the Church; divine law; Luther; morality; Puritanism
repression, 9-10, 32-33, 78, 84-85, 88, 91-96, 102, 122
resistance, 108-10, 150-52, 154-55. *See also* rebellion; revolution
revenge, 10, 14, 29, 33-39, 81, 127, 136, 138-40
revolution (and revolutionary), 5, 6, 10, 11, 16, 20n. 24, 48-49, 71, 136, 143-44, 149-52, 154-55
Ribner, Irving, 96
Richardson, Samuel, 16, 106
Richelieu, Cardinal, 70, 71, 101-102, 105
Rome, 136-37, 144, 149, 153, 154
Romelio, 115, 118, 120-22, 125, 126, 127, 128, 131, 141-42, 148
royal prerogative, 8, 48, 71, 105, 108, 148

St. German, Christopher, 72
Sanitonella, 122, 123
satire, 1, 12, 13, 15-16, 24, 52, 83, 90, 113, 117, 126
scepticism, 4, 6, 12-16, 28, 66-70
Selden, John, 124
sententiae, 13-16, 28, 114-15
sexual passion (love), 8, 16-17, 22-23, 25-27, 28-33, 72, 73-74, 78, 79-80, 82-84, 89, 91-96, 102, 106, 116-19, 132, 134
Shakespeare, William, 6, 7, 8, 16; *Antony and Cleopatra*, 8, 9, 31, 104; *Coriolanus*, 8; feminist criticism of, 111n. 11; *Hamlet*, 81; *King Lear*, 73, 98n. 15; *Macbeth*, 75, 98n. 15; *Measure for Measure*, 120, 125; *Othello*, 9; *Richard II*, 133; *Romeo and Juliet*, 40n. 13
Shelley, P. B., 85

Index

Shepherd, Simon, 21n. 31, 110n. 10, 112n. 22, 145
Shirley, Frances A., 129n. 1
Sirluck, Ernest, 67, 150
social contract, 10, 71, 150
Spencer, Theodore, 66
Spenser, Edmund, 5, 122n. 22
the State, 3, 8, 23, 24, 29, 55, 59, 64, 65-66, 70-71, 73, 74-75, 100, 106
Stilling, Roger, 21n. 31
stoicism, 8, 15-16; Christian, 152
Stoll, Elmer, 51-52
Stone, Lawrence, 23-24, 25, 79-80, 107
Stuart, Arabella, 97

Tarleton, Richard, 6
Thomson, Peter, 61n. 38, 63n. 50
Tillyard, E. M. W., 66
tyranny, 10, 70-71, 75, 102, 105, 106, 141, 142-45, 148, 150; and sexual aggression, 151-52

Vere, Sir Henry, 152
Villiers, George, Duke of Buckingham, 152
Vindice, 81
Virginia, 132, 133, 134, 135, 138, 142, 143, 145, 152, 154
Virginius, 133, 134-39, 140, 141, 142, 143, 144, 145, 149, 151, 152, 153
Vittoria, 14, 17, 22-23, 24-27, 28, 29, 30, 31, 32-33, 35, 36, 37, 38, 39, 45, 50, 51, 52-60, 63n. 50, 72, 73, 74, 75, 78, 94, 107, 118, 120, 128, 131, 145, 150, 151

Walwyn, William, 6
Webster: authorship, 9-10, 20n. 21, 133, 146n. 1, 155n. 22; biography, 7, 114; characters, 33, 35, 97n. 7, 123; chronology, 9-10, 19n. 20, 147-48; criticism, 1-7, 9, 13, 50, 58, 61nn. 34, 38, 62n. 39, 63n. 50, 81-82, 98n. 15, 104, 108-109; historical position, 3-9, 10-13, 16. Works: *Anything for a Quiet Life*, 115-16, 119; *Appius and Virginia*, 10, 11, 17, 20n. 20, 39, 113-14, 122, 127, 128-29, 131-46, 147, 149-55, 155n. 20; *The Devil's Law Case*, 10, 11, 19n. 20, 39, 113-30, 131, 141-42, 144, 145, 147, 148, 149; *The Duchess of Malfi*, 7, 9-11, 15-16, 17, 18n. 6, 19n. 20, 78-99, 100-12, 116, 122, 127, 131, 141, 145, 147, 151, 154; *The Famous History of Sir Thomas Wyat*, 148, 154-55; *Monuments of Honour*, 153; *Westward Ho*, 41n. 37; *The White Devil*, 1, 9, 10, 11, 14-15, 17, 18n. 6, 19nn. 16, 20, 22-42, 43, 45, 48-60, 64, 72-75, 78-79, 81, 89, 94, 100, 106, 107, 116, 117, 118, 122, 127, 131, 147, 151. *See also* individual characters
Wentworth, Sir John, 44
Whitman, Robert, 61n. 35
widows, 79-80
women, 16-17, 21n. 31, 96, 104, 110n. 10; and chastity, 25, 91-92, 106-107, 112n. 22, 116-17, 151; femininity, 17, 104, 112n. 27; as heroic, 17, 106-107, 111n. 11, 145; infidelity of, 14, 17, 25-27; and male sexual aggression, 17, 133-35, 145, 151-52; maternal feelings, 32, 103, 115-17, 118, 148; position of, 16-17, 22-23, 25, 55, 63n. 51, 73, 79-80, 102, 126; and Puritanism, 4-5, 16, 105-107; sexuality of, 25-27, 79-80, 91-92, 102, 111n. 10, 116-17, 118-19
Wriothesley, Henry, third Earl of Southampton, 45

Zagorin, Perez, 20n. 24
Zanache, 38